# THE REAL TOSCANINI

# The Real Toscanini

## MUSICIANS REVEAL THE MAESTRO

## Cesare Civetta

AMADEUS PRESS

AN IMPRINT OF HAL LEONARD CORPORATION

Published in 2012 by Amadeus Press
An Imprint of Hal Leonard Corporation
7777 West Bluemound Road
Milwaukee, WI 53213

Trade Book Division Editorial Offices
33 Plymouth St., Montclair, NJ 07042

All photographs are copyright Estate of Robert Hupka/Arthur Fierro, executor, 172 Gordon Avenue, Totowa, NJ 07512.

All excerpts from the NBC Radio series *Toscanini: The Man Behind the Legend* are courtesy of NBC.

Other credits and expressions of gratitude may be found in the Acknowledgments section of this book.

Printed in the United States of America

Book design by Mark Lerner

Library of Congress Cataloging-in-Publication Data

Civetta, Cesare, 1959-
The real Toscanini : musicians reveal the maestro / Cesare Civetta.
    p. cm.
Includes bibliographical references and index.
ISBN 978-1-57467-241-1
1. Toscanini, Arturo, 1867-1957. 2. Conductors (Music)--Biography. I. Title.
ML422.T67C48 2012
784.2092--dc23

www.amadeuspress.com

*To my mentor, the Buddhist philosopher Daisaku Ikeda, whose efforts in peace, culture, and education inspire my work in music*

# Contents

*Preface*  xv

*Acknowledgments*  xix

*Biographical Sketch of Arturo Toscanini*  xxi

**1  TOSCANINI DEFIES MUSSOLINI AND OPPOSES HITLER**  1

Toscanini Defies Mussolini  2

Bayreuth  2

Bologna Incident  3

Second Visit to Bayreuth  4

Vienna Philharmonic  5

Palestine Orchestra  5

Salzburg Festival and Break with Furtwängler  7

Second Visit to Palestine  8

Establishment of the Lucerne Festival  8

Frustration and Despair over the Tyranny of Mussolini and Hitler  9

Return to La Scala after World War II  11

**2  INNER POWER AND CHARISMA**  15

Musicians' First Rehearsals with Toscanini  15

Additional First Impressions  17

Audience Reaction, Electricity  18

Off the Podium and Eye Contact  19

Magnetism  20

Fire and Charisma    22

Outdoing Themselves    22

Personal Force    26

Hypnotic    26

Inspiration    27

**3    WORK**    31

Practicing Outside of Rehearsals    31

Hectic Schedule    32

Study    33

Little Sleep    34

*Falstaff*    35

1935 *Falstaff* at Salzburg    35

1950 Concert Version of *Falstaff* at NBC    36

1946 Concert Version of *La bohème* at NBC    37

1947 Concert Version of *Otello* at NBC    37

1935 Salzburg *Fidelio*    38

Nervousness    38

Concentration and Self-Discipline    39

Repertoire    40

Knowledge    40

Self-Improvement    42

Rethinking    44

Restudy    47

Preparation    50

Shostakovich's Seventh Symphony    51

Memory and Ear    52

Memory    53

Bayreuth    55

**4   TEMPO**  59

Composers  59

Some Tempos Have Become Slower  60

Playability  61

Steady  62

Clarity  63

Sense of Timing, Rhythm  63

Words  64

Consistency of Tempos  65

Tempo Relationships  66

Transitional Modifications  67

Setting a Single Tempo for an Entire Movement  68

Control  69

Toscanini and the Metronome  69

Rubato  70

Rethinking  74

Slow Music  75

Young  75

Italian Tempo Markings  76

Slow Movements  77

*Die Zauberflöte*: "Ach, ich fühl's"  78

Acoustics  79

Following the Orchestra  80

Accompanying  80

Critics  82

Generalizations  83

Breathing  83

Life—Sonority  84

**5  OPERA**  87

Passion for Opera  89

Puccini  90

Rehearsals for the Twenty-fifth Anniversary of *Manon Lescaut* at
    La Scala  90

Singers  91

Singers' Repertoire  94

Recitals  94

Flexibility in Performance  95

Staged vs. Concert Version  96

Singers and Rubato  96

Holding High Notes  97

Tradition and Style of Cadenzas  97

Transposition  98

Word Changes  99

Education of Young Singers  100

Breath Support  101

Diligence and Perseverance  101

Covered vs. Open Sound  102

Singing Lightly  102

Vocalizing with *Ernani*  103

Vocalizing at the Piano  104

Scotti and De Luca  104

Conserving the Voice  105

"Do Not Push the Voice!"  106

Singing Full Voice at Rehearsals  107

*La forza del destino*  108

Drama and Text  109

Stage Direction  110

Period  112

Wigs  112

Costumes   113

Acting and Characterization   113

Prompters   115

Diction   115

*Otello*   116

Intonation Tip   119

Smaller Operatic Roles, or *Comprimari*   119

Recording of *Otello*   120

*Aida*   121

Balance   123

World Premiere of *I pagliacci*   123

*Madama Butterfly*   124

Critics and Audiences   124

Importance of Endings   125

Spontaneity   125

*Falstaff*   125

Characterization of Falstaff   128

**6   MUSICAL ARCHITECTURE**   133

Proportions, Climaxes, and Crescendos   134

Convincing   134

**7   BALANCE**   139

Clarity   139

Preparation and Ear   144

Orchestra Size   145

Doubling and Retouching   145

Dynamics   150

Small Theatre   151

Acoustics   151

*Oberon* Overture   152

**8   BATON TECHNIQUE   155**

Inexplicable   155

Immediate Response   156

Beautiful Beat   156

Age   156

Standing   157

Didn't Talk   157

Phrasing   158

Didn't Dance   159

Clarity   161

"Never Stop the Beat!"   163

Subdivisions of the Beat   163

*Parsifal*   164

*Oberon* Overture   164

Economy of Gesture   165

Pain   165

Humility   165

Description   165

On the Beat   166

Facial Expressions   167

Eyes   167

Mysterious   168

Rehearsal vs. Performance   169

Dress Rehearsals   170

Chemistry   171

Complete Command and Control   171

Unorthodox Baton Technique   171

Position of Arms   173

Different Gestures for Different Sections of the Orchestra   173

Placement of Gestures   173

No Lessons   174

Mood and Result   174

Tone Color   175

**9   PHILOSOPHY**   177

Composers   178

Humility   179

Ideals   181

*La mer*   181

Sincerity   182

Channel   184

Tchaikovsky's "Pathétique" Symphony   185

Music and Painting   186

**10   REHEARSAL STYLE**   189

"Sing!"   190

Beauty of Sound   193

Vibrato   193

Oboe Sound   193

Self-Dissatisfaction   194

Perfection and Ideals   195

Tantrums   196

Intense Concentration   198

Line   199

Afternoon Rehearsals Preferred   200

No Recriminations after Performances   201

Psychology   201

Forgiven by Musicians   203

Humanism   205

After Toscanini   208

**11   RECORDINGS**   211

Alteration of Acoustics   212

Dynamics Destroyed   212

Equalization   213

Microphone Placement   213

Single Mic vs. Multiple Mics   214

Balance   214

Clarity   215

Dubbing   216

Self-Dissatisfaction   216

Recording in Five-Minute Segments   217

Listening at Home   218

Recorded Legacy   219

**12   CONCLUSION**   221

Toscanini's Opinions of Other Conductors   221

Influence   224

Inspiration   224

Lessons Learned   226

*Appendix of Names*   227

*Notes*   239

*Bibliography*   247

*Index*   251

*About the Author*   259

# Preface

Arturo Toscanini (1867–1957) was a major force in raising symphonic and operatic performance standards of the late nineteenth and twentieth centuries. Most of the performers who worked with Toscanini considered the experience to have been the pinnacle of their careers. He conducted the world premieres of *I pagliacci, La bohème, La fanciulla del West, Turandot,* Respighi's *Feste romane,* and Barber's *Adagio for Strings;* the American premieres of *Boléro, Boris Godunov,* and Shostakovich's "Leningrad" Symphony; the Italian premieres of *Salome, Le martyre de Saint-Sébastien, Pelléas et Mélisande, Eugene Onegin, La damnation de Faust, Euryanthe,* Brahms's *Tragic Overture,* and three of Verdi's *Quattro pezzi sacri;* and he introduced several works to Argentina. Toscanini rehearsed and performed 117 operas and 480 symphonic compositions from memory, and during the first four decades of his career, was a champion of contemporary composers.*

Many composers admired Toscanini's interpretations of their works. Toscanini enjoyed a professional relationship with Verdi, who applauded enthusiastically when he heard him conduct Franchetti's *Cristoforo Colombo* in 1892. Verdi praised Toscanini for his interpretation of the composer's Te Deum when he heard the conductor play it on the piano, and he sided with him in disputes with singers over tempos.† After a concert in 1896, Saint-Saëns immediately went backstage to tell Toscanini that it was the first time he heard his *Danse macabre* performed in the tempos he had indicated. Richard Wagner's son, Siegfried, wrote about how impressed he was by Toscanini's performance of *Tristan und Isolde* at La Scala in 1901; he told the conductor that the production excelled even those of Munich and Berlin. Puccini gave

---

* At the 1898 International Turin Exhibition, he conducted 133 compositions by fifty-four composers, of which thirty-six were contemporary composers.

† Francesco Tamagno sang the title role in the world premiere of *Otello.* Antonio Pini-Corsi sang the role of Ford in the world premiere of *Falstaff.* Both productions were prepared under Verdi's supervision. In subsequent productions, conducted by Toscanini, these singers disagreed with the conductor about certain tempos, and when they sought out the composer to decide the disputes, Verdi sided with Toscanini's choices of tempo.

Toscanini complete freedom regarding interpretation and alterations of orchestral and compositional details, telling the conductor, "You are a better musician than I, and I take any correction from you."* Debussy gave Toscanini permission to alter the orchestration of *La mer*;† Toscanini recalled, "I tell Debussy are many things not clear; and he say is all right to make changes."[1]

Toscanini's performances attracted the praise of even the most highly esteemed conductors of his time. Leopold Stokowski, upon being offered a free ticket to a Toscanini concert in 1920, insisted on paying for the ticket, saying, "Everyone must pay to learn something."[2] Otto Klemperer wrote about a performance of *Die Meistersinger* he heard Toscanini conduct at La Scala in 1922: "He is the king of conductors . . . I have never heard a similarly musical presentation of the work in any theatre in the world."[3] Richard Strauss said about Toscanini, "When you see that man conduct, you realize that there is only one thing for you to do: break that little stick of yours into pieces, throw it away, and don't conduct ever again."[4]

Although Toscanini was one of the most revered conductors of the twentieth century, some writers began to criticize his work after his death, based on several of the recordings made near the end of a career that spanned from 1886 to 1954. Unfortunately, his recordings are not always musically representative of his best work. And some of them are sonically damaging to his art.‡ B. H. Haggin responded to the negative criticism in 1967 by publishing *The Toscanini Musicians Knew*, a collection of interviews he had conducted with nineteen artists who had worked with the maestro.

Intrigued by these interviews and by the recollections of my high school band director, Robert Cusumano—who himself had played trumpet with the maestro—I began listening to Toscanini's Beethoven recordings. It seemed that the unanimous

---

* Please see pages 90–91 for more about Puccini's praise of Toscanini.

† Edwin Bachmann, principal second violinist of the NBC Symphony, described Toscanini's relationship with Debussy and *La mer*: "Debussy sent Toscanini the score of *La mer*. The dedication is one full page in which Mr. Debussy said, 'Up until now I thought I have written a very fine composition to the best of my ability. Now I know that I have created something better than that with your help.' He said 'with your help' because Toscanini told Debussy that there were many things unclear in the score and told him about the changes he made especially in orchestration, all of which Debussy approved."

‡ Virtually all of the recordings of Toscanini's conducting were made during the final eighteen years of his career. He was often reluctant to consider a recording to be good enough to be published, and there are several reports of the maestro regretting having approved certain recordings for publication. See chapter 11, "Recordings," for a discussion of Toscanini's recordings.

praise from legendary composers and the distinguished artists in *The Toscanini Musicians Knew* contradicted the results I was hearing on the recordings. As a young conductor inspired by the artists' accounts, I decided to clarify this discrepancy by interviewing the musicians who had worked with Toscanini that were still alive in 1976.

Early in my journey, I met Robert Hupka, a Viennese photographer and former employee of RCA who took over 1,500 photographs of Toscanini at rehearsals and recording sessions. Hupka had obtained private recordings of rehearsals and concerts that were made using what he called "the optimum placement of a single microphone."

Hupka played these recordings for me, which he described as being "an accurate representation of what Toscanini's orchestra sounded like."* By playing these recordings on an enormous speaker system in a small, reverberative hall, Hupka succeeded in re-creating an approximation of the power and beauty of the maestro's performances. As I listened to these recordings, the enthusiastic praise of composers and performers now matched what I was hearing! As a sixteen-year-old budding conductor, I was inspired to discover the existence of infinite artistic possibilities.

It was Hupka who introduced me to some of the fifty artists to whom I spoke in the late 1970s. The interviews were broadcast on Fordham University's radio station, WFUV, in New York City during a thirty-five-part series I produced, entitled *The Toscanini Legacy*.† Each week, the programs featured interviews with one or more of the artists. They included composers; conductors; soloists and instrumentalists who performed with Toscanini and the Vienna Philharmonic, the Lucerne Festival Orchestra, the Palestine Orchestra (now the Israel Philharmonic), the New York Philharmonic, and the NBC Symphony; and singers who performed with Toscanini at La Scala, the Metropolitan Opera, and Carnegie Hall and with the NBC Symphony.‡

My questions focused on the technical aspects of music making, rather than biographical, nonmusical topics. The interviews were usually recorded at the artists' homes or studios, where I encouraged them to ramble and reminisce. In this

---

\* Hupka made this evaluation by attending Toscanini's concerts, and then going into the control room immediately afterward to listen to the recordings of the performances that had just taken place while the sound was still fresh in his ears.

† Please see the Appendix of Names for a comprehensive list of the interviewees.

‡ For this volume I have also included accounts from various artists who worked with Toscanini at Salzburg, Bayreuth, Madison Square Garden, the Philadelphia Orchestra, the Philharmonia Orchestra, and the BBC Symphony; and reminiscences from composers, soloists, conductors, orchestral librarians, producers, audio engineers, assistants, friends, family, and members of Toscanini's household.

relaxed atmosphere, the musicians opened up and freely shared their memories, impressions, explanations, and convictions about working with Toscanini. I was struck by the vividness of their recollections and the enthusiasm with which they recalled events they had participated in thirty to forty years before. After working as a conductor internationally with more than sixty orchestras and opera companies since 1980, I decided to share the insights I had gained from these artists with another generation of music lovers and professionals by publishing these testimonies.

In *The Real Toscanini: Musicians Reveal the Maestro*, the transcripts of the musicians' interviews are organized based on various aspects of Toscanini's art. Discussions about his inner strength, charisma, tempos, balance, rehearsals, opera, and other topics become a virtual panel discussion. Each topic is given a full chapter divided into specific sections. For example, chapter 4, "Tempo," includes discussions of rubato, the evolution of Toscanini's tempos within a composition, the effect of a hall's acoustics on tempos, tempo relationships, timing, his use of the metronome, and his relationship to the composers' metronome markings. It is my hope that the artists' perspectives clearly reveal Toscanini's philosophy, opinions, musical style, and techniques.

## Editor's Note

Passages from baritone Giuseppe Valdengo's book (with Renzo Allegri) *Scusi, conosce Toscanini?* (Excuse Me, Do You Know Toscanini?) were translated from Italian by Laurie Tanner and are being made available here in English for the first time. All uncited quotations attributed to Valdengo or to Toscanini via Valdengo are from Tanner's translation of *Scusi, conosce Toscanini?*

All other quotations throughout this book without citations are from the author's original interviews.

# Acknowledgments

I wish to express my gratitude to:

Iris Bass, copy editor, for her patience and flexibility;

Jessica Burr at Amadeus Press, for her utmost professionalism and care;

John Cerullo, publisher at Amadeus Press, for the opportunity to share these firsthand impressions of Toscanini;

Donald Drewecki, for his painstaking efforts in transcribing the recordings of many of the interviews;

Arthur Fierro, for his consistent, reliable guidance regarding many aspects of Toscanini's art and recordings, and for his kind permission to include some of Robert Hupka's photographs of Toscanini;

Mortimer Frank, for his encouragement, for interviewing Martin Bernstein, Harry Glantz, and Raoul Poliakine on my behalf, and for his kind permission to include quotations from these interviews;

Loredana Genova at Musumeci Editore, for permission to quote from Giuseppe Valdengo's *Scusi, conosce Toscanini?* (Excuse Me, Do You Know Toscanini?);

Elaine J. Gorzelski, publisher, at Harmonie Park Press, for her kind permission to quote from *Mischa Mischakoff: Journeys of a Concertmaster* by Anne Mischakoff Heiles;

the late Robert Hupka, for his lifetime of dedicated immersion and understanding of Toscanini's work, his photographs of the maestro, introducing me to several of the musicians interviewed in this book, playing recordings of many of Toscanini's concerts and rehearsals for me, and pointing out the attributes that make them what they are;

Ellen Klemme, for her meticulousness in assisting with the preparation of the manuscript;

Walter Levin, founder and first violinist of the La Salle Quartet, for his unbridled enthusiasm and guidance in understanding the Toscanini rehearsal recordings;

Donald E. McCormick, former curator of the Rodgers and Hammerstein Archives of Recorded Sound at the New York Public Library at Lincoln Center;

Danny Nagashima, for insisting on the publication of this book and never giving up on me;

Harvey Sachs, for his invaluable research on Toscanini, and the objective style with which he has shared it in his books about the maestro;

Laurie Tanner, for her wonderful English translation of Giuseppe Valdengo's material;

and Seth B. Winner, technical curator of *The Toscanini Legacy* at the Rodgers and Hammerstein Archives of Recorded Sound at the New York Public Library at Lincoln Center.

# Biographical Sketch of Arturo Toscanini

Toscanini was born in Parma, Italy, on March 25, 1867. He studied at Parma's Royal School of Music for nine years and received honors in piano, composition, and his primary instrument, cello. Toscanini made his conducting debut in Rio de Janeiro at age nineteen. The next several years were spent playing cello—including at the world premiere of *Otello*—and guest conducting in many of Italy's opera houses.

In 1895, Toscanini became the artistic director of the Teatro Regio in Turin, where, a year later, he conducted the world premiere of *La bohème*. In 1897 he married Carla de Martini, with whom he had four children: Walter; Wally; Giorgio, who died at age four; and Wanda, who married pianist Vladimir Horowitz. Toscanini was the artistic director of La Scala from 1898 to 1903, and from 1906 to 1908.

Between 1901 and 1906, he conducted four seasons of opera in Buenos Aires. For the 1908–1909 season, Toscanini was co-principal conductor of the Metropolitan Opera with Gustav Mahler, and from 1909 to 1915, its artistic director.

From July 1915 until the end of World War I, Toscanini conducted only benefit performances in Italy, especially to aid unemployed musicians. In fact, he was so generous that he was forced to sell his home.

From 1921 until 1929, Toscanini was again the artistic director of La Scala, where his achievements during that decade amounted to one of the most glorious periods in the history of opera.

Toscanini's first guest appearances with the New York Philharmonic were in 1926; he was made co-conductor with Willem Mengelberg in 1927, and from 1929 until 1936, he was its principal conductor. Between 1935 and 1939 he conducted several performances and recordings with the BBC Symphony in London.

Toscanini was a vehement anti-Fascist and anti-Nazi. His uncompromising brushes with Mussolini and Hitler attracted international attention and are detailed in chapter 1. At the invitation of Siegfried Wagner, Toscanini became the first foreign conductor to perform at the Bayreuth Festival in 1930 and 1931. Protesting Hitler's ban on Jewish artists, he canceled a further scheduled season in 1933 and never returned to Germany.

From 1933 until the end of World War II, Toscanini refused to conduct in Fascist-controlled countries and performed instead in Austria, Belgium, Denmark, England, France, Holland, Sweden, and Switzerland. In 1933 he began conducting the Vienna Philharmonic, with which he appeared at the Salzburg Festival from 1934 until the Austrian government's concessions to Hitler in 1938. In 1936, Toscanini donated his services to conduct the inaugural concerts of the Palestine Orchestra—now the Israel Philharmonic—comprised of Jewish refugees from Nazi persecution. He returned in 1938, as with the first visit, at his own expense. He helped launch the Lucerne Festival in 1938 conducting an orchestra largely composed of refugees from Nazism to which he returned in 1939 and 1946.

In 1937, Toscanini began conducting the NBC Symphony in New York in weekly concerts and frequent recording sessions, until his retirement in 1954 at age eighty-seven. The concerts were heard live via radio by millions of people throughout the world. All of the broadcasts were recorded and many of them have been published. Several were televised and are now available on DVD.

After his sixty-eight-year career, Toscanini listened to recordings of his performances to review what he would approve for publication. He died at his home in Riverdale, New York, on January 16, 1957, two months before his ninetieth birthday.

## Reforms

Throughout his career, Toscanini raised the standards of orchestral and operatic performance by insisting on accurate intonation, proper rhythms and balances, and tempos that the composers specified. His example continues to influence several aspects of contemporary performance practice, especially symphonic music, where an increased fidelity to the composer's instructions is often emphasized.

In the opera house, Toscanini banned encores, lowered the house lights during performances, and insisted on the construction of orchestra pits in Turin and Milan. Please see chapter 5, "Opera," for more details about his operatic reforms.

## Toscanini's Generosity

Toscanini was very generous financially, and conducted many performances gratis throughout his career. During World War II he conducted numerous benefit concerts for U.S. Treasury bond drives, the Red Cross, and several other charities. After World War II, he conducted a concert in New York that raised $30,000 for the benefit of several Italian welfare societies, including the War Orphans Committee. Toscanini contributed regularly to the Casa di Riposo, a rest home for aged singers and instrumentalists founded by Verdi. In 1949, on the anniversary of Verdi's death, he donated $6,000 to the needy musicians of Milan. The Toscanini family also assisted large numbers of refugees from Europe in securing American entry visas, jobs, and homes.

Giuseppe Valdengo, baritone: "In diaries that I kept at that time, I find incidents . . . regarding his solidarity and generosity toward orchestral players and singers, his innate modesty, integrity and kindness of spirit that constituted the true and genuine foundation of his personality . . .

"In Parma, there were friends of Toscanini whose finances were limited. Every now and again they would receive checks from an anonymous source. For those disinherited by fortune, these checks truly represented good luck. That good luck came from none other than the Maestro, who secretly but generously came to the rescue of his friends!

"In 1921, the management of La Scala, to demonstrate their gratitude to the Maestro, gave him 100,000 *lire* as a bonus. Toscanini refused the money because he felt that he had done nothing to justify such a gesture. The managers insisted that he accept it, and in the end he gave in, but he arranged that the amount be paid into a grant to benefit the theatre and that the donor's name not be made known."

Toscanini instructed his wife to assist musicians from La Scala whenever any of them were in financial distress. And in his will, he stipulated that his wife should generously contribute to the Toscanini Institute, a fund to which he made substantial contributions to help finance health care, fresh-air camps, and educational projects for the children of La Scala's employees.

# THE REAL TOSCANINI

**CHAPTER 1**

# Toscanini Defies Mussolini and Opposes Hitler

*I would like to spit* poison *in the face of all mankind . . . I think of those poor young men who are going off, fooled or forced, to get themselves killed . . . Not for their country, but for delinquents named* Mussolini, Hitler, Stalin.
　　—Toscanini, 1937[1]

Daisaku Ikeda, Buddhist philosopher and peace activist: "Toscanini was not able to separate art from daily life. For him, pretending not to see injustice was not only stifling to his humanity but fatal to his art. When one's spirit is twisted, one's backbone is twisted as well. It was Toscanini's solid conviction that his daily actions must reflect his conscience."[2]

William Carboni, violist: "You knew that as a man he had principle and character: What he felt was right was right; and you could kill him but it would still be right . . . You knew he couldn't be pulled or swayed by management—that if NBC didn't do what he liked he'd stay home: For $6,000 a concert he'd tell them to go to hell. Someone else would be influenced by the money; but it didn't influence him; so you had respect for him—great respect for the Old Man."[3]

## Toscanini Defies Mussolini

> Toscanini, 1938: "I'll never be able to remain silent about the truth and not defend it . . . I can't exempt myself from expressing what I think . . . Everyone ought to express his own opinion honestly and courageously—then dictators, criminals, wouldn't last so long."[4]

Toscanini supported Benito Mussolini in 1919, when the politician advocated a socialist platform, but withdrew his support when Mussolini moved to the extreme right and began destroying civil liberties and resorting to violence. In 1924, Mussolini decreed that all Italian theatres were to prominently display photographs of himself and the king. Toscanini, as director of La Scala, refused to comply.

In 1928, after nearly a decade at the helm of La Scala, Toscanini became the principal conductor of the New York Philharmonic. This, combined with the difficulty of functioning freely in Mussolini's Italy, caused Toscanini to decide to stop conducting at La Scala a year later. In 1934, Mussolini offered him the directorship of the Royal Opera Theatre in Rome and general directorship of all Italian theatres. Toscanini refused.

## Bayreuth

Toscanini's love for Richard Wagner's music quickly developed in his youth. After playing cello in the 1884 Parma production of *Lohengrin*, Toscanini abandoned his ambition to be a composer—even though several of his compositions had already been published.

Wagner designed and supervised the construction of a theatre with magnificent acoustics, built for the exclusive performance of his operas, in Bayreuth, Germany. Toscanini attended performances in Bayreuth conducted by Hans Richter and Siegfried Wagner, the composer's son, in 1899 and proclaimed that Wagner was the greatest composer of the century.

Siegfried Wagner heard Toscanini conduct *Tristan und Isolde* at La Scala in 1901 and wanted to invite him to conduct at Bayreuth. It was not until 1930, however, that Siegfried overcame the opposition to engaging a non-German-school conductor. That summer, Toscanini made his Bayreuth debut, refused to accept payment, and conducted three performances of *Tristan* and five of *Tannhäuser*, both staged by Siegfried.

Lauritz Melchior, tenor: "Arturo came, as all of us, as a pilgrim. Richard Wagner was his pope—[He] came full of respect and . . . cried tears when he stepped inside the Festspielhaus . . . We saw it, and we were all full of emotion . . ."[5]

"The first rehearsal of the new *Tannhäuser* . . . had taken place while Siegfried was hospitalized, and Toscanini wept through it."[6]

Siegfried Wagner suffered a heart attack and died during the 1930 festival.

## Bologna Incident

On May 14, 1931, at the age of sixty-four, Toscanini was to have conducted two concerts in Bologna dedicated to the memory of an old friend, composer Giuseppe Martucci. He offered his services gratis. As he was about to enter the theatre before the first concert, Toscanini was attacked, beaten in the face, and injured by a group of Fascists for refusing to conduct the Fascist anthem at the event. Two days later, Mussolini ordered the confiscation of his passport. In the press, the Fascists accused Toscanini of being unpatriotic. Toscanini wrote about the beating:

> The lesson which they wanted to teach me . . . was to no avail . . . because I would repeat tomorrow what I did yesterday . . . The conduct of my life has been, is, and always will be the echo and the reflection of my conscience—reinforced by a proud and scornful character, yes, but as clear as crystal and just as cutting—always and everywhere ready to shout the truth loudly.[7]

Soon after the attack, pianist Ossip Gabrilowitsch visited the conductor, who said to Gabrilowitsch:

> Truth we must have at any price, and freedom of speech, even if that price should be death. I have said to our Fascists time and again: You can kill me if you wish, but as long as I am living I shall say what I think.

Gabrilowitsch: "He was in no way the broken man one might have expected to see. On the contrary, he was full of vigor and dynamic energy."[8]

Toscanini's telephone was wiretapped and his house was under twenty-four-hour surveillance, and it hurt the maestro that because of this, many of his friends stopped calling and visiting. Reports were given to Mussolini of the names of the friends that did continue to call and visit.

Valdengo: "When the Fascist fury unleashed itself toward him and solidarity with the maestro was judged to be an act of conspiracy against the regime, many friends stayed close to him . . . Toscanini considered friendship a sacred bond. Even here, as in the domain of his artistic activity, he didn't allow halfway measures, compromises, or mental reservations."

> Toscanini: "Protect yourself, Valdengo, from people who profess friendship, and yet when the right moment comes to demonstrate it, they will no longer be at your side. Don't bear them grudges, but don't ever again allow them into your circle of friends. Remember: Someone who has not fulfilled his duty in friendship one time will be ready to desert you again, at the first opportunity. Don't trust him again! The world is full of false friends!"

Valdengo: "After the fall of Fascism, the perpetrator of the notorious aggression suffered by Toscanini in Bologna was identified. Toscanini said to a reporter, 'I have forgotten the name of the person who offended me. I feel no ill will toward him. The responsibility of having betrayed the country, stamping out every principle of civil liberty, belongs to others, not to him.'"

## Second Visit to Bayreuth

Toscanini returned to Bayreuth in 1931 to conduct five performances of *Tannhäuser* and five of *Parsifal*. There was no festival in 1932, and in 1933, Toscanini agreed to conduct five performances of *Parsifal* and eight of *Die Meistersinger*.

However, as Adolf Hitler gained power in the early 1930s, Toscanini's moral conscience prevented him from returning to Germany. On April 1, 1933, Toscanini and eleven other prominent musicians sent a cable to Hitler that was published on the front page of the *New York Times*, protesting the boycott of Jewish musicians and the German dictator's racist policy. On April 3, Hitler wrote to Toscanini, personally inviting him to Bayreuth that summer "to thank you . . . the great representative of art and of a people friendly to Germany, for your participation in the great Master's work."[9] The next day, the conductor's recordings and broadcasts were banned by the German state radio. Toscanini sent a noncommittal response to Hitler on April 29: "It would be a bitter disappointment to me if any circumstances should interfere with my purpose to take part in the coming Festival Plays."[10] On May 28, he notified Siegfried Wagner's widow, Winifred, that he would not return to Bayreuth.

Several years later he referred to giving up Bayreuth as the "deepest sorrow" of his life.[11] He never set foot in Germany again.

## Vienna Philharmonic

Toscanini's refusal to return to Bayreuth attracted worldwide attention. He knew that by performing in non-Nazi Austria, he could make a stronger protest against Hitler. Thus, in 1933, Toscanini accepted a long-standing invitation to conduct the Vienna Philharmonic, with which he worked until 1937.

Toscanini loved conducting this orchestra in Salzburg during the summers of 1934 to 1937. He paid to attend other conductors' concerts, purchased tickets for his family and friends, and contributed his own money toward the reconstruction of a theatre in Salzburg.

## Palestine Orchestra

When the Polish violinist Bronisław Huberman founded the Palestine Orchestra, composed of Jewish refugee musicians who had escaped persecution, he asked Toscanini to conduct a benefit concert in New York for the new orchestra. Toscanini decided to travel to Palestine in December of 1936, train the orchestra, and conduct the first concerts of what later became known as the Israel Philharmonic. The news of Toscanini's plans attracted more musicians to join the orchestra and resulted in very successful fund-raising for the new venture. Toscanini stayed for more than a month, and refused to accept a fee or reimbursement for his travel expenses. It was his conviction that everyone had a responsibility to help, according to one's means.

The dress rehearsal for the first concert was open to artists and workers. "The public's response was one of overwhelming emotion. The president of the Hebrew

University broke into uncontrollable tears."[12] There were nine sold-out concerts in Tel Aviv, Jerusalem, and Haifa, and concerts in Cairo and Alexandria. In Tel Aviv, crowds stood outside near the windows and some people even climbed onto the roof attempting to hear. At the end of the first concert, the ovation lasted for more than thirty minutes.

Toscanini was very interested in the extramusical affairs of Palestine. In addition to rehearsing the Palestine Orchestra and conducting its inaugural concerts, Toscanini expressed his humanitarianism through bonding with the Jewish refugees.

He was enthusiastic to see Palestine's potash plants and agricultural settlements. He visited Bethlehem, Nazareth, the *kibbutzim* and experimental farms. He attended a Passover feast, a Seder, and visited the Hebrew University where he attended a lecture on Hebrew literature. When he asked his chauffeur why he seemed depressed, Toscanini was told that because his wife was expecting their baby, she was unable to attend the concerts. In response, the Toscaninis visited the young couple at their home.

In his first weeks in Palestine, Toscanini experienced what he called "a continuous exultation of the soul."[13] He called it the land of miracles, where Jews who had been doctors, lawyers, and engineers in Germany had become farmers who transformed sand dunes into olive and orange groves. Toscanini was given a piece of land upon which a common-house dedicated to him was to be built.

He went twice to Ramot HaShavim.* "The farmers were overjoyed to be able to present Mrs. Toscanini with a basket of eggs from their henhouses . . . The Toscaninis and Huberman planted trees on this piece of land at a special ceremony, and school children sang folk songs and children's songs for them. Toscanini said it was difficult for him to speak because of the power of the impressions he had received, and Signora Carla wept openly."[14] Carla Toscanini wrote to their daughter, Wanda: "When we left we were both crying. If you stop to think of what they have achieved through sheer labor, it is nothing short of miraculous."[15]

Because of the many music lovers who couldn't procure tickets to the concerts, Toscanini opened some rehearsals to the public at a small admission charge for charity. Upon arriving at the venue for the public rehearsal thirty minutes early, he was surprised to find no one outside entering the hall. The audience had arrived before; the hall was packed to capacity. Children were in the arms of their parents. The quiet and interest of the audience almost caused him to weep.

---

* Established in 1933, Ramot HaShavim was the first agricultural community to be founded in Israel by immigrants from Germany.

## Salzburg Festival and Break with Furtwängler

The 1937 Salzburg Festival marked Toscanini's last performances with the Vienna Philharmonic. Toscanini deliberately conducted Mendelssohn's music there, which had been banned in Germany because the composer was a Jew. The Salzburg performances were to have been broadcast in Germany, while performances at Bayreuth were to have been broadcast in Austria. However, the broadcasts of Bruno Walter's performances from Salzburg were canceled because he was a Jew. Toscanini implored Walter to leave Austria for his own safety. The Nazis also prohibited singers who were scheduled to sing in Toscanini's Salzburg productions from leaving Germany.

Toscanini and Wilhelm Furtwängler have often been misunderstood to be musical opposites. In reality, their conducting could at times be strikingly similar—including the way they performed Wagner. Toscanini demonstrated respect and high esteem for his colleague's work by inviting Furtwängler to conduct at La Scala in 1923 and recommending Furtwängler as his successor when he resigned from the New York Philharmonic in 1936. Toscanini broke with Furtwängler in 1937 because of the latter's decision to remain in Germany and conduct for the Nazis, including Hitler. During their last encounter in Salzburg that summer, Toscanini said to him, "In London you lunch with Jews to make a good case for yourself so that you won't lose your position in the West. In Germany, you work for Hitler."[16]

Harvey Sachs, author: "Toscanini told him, in effect, that he should not expect to be able to keep one foot in Nazi Germany and the other in the free world."[17]

Toscanini referred to Furtwängler as "that opportunist" because he chose to conduct under the Nazi banner.[18]

Toscanini had planned to conduct a concert at Carnegie Hall for the benefit of the Salzburg Festival on March 4, 1938. However, on February 16, he announced that the concert's beneficiaries would be the Unemployed Musicians Fund in New York and the Casa di Riposo, the rest home in Milan for aged musicians and singers, founded by Verdi. On the same day, he cabled the director of the Salzburg Festival: "The current political events in Austria oblige me to renounce my Salzburg participation."[19]

Gaetano Salvemini, anti-Fascist politician and historian, wrote to Toscanini on February 18, 1938: "You are the only one who, at those important moments when we were lost in the darkness of despair, shouted words of faith, duty, and hope at us."[20]

One week after the concert, the formation of an Austrian National Socialist government was announced, and a day later, Hitler's troops entered Vienna. Toscanini was so enraged that he couldn't contain his frustration and stormed out of that day's rehearsal at NBC, locking himself in his dressing room. "There he barred the door to his family and friends. He threw scores on the floor, turned over chairs, kicked the table, tore at his clothes, and wept. For hours he went through this solitary lamentation."[21]

## Second Visit to Palestine

Toscanini planned a second series of concerts with the Palestine Orchestra in 1938. Huberman and Chaim Weizmann—who later became the first president of Israel—tried to convince him to cancel this visit, explaining that conditions had worsened and that there was increased danger of an Arab attack. Undeterred and convinced that his visit would greatly encourage the young Jewish refugees, Toscanini returned to Palestine in April, again at his own expense. Fortunately, Toscanini and his wife escaped a bomb thrown at their car.

The Toscaninis returned to the agricultural village of Ramot HaShavim, where a piece of land had been dedicated to him during his first visit in 1936. Upon their return to Ramot HaShavim, they wept when they were given oranges from this plot. Every year thereafter, a basket of oranges was sent to Toscanini on his birthday.

He conducted the two *Lohengrin* preludes despite the fact that the music of Wagner, a self-proclaimed anti-Semite, had been banned.

While Toscanini was in Palestine, Italy announced its anti-Semitic policy, adopting German racial laws that deprived Jews of their citizenship. He referred to the new policy as "medieval stuff."[22]

At a banquet given by the orchestra the end of his visit, Toscanini told the musicians: "Thank you all my dears. I was happy here." He encouraged them to maintain the highest musical standards and expectations, saying: "Don't be satisfied with yourselves."[23]

## Establishment of the Lucerne Festival

When Austria was absorbed into the German Reich, Toscanini abandoned Salzburg for Switzerland and inaugurated the Lucerne Festival during the summer of 1938. The orchestra was comprised of Jewish musicians expelled by Hitler and Mussolini and others who joined them in solidarity. The concerts were held as benefits for the musicians, and Toscanini refused to accept a fee. In the summer of 1939, he returned to the Lucerne Festival, where, on August 29, he conducted his final performance in Europe until after World War II.

## Frustration and Despair over the Tyranny of Mussolini and Hitler

Toscanini placed inestimable value on truth, freedom of speech, and spiritual and moral independence. He often spoke out against Mussolini, calling him a tyrant and a criminal. Toscanini's home was placed under twenty-four-hour police surveillance; a list was made of his visitors, including vehicle license plate numbers. Incoming and outgoing mail of the conductor and his family was opened. Italians who wrote him letters had their homes entered and searched. His phone was tapped and his conversations were recorded. Threats were made that his property would be seized, and in 1931 his passport was confiscated.

However, this did not stop Toscanini from freely speaking out against the tyrant, even when it meant risking his life. Toscanini's passport was again confiscated by order of Mussolini in 1938. This time, when it was returned, Toscanini left Italy and did not return until after World War II.

Toscanini realized that he wouldn't be able to continue living in Italy under Mussolini's reign. And no one could predict for how long the regime would remain in power. He considered the possibility that he might not ever again see his beloved Italy "fearfully horrible."[24]

One month after leaving Italy, Toscanini conducted Tchaikovsky's "Pathétique" Symphony in New York. He wrote about how the tragic theme in the last movement brought his emotions to the surface: "I wept like a *man in despair* . . . I couldn't contain myself. Tears flooded my face."[25]

By 1938, Toscanini refused to conduct in Italy, Austria, and Germany. Instead, he conducted in France, Belgium, Denmark, Holland, Sweden, Switzerland, England, the United States, and Palestine.

Howard Taubman, author and critic: "Though he no longer conducted in Italy, he watched events there with pain and shame. He felt personally humiliated when La Scala played a joyous *Aida* on the day Italy attacked Ethiopia. He suffered when his cherished theatre [performed *Aida*] to celebrate Hitler's visit to Italy to meet Mussolini. And in 1940, when Italy launched its jackal invasion of France, Toscanini, who was on route to South America, locked himself up in his cabin, and in a frenzy of grief tore at his clothes and wept."[26]

When France surrendered to Germany a week later, Toscanini sat in his cabin moaning, refusing to eat or to see the musicians. After returning from the tour of South America with the NBC Symphony, Toscanini wrote:

> While millions and millions of beings are being swept away . . . I sit here, a ridiculous spectator, with my hands folded, sighing, hating . . .[27]

A month later, he wrote:

> I feel so humiliated to be a useless tool at this moment that I'm ashamed of the air I breathe![28]

Toscanini's mood worsened in the fall of 1940 as the Nazis began bombing London in September, when Hitler and Mussolini met in October, and as the Germans massacred the Jews of Warsaw in November.

> Life no longer holds any interest for me, and I would pray God to take it from me if it weren't for my firm, *never-diminished hope* to see the *delinquents* swept off the face of the earth before I go . . .[29]

On July 19, 1942, he conducted the American premiere of Dmitri Shostakovich's Seventh Symphony ("Leningrad"). Known as a symbol of resistance to Hitler's invasion of Russia and the nine-hundred-day Siege of Leningrad (now Saint Petersburg), it became a musical testament to the millions of victims who lost their lives.

Toscanini conducted numerous benefit concerts gratis during World War II in support of—or made donations to—Italian welfare societies, U.S. Government war bonds, U.S. Treasury bond drives, Roosevelt Hospital, the National Foundation for Infantile Paralysis, and the Paris-based Giustizia e Libertà. On April 25, 1943, over ten million dollars in bonds were sold at one concert. At a benefit concert for the Red Cross with the New York Philharmonic in November 1942, he gave a signed blank check to the orchestra's management to ensure that a minimum of $20,000 would be raised. Another concert for the Red Cross in Madison Square Garden raised more than $100,000. At the benefit concerts, he always insisted on paying for a box for his family.

Toscanini made a strict distinction between the Fascist party and the citizens of his beloved Italy, who were victims of Mussolini's barbaric reign. The editorial page of the September 13, 1943, edition of *Life* magazine was an open letter from Toscanini, "To the People of America." It was originally intended as a letter to President Roosevelt and reads in part:

> Do not forget that we Italians have been the first to endure the oppression of a tyrannical gang of criminals, supported by that "fainthearted and degenerate King" of Italy*—but that we have never willingly submitted to them. Countless thousands of men and women in Italy shed blood, met imprisonment and death, striving fiercely against that horde of criminals, enduring also the apathy and indifference of the world then full of admiration for Mussolini.[30]

## Return to La Scala after World War II

Ikeda wrote: "It was the warrior of art who triumphed in the end. Mussolini was eventually executed, his body hung upside down from a tall pillar on Milan's central plaza. A year later, the seventy-nine-year-old Toscanini led a victory performance at the wonderfully restored La Scala."[31]

When La Scala's orchestra invited Toscanini to return home, he donated one million *lire* toward the reconstruction of the theatre, which had been bombed during the war, and insisted that the Jewish musicians who lost their jobs at La Scala in 1938 be reinstated, including the chorus director, Vittore Veneziani. He returned to Italy in 1946.

At the reopening of the opera house, Toscanini suggested that a group of old musicians from the Verdi Rest Home sit in the former Royal Box.

The program was a marathon!

---

* Reference to Shakespeare's *Henry VI*.

Rossini:
  *La gazza ladra*: Overture
  *Guillaume Tell*:
      Act 1: "Coro dell'Imeneo" ("Cinto il crine di bei fiori")
      Act 1: "Passo a sei"
      Act 3: "Passo dei soldati"
  *Mosè in Egitto*: "Preghiera, 'Dal tuo stellato soglio'"

Verdi:
  *Nabucco*:
      Overture
      "Va, pensiero, sull'ali dorate" (Chorus of Hebrew Slaves)
  *I vespri siciliani*: Overture
  Te Deum

Intermission

Puccini:
  *Manon Lescaut*: Act 3

Boito:
  *Mefistofele*: Prologue

The concert was broadcast live throughout Italy, and via shortwave throughout the world. The ovation at its conclusion lasted thirty-seven minutes. Finally reunited with his audience and orchestra at La Scala after the lengthy years of exile, Toscanini considered the concert to have been the most moving moment of his career.[32]

Renata Tebaldi, soprano, remembered that the entire audience was in tears, as were the singers.[33]

Ikeda: "The war was over at last! Art and culture were finally triumphant! The excitement of the victory concert reached a crescendo when Toscanini conducted 'Va, pensiero, sull'ali dorate' (Fly! Thought, on golden wings). Not only the chorus but the whole audience joined in singing. Those standing in the aisles sang. Outside, crowded in the Piazza della Scala, the Piazza del Duomo, and the Galleria arcade,

20,000 citizens unable to fit in the opera house sang too, accompanying the voices being broadcast over loudspeakers.

"'Fly! Thought, on golden wings.' In these thoughts—thoughts of love for others, of love for one's country, of love for peace—there is no distinction between east and west, there is no distinction between old and new. For these eternal thoughts of humanity to soar, they require the golden wings of art . . .

"To give these thoughts expression, the word *effort* does not suffice—no, it requires the will 'to fight.'"[34]

# CHAPTER 2

# Inner Power and Charisma

*When I came onstage to play and heard the music and saw the man conducting, my jaw dropped; I couldn't close it. I could hardly play because of the grandeur of the sound. I was bewildered. It was the most wonderful thing I ever heard in my life.*
—**Michael Krasnopolsky**

Many of the performers spoke of having dramatic reactions to their first encounter with Toscanini.

Civetta: "When did you first hear Toscanini?"
Arthur Lora, principal flutist, NBC Symphony: "It was in the late twenties. I remember particularly my reaction to his New York Philharmonic broadcast of Ravel's *Boléro*. The crescendo and rhythmic impact was such that before it ended I found myself stamping savagely around my living room in sympathy with the music. It was intoxicating—almost frenzied."

## Musicians' First Rehearsals with Toscanini

In 1937, the National Broadcasting Company assembled a first-rate orchestra for Toscanini, which he conducted primarily in live radio broadcasts until his retirement in 1954.

David Walter, bass player: "When I joined, we had eight bass players, six of whom had left the first chair of other orchestras to join the NBC Orchestra. In our violin section we had many erstwhile concertmasters and so on."

Alan Shulman was a young cellist who played at Toscanini's first rehearsal with the orchestra: "Oh, we were geared. We were like racehorses that had been trained and ready for the race. And there was electricity in the air. Maestro came in and said, 'Brahms,' and we went to work on the C Minor Symphony. We were all just dumbfounded by the dynamism of the man, the electricity, and the fact that every part of his body lived and breathed music. He was an incredibly energetic man."

Paul Winter, violinist, was also at that first rehearsal: "I found the very first time I played with him that I reached levels I had never known before. Near the end of the last movement of the Brahms First Symphony there's a tremendous climax. He kept building until you thought you'd never get a bigger climax, and he just kept going until we reached this absolutely hair-raising climax. This happened almost every week; you'd get a chill almost every week. The only trouble was that it spoiled me for the rest of my life for every other conductor. Nobody came close to Toscanini, not even Bruno Walter, who was so famous for Mozart. He never gave us the thrill that Toscanini gave us in Mozart."

Mischa Mischakoff was the NBC Symphony's concertmaster from 1937 to 1952. In the early months of working with Toscanini, Mischakoff commented: "His energy is boundless. Although he is seventy-one years of age, he is stronger and more vigorous than most men in their prime. He is slight in build, with delicate sensibilities, yet I defy any man to drive a great orchestra as he does, to inspire it to such heights of perfection and musical grandeur."[1]

Toscanini was delighted with this new, youthful, virtuoso orchestra.

Mischakoff: "I must say the Maestro appreciates the strings because he invariably chooses, for each concert, one work to show them off to advantage. Words can hardly express the deep satisfaction it gives me, and all of us. He has been most appreciative of the organization. He has said 'bravo' to us a number of times and he has been sympathetic, patient, and so constructive in his criticism that the most experienced men consider it the highest privilege to work with him. WHAT imagination he has!"[2]

When an orchestra played up to its own potential, Toscanini immediately demonstrated his respect and appreciation with incredible energy and enthusiasm.

When he guest conducted Walter Legge's Philharmonia Orchestra in London in 1952 for a Brahms cycle, he was so pleased that he conducted straight through one of the symphonies at the first rehearsal, making only two small corrections between movements.

## Additional First Impressions

Starting at the beginning of the second season in 1938, three brothers— Arthur, Harry, and Jack Berv—transferred from the French horn section of the Philadelphia Orchestra under Leopold Stokowski to the NBC Symphony to play with Toscanini.

Harry Berv: "From that very first moment we knew that we were in the presence of a really great master. I was young at the time, and I'm sorry that I was, because I wish I had been older and more mature to realize in whose presence I was. Every rehearsal, every performance was a great experience."

Civetta: "Do you remember your first impression?"
Frank Brieff, conductor and violist: "Well, it was shattering, because I remember we were doing the 'Eroica' Symphony. The impact of that man's personality, his enormous faith, his great feeling of what the music should really sound like was, to me, one of the great thrills of my life. I had chills running down my back in the slow movement, where the basses come in with that tremendous *fortissimo*. It was like a bomb explosion to me. I'll never forget the shattering impact that 'Funeral March' made on me. And this is the way I always was under Maestro."

Michael Krasnopolsky, double bass player, recalled his first rehearsal with Toscanini: "When I came onstage to play and heard the music and saw the man conducting, my jaw dropped; I couldn't close it. I could hardly play because of the grandeur of the sound. I was bewildered. It was the most wonderful thing I ever heard in my life. I never heard such sounds and I was never so inspired, from that first moment to the last moment of my playing with him. It was the greatest opportunity for any musician to be there to witness the enthusiasm, the love and the cooperation of the musicians. It was a great exaltation. It was the greatest experience in my musical life."

## Audience Reaction, Electricity

Toscanini's impact on audiences was also electrifying.

H. Berv: "He had tremendous charisma. You could tell right away that there was something electric up there. There was such a dynamic, electric quality about this man, that when he walked out on the stage the audience knew it. It was concentration right to that one point."

Edwin Bachmann, principal second violinist, NBC Symphony: "Other conductors don't have this electricity. They don't have this natural outburst of music."

A. Shulman, to Haggin: "The electrifying, incisive rhythm is something you don't hear today. I've heard musicians talk about Furtwängler; and I've heard his old recording of Tchaikovsky's 'Pathétique' with the Berlin Philharmonic, which is very beautiful. But the tempos are a bit on the slow side; so I don't feel the excitement of the march in the third movement. Whereas, my God, when Toscanini finished that movement you'd want to jump out of your seat, and the audience always broke out into applause—they couldn't help it: It was electrifying. And it didn't run away."[3]

A. Shulman, to Civetta: "He had the audience roaring even though the fourth movement was coming up and he would have to quiet them down. He'd hold his hands up but to no avail. They'd start screaming and applauding because he lifted the audience right out of their seats. I will never forget the march of the 'Pathétique.'"

George Koutzen, cellist: "It's impossible for me to convince people of how much electricity Toscanini was able to generate in the orchestra, in the audience, in the whole thing—it was just complete excitement. I remember on the 1950 transcontinental tour when we went down south and played 'Dixie' as an encore. Wow! That really brought down the house. I can still feel the electricity in the air. A little thing like that—they went wild."

A. Shulman, recalling Toscanini's 1940 tour of South America with the NBC Symphony: "When we got there, the Latins went wild; they went absolutely wild. It was almost frightening to hear that kind of an ovation from the audience because the Latins are not afraid to show their emotions and they screamed and I thought the roof would come off."

Winter: "What we will never see again is the drama he created. I have never seen an audience react that way to a performance. People would jump up out of their chairs and scream like they were at a prizefight. A roar would go up at the end of a piece. No conductor has that hold on an audience today. I think that's something we will never see again. If you see another Beethoven, maybe you'll see another Toscanini."

Joseph Novotny, tuba player: "A Toscanini performance became an emotional experience not only for the musicians, but the audience itself became involved. He was so totally involved, so you were in the orchestra and the audience also. They actually participated in the performance without being aware of the fact. That's why they reacted the way they did at the conclusion of these performances."

## Off the Podium and Eye Contact

Remo Bolognini, violinist and conductor, was the assistant concertmaster of the New York Philharmonic with Toscanini for four years in the 1930s and the third assistant concertmaster of the NBC Symphony for the seventeen years of its existence. He said of Toscanini: "First of all, he had—electricity, a dynamic. When the orchestra and the artists knew he was in the audience at a concert or an opera, it changed the atmosphere."

Robert Bloom, principal oboist, NBC Symphony, 1937–1943: "He did have an aura about him. He just wasn't 'one of the boys.'"

Robert Hupka, photographer: "The first time I saw him face to face was in Salzburg. The Maestro was walking through the city, and it was like the expression, 'God is walking through the woods,' because the traffic stopped; everybody stood still and simply stared. The greatness of that man was radiating all around."

Frank Guarrera, baritone: "He did something very interesting with his eyes and face: When he talked to you, I never saw him look away. He looked right at you, like he was hypnotized. And it didn't make you feel ill at ease at all. You just felt that this communication was there with this man at all times, even in a social way, even when he wasn't talking about music."

Gabor Carelli, tenor: "He was completely interested in what you had to say in that moment, and went from eye to eye. You were convinced that he was 100 percent involved in that conversation."

## Magnetism

Harry Glantz, who played principal trumpet with Toscanini for twenty-two years: "He would inject himself into the orchestra and it was like a magnet. I mean you just couldn't help giving. He had that magnet in his baton. He would draw the gift that you were endowed with out of you."[4]

Lotte Lehmann, soprano, recalled the effect Toscanini had on baritone Hermann Nissen during the general rehearsal of *Die Meistersinger* at Salzburg in 1936. Nissen, according to Lehmann, had a calm personality and was not easily carried away by emotion. "Even this man was stirred to his very depths by the great Maestro. I can still see him, his eyes overflowing with tears, as he turned around after the 'Wach auf' chorus in the general rehearsal, saying, 'My God, how shall I be able to sing now? This damned demon down there has absolutely devastated me with his fire.'"[5]

Giuseppe De Luca, baritone, in conversation with Valdengo: "Tell me the truth, Valdengo: Toscanini must have in himself something magnetic that transmits to the performers, while instructing and conducting."
Valdengo: "Dear De Luca, it is really so: An aura emanates from his being, making you do what he wants."
    Valdengo elaborated further: "During performances, in the moment in which one had to overcome difficult passages, Toscanini concentrated and stared hard at us, as though he wanted to transfuse to us all the force of his thought and feeling. At those times, we perceived something like an aura that emanated from him. In particular, I had the exact impression in those moments that the maestro succeeded

in making me do what he wanted, and I always had a single and great conviction: 'With Toscanini I can't make a mistake; he will guide me and everything will go well.' Singing with him, I was always conscious of this truth, which comforted and tranquilized me in the most difficult moments."

Brieff: "There issued from that man a magnetism that went to the orchestra, and from the players to the audience, and everyone felt it. It was a great era. He was a mesmerizer."

Sylvan Shulman, violinist: "There was a magical quality about him that I don't think anybody is able to put their finger on, but, by God, you were transported to another world. It was really heavenly."

Civetta: "How did he compare with the conductors of his own generation?"
Harold Coletta, violist: "The other ones I knew of his generation were Stokowski, Bruno Walter, Monteux, Koussevitzky, Rodzinski, and Reiner—I played under all of them. Toscanini soared above all of them. There was a certain spirit and personality in Toscanini, just like when you see a film, and someone who has an outstanding personality enters the scene, and you're mesmerized. The Old Man had that magnetic quality, not only because of his handsomeness, but because of the respect you had for what he knew, and also his fervor and love for the music.

"This man had an undying passion for music from the time he was first exposed to it, and it sustained him into living to age eighty-nine. I equate this passion with a man like Stradivarius, who lived to be ninety-three, when the average person lived thirty-three, thirty-four years. And I feel Michelangelo—all the great ones, were absorbed in their work, and so impassioned with their work that they lived almost forever, because they were married to their art. They were sustained by it. They couldn't wait to get up in the morning to tackle their work, and Toscanini was always studying and restudying scores."

S. Shulman: "When that man stood up, that profile of his, that beat of his, that elegance created elegance in your playing. There was an excitement. There was something in the physical makeup of Toscanini that very few people can match. I don't know of any other conductor that can match that. For example, Solti is certainly a marvelous conductor, but if you watch him you do not get the feeling of excitement that you got with Toscanini."

## Fire and Charisma

Arthur Berv: "He'd get the orchestra to play with such fire that it was unbelievable."

David Sarser, violinist: "The first time we did the Verdi Requiem was the most exciting. In the Dies Irae, whatever hair you had went to the ceiling."

Emanuel Vardi, violist: "I was very young and very much in awe of him. It was like God walked out, you know. I found out subsequently that he was a human being, but that he had all the attributes of a big leader, a great leader. A conductor has to have not only the knowledge but he's got to have that charisma, that something that makes a hundred or a thousand people do the same thing at the same time. And he had it. When he came down with the beat it was something that pulled that orchestra together; there wasn't any question of what he wanted."

## Outdoing Themselves

The artists' perception of experiencing levels of achievement with Toscanini above what they imagined to be possible is a common theme throughout many of the interviews.

H. Berv: "He knew exactly how to get the best out of all of his musicians and I don't think there's anyone today [1976] on the scene that could do a thing like this."

Carelli: "Maestro Toscanini used to say, '*Io faccio cantare pure cane!*' (I can even make a dog sing!) He thought that his suggestive powers would bring out really the best, better than what you ever thought you could do."

Jarmila Novotná, soprano, said in an interview for the film *Toscanini: The Maestro*, produced and directed by Peter Rosen: "There was some magic in it because everybody tried to give his best, and everybody was better. And that's why all the performances were so fantastic. That was his genius."[6]

Ray Crisara, trumpet player: "Invariably, your effort would be to play as well as you possibly could, just because of the atmosphere he would create. You sensed that this man could draw from you as much as you could possibly give to him. I would assume that many of the others have said to you that numerous times, they played really above what they normally would play, just through his inspiration."

Guarrera: "He made you sing better than you thought you could. He would bring the best out of everyone. He had this magic about him. He would almost hypnotize you into performing better than you knew how."

Sarser: "No words were necessary. You just played and he seemed to draw things out of you that you never could do alone. He made you play better than you could play when he wasn't there. He was the greatest teacher I ever had."

Bachmann: "He was the only one who made you play better and always more beautifully than you thought you were able to do. He brought out this hidden talent and expression in you. No other conductor was able to reach that height."

A. Berv: "He had the magnetism. There was something about this man, that you'd have to give more than you were able to give. You could never relax. If you had any musicianship in your body, you could sense that the man was giving everything of himself and you'd have to give that much or more. The performances always seemed to have the utmost magnetism, fire—never a dull moment."

Selig Posner, violist: "He had the uncanny ability to inspire the musicians; he had the ability to bring out that tremendous excitement. If you had to play with vibrato, if he vibrated a little bit, you were going to vibrate twice as fast.* One of the big reasons was, in conducting—great conducting—you have to be everything: a great actor, a great musician, a great scholar. He had everything. He had a fascinating face, a kind of face that if you looked at him and saw he was so involved, you just couldn't help responding if you had anything in you. That's what happened; most of us responded to his face, his gestures, his manner, to his whole personality, a fantastic personality."

Felix Galimir, violinist: "I really have played with most of the so-called great conductors of that time: Furtwängler, Walter, and Klemperer. With every conductor

---

* Toscanini sometimes vibrated a finger of his left hand held against his chest as if playing the cello—a gesture that reminded string players to vibrate or vibrate more.

there were great moments, and maybe one conductor did this particular piece better than the others. But I would say the greatest experience of playing with a conductor was with Toscanini. There was something that electrified you to the point where you had the feeling you played better than you can play. It was really an unusual experience to play with him. No matter what instrument or where you were playing, if there's anything that anybody will tell you—and this is the great thing about Toscanini, aside from interpretation—it's that he made the players play better than they played. With his own enthusiasm for music, he could inspire every single player to play better than he actually would play normally, which was a wonderful thing. You went off the stage and said, 'Ah! Today I really played well!'"

Civetta: "This happened often?"

Galimir: "Every time you played with him! Usually you didn't play that well when you were by yourself. You felt that way; you gave always your utmost best."

The film *Toscanini: The Maestro*, directed by Peter Rosen, has the following statement by Herva Nelli, soprano: "You achieved something that you probably wouldn't with any other person. He had ways of getting things out of the artist which others couldn't do."[7]

Mortimer Frank: "How did he enable individual members of the orchestra to play better than they knew they were capable of playing?"

Raoul Poliakine, violinist: "His sheer personality—he was in the music. You felt he was so sincere, and he knew his music, and he knew exactly what he wanted to get out of everyone, and you had give it to him, otherwise he wouldn't be satisfied. You felt you had to do your best, and with Toscanini I felt I gave 120 percent."

Frank: "How would you compare Toscanini with Bruno Walter?"

Poliakine: "It was less impelling with Walter. He was a great man, a great conductor, a nice man; but the performance was less impelling. You didn't give 120 percent. And yet you knew he was a great conductor, a great musician. But it's the personality of the conductor that reflects the reaction of an orchestra. The sheer force of a conductor—that's what determines the reaction of an orchestra. Like Mitropoulos: a great musician, tremendous musician, but the orchestra sounded really bad because he didn't have the personality. Toscanini was the strongest-willed man I ever worked for. Stokowski and Reiner could get tremendous results out of an orchestra, but Toscanini had an edge over them as far as getting from an orchestra what he wanted."[8]

Frank Falcone, trumpet player: "He brought out the good in a lot of mediocre musicians. There were a couple of passages in a work played by one of the basses, which just awed everybody. This man, who was considered a mediocre player, sounded like he never sounded again. Toscanini brought everything he had out of him, and Toscanini just took it for granted. It was just as if somebody touched him on the shoulder and said, 'Here, play this, and play it good.' It sounded fantastic. This was something."

Glantz: "Each rehearsal was like a wonderful concert. He absolutely captivated not only the audiences but also the musicians. Sometimes I'd come home from a concert and say to my wife, 'I never dreamt I could play the way I played tonight.' He drew it out of me. He had that gift that no other conductor in the world that I have ever played with had—to be able to instill in you his passion, his love, his gift and fire of music. That's why every orchestra he ever conducted sounded so fantastic."[9]

Brieff: "There was never a dull moment. In fact, there was never a moment in all the years I played with him that I did not thrill and learn. Oh Lord, did I learn! The aura surrounding this master—I thought that maybe this thing would wear off, but it never did. As time went on, and I played more and more with him, I was always astounded and amazed and thrilled. My wife always tells the story that it took me a few days after I came home from rehearsals or concerts to get down to earth. You played like a demon for this guy. I don't know why, but I reacted to it, and a lot of my colleagues did, too. You just dug into your instrument and played as if your life depended on it. And this is the difference between the excitement he got out of an orchestra vis-à-vis other conductors. He was a magician. At rehearsals, he was always a demon, demanding things, impossible things. But he also demanded impossible things from himself."

Bachmann: "Once when Toscanini was rehearsing the Philadelphia Orchestra as a guest conductor, I was listening to the rehearsal with the orchestra's conductor, Eugene Ormandy, who turned to me and said, 'Eddie, tell me. Is this my orchestra? Because if it is, I don't want to talk to them. If they can play for him like that, why can't they play for me like that?'"

Krasnopolsky: "He made all of us rise above what we thought we were. Usually I have to practice two hours a day. I practiced three hours a day to make sure that I wouldn't get in trouble."

## Personal Force

Brieff: "When the Maestro got up on that stage, you knew there was a great master there, and you paid all the attention in the world to everything he said and did."

Robert Shaw, conductor: "He was possessed enough of this arching sound dream, from this instant until whenever it stopped, that he had enough psychic energy to carry people along with him."

Jascha Bernstein, cellist: "He comes in, and the man has this fantastic power which goes over you, terrific projection power."

## Hypnotic

Bachmann: "The moment he came down with the baton he electrified the orchestra. But he also electrified the audience. He hypnotized them like he hypnotized himself. It was a self-hypnosis."

Hupka: "Watching the Maestro, it was magnetism, hypnotism, call it what you want. It was just beauty that completely captivated you."

David Weber, clarinetist: "Sometimes, I was playing in spite of myself. Did I actually play it? Did it actually happen? Did I do it? It seemed that he would hypnotize you to a certain extent, that you became so involved with what you were doing."

Civetta: "What was his most outstanding attribute?"
Lora: "As a personality, his tremendous charisma, the basic sexuality of the man. He was simply hypnotic."

Galimir: "This is one of the few things that a conductor must have. He must have a good ear. He must have personality and musicality, etc. But he also has to have something with which to fascinate or almost hypnotize the players. He had something that almost hypnotized the players, which was sometimes quite scary, I must say. When he looked at you in a mad way, it was not too comfortable."

Brieff: "When he got up to conduct, he held you in such a grip that you were almost enslaved by this tremendous man. He imposed a will on you, a will that you were certainly accepting. When you were under that spell, nothing else mattered in the world but to do that, and listen to that, and to feel that you had experienced some of the most beautiful moments in your life."

Some of the musicians stated that they felt taken outside of themselves.

Sol Schoenbach, principal bassoonist, Philadelphia Orchestra: "I was carried away almost to the point where I'd forget to come in and play."[10]

Weber: "Sometimes I felt I was playing out of myself. It seemed like when you were playing for him, you were so carried away or so mesmerized by his conducting, that you were listening to yourself rather than feeling that you were doing it. It was hair-raising. Every concert was an experience."

Joseph Gingold, violinist: "My wife likes to tell the story about the day I had some bug and wasn't feeling well enough to go to a rehearsal, but there was something on the program that I wanted to play, so I said: 'I'll bundle up and go, and I'll play that one piece and then come right home.' I went there feverish and in no condition really to play; but once the Maestro began the rehearsal, I became so absorbed in what we were doing that I forgot I was sick, I forgot about myself entirely; and at the end of the rehearsal I was feeling completely well. This was the effect Toscanini had: When you were playing with him your mind never wandered for one moment; you were completely absorbed in music-making and at one with him and with the composer."[11]

Lehmann: "I shall forever remember the feeling of intoxication and utter abandon as I sang the last words of Isolde . . . The music was like an overpowering surf, in which I sang, lost in the splendor of sound. And so I feel that the overpowering strength of his magical personality is akin to the power of the ocean."[12]

# Inspiration

Krasnopolsky: "No human language can adequately describe the exultation and inspiration felt by the musicians who played under his leadership."

J. Bernstein: "I remember once we had a recording session. He was standing there with his white handkerchief around his neck like a Rembrandt picture. It was fantastic! Not everybody's so inspired by music, but when they looked at this face, they had to play."

Brieff: "The man's eternal search for the truth in music is one of the things that I shall forever carry with me, and it inspired me in many ways. It gave me a tremendous goal to strive for."

Civetta: "A lot of people have spoken about an electricity or magnetism about him. Did you feel this yourself?"
Crisara: "Oh, very much, very much! That was part of the privilege of being there. I remember sitting in the orchestra many times, just having goose flesh, because of the sounds that were coming out and the way things were being shaped and everything else. It was an extraordinary thing. I played for a lot of conductors. I can't think of anybody that has inspired me to a like degree."

# CHAPTER 3

# Work

*I shall tell you my secret: All my life I have been studying scores.*
—Toscanini

## Practicing Outside of Rehearsals

Manoug Parikian was the concertmaster for Toscanini's all-Brahms concerts in 1952 with the Philharmonia Orchestra in London. He remembered a most unusual occurrence: twenty minutes before the first rehearsal, 90–95 percent of the musicians were already seated, tuned, and ready to begin.[1]

Galimir recalled a Toscanini rehearsal with the Vienna Philharmonic in 1933: "We heard in the conservatory that it was something special, so we tried to sneak into the rehearsals, and I got into one. And before the rehearsal—this was an historic event—all the violinists of the Vienna Philharmonic were actually practicing their part—which had never happened since Gustav Mahler left!"[2]

D. Walter, to Civetta: "Even the most expert orchestra musicians became more alert and sensitive playing with him."

D. Walter, to Haggin: "Even for a good conductor whom he respects and likes, the average player does about 50 percent of what he is capable of; but with Toscanini you felt you had to do your best every moment . . .

"Actually you did more than your best for Toscanini: He got you to extend yourself, so that however well you played, with him you found yourself playing better. In Rossini's overture to *Cenerentola* there is a fast passage for the basses that is extremely difficult to finger; and in most performances one or two men may make an enormous effort and play it accurately; but with Toscanini the section played it perfectly, and in his faster tempo."[3]

Civetta: "Why did one play beyond one's ability?"
D. Walter: "You played beyond the limit of your ability—out of fear of his knowledge and fear of his anger, but also out of fear of not fulfilling yourself. It was the thought that he studied that work, by God, for the last two weeks, night after night, even though he had done it a thousand times before; the least you could do was to take your music home and study. I think that not ever in symphony history did so many musicians take their parts home to practice. Partly, it was a fear of incurring his wrath because you weren't doing your job. Partly, it was a great pride to be associated with him, to be on what was the best symphony 'gig' that there was around, and also to know that you were playing with an exceptional group of people. You just wanted to try hard and wanted to give, and it was interesting and exciting. So when you play in that kind of ambiance, you play music that's interesting, and you play with a very exciting conductor, of course you want to play well. And there was the other factor: If you didn't, he caught you at it."

D. Walter, to Haggin: "So the men took their parts with them to practice at home, and came to rehearsals early to practice them some more. I remember arriving for a rehearsal and finding the woodwinds practicing those enormously difficult passages in the Scherzo of Tchaikovsky's *Manfred*, which usually have to be taken a little more slowly than they are marked; with the result that at the rehearsal the passages were played brilliantly in the right tempo."[4]

## Hectic Schedule

It was not unusual for Toscanini to maintain a very hectic performance schedule. For example, on the evening of February 3, 1910, he conducted

*Tristan und Isolde*; the next day, a matinee performance of *La fanciulla del West*; followed that evening by a performance of *Madama Butterfly*. And between November 16 and November 22, 1927, he conducted the dress rehearsals and opening nights of *Mefistofele, Fidelio, Manon Lescaut*, and *Otello!*

In 1920, Toscanini assembled and trained a new orchestra at La Scala and then took it on an enormous tour. In thirty-five days, they performed thirty-three concerts in twenty-one Italian cities. Two days later, they departed for a 112-day tour of the U.S. and Canada, where they gave sixty-eight concerts in forty-one cities, and played several recording sessions. Returning to Italy, they performed another 56-day Italian tour of thirty-six concerts in nineteen cities.

## Study

Toscanini said to a young conductor seeking advice: "I shall tell you my secret: All my life I have been studying scores."[5]

Wilfrid Pelletier, conductor and friend of Toscanini's: "It was a great mind. Toscanini never belittled anything. If you asked him for advice, he listened very well, and then he'd say, 'Well what I'd do is not the same as your choice of what you should do, but this is the way I feel it.' He was always nice. I don't know any conductor that worked as hard as he did. His interpretation was as pure as could be. He never sought an effect for a conductor. He always went with what the composer wanted to do. I don't know anyone who worked as hard on a score as he did. One day I was telling him, 'I don't know, Maestro; I reached a point where I'm obliged to write all my problems on paper.' He said, 'Do you think you're the only one? I've done that many times.' He said, 'No. No. You have to study. Study your music until the notes lift themselves from the score. Don't forget that when you know a score the music becomes alive. Until then, you're just in the process of learning. Hard work.' I said, 'Maestro, it takes me so long.' He said, 'It takes you a long time to study a score. So what? I had the great facility in my youth. I could take a score and learn a whole opera overnight if I wanted, but we're not interested in that. The public that listens to you is not interested in how fast you learn a thing. What do you say with the music? If you have to go over it two hundred times, do it; but don't take a chance, saying, "Well, it's about right." There's nothing "about right" in music. It must be perfect or not at all.' He was the greatest inspiration I had."[6]

Civetta: "Was he depressed often?"
Joseph Mordino, tenor: "Yeah. He would be moody, and he didn't want to eat; he was not an eater. He would have a little portion, and as he was chewing away he'd be conducting with his hand. He was always in the music."

## Little Sleep

Toscanini liked to be alone for several hours at a time; often, he even preferred to spend nights in his study instead of in his bedroom.

Leo Rostal, cellist: "Nights, he couldn't sleep, so he was always studying the score."

Bolognini: "He used to study everything. He studied. Sometimes he used to get up at three or four o'clock in the morning and go to the piano and study certain things."

Mordino remembered hearing the loudspeakers from Toscanini's Milan residence in the middle of the night: "When I was living next to his home in Milan, he put it on loud and, God, none of us could sleep; he had it on until four or five in the morning, and none of us would sleep. Then I had to be in school at La Scala early, and only then he'd go to bed, but I'd be dead because he was up all night. He wasn't in his bed. He was in the room where the music was. And who could sleep? It was on loud, loud."
Civetta: "This was occasionally?"
Mordino: "No. Every morning, while he was there, he was listening to this music."

Valdengo: "Toscanini had given me his private telephone number because he liked it when I called him at night. He wanted to chat and hear news from me. Often the 'chat' lasted for more than an hour! I recorded some of those conversations and I confess that, hearing the voice and words of that great one again, I am deeply moved, even now. I would phone him at midnight, when, that is, I was certain that he had already retired to his bedroom.

"The maestro slept very little. He studied even at night. When I would ask, 'What are you doing, maestro?' He would respond, 'What do you think I do at my age?

I study . . . I always study . . . I review my errors in past performances and seek to correct them.'

"'What do you think I do? I study,' was, for me, always an incitement to continuous study."

## Falstaff

Mariano Stabile, baritone, recalled his audition for the 1921 La Scala *Falstaff* production. He first sang excerpts from the opera for Toscanini at La Scala in the empty theatre. After confirming that Stabile was then currently free of engagements, Toscanini instructed the singer to show up at his home the next morning at ten.

The coaching with Toscanini at the piano began precisely at 10 a.m. with the monologue from the third act, "Mondo ladro." Stabile remembered: "From then on until one thirty I repeated those few words, because he wanted me to pull forth the regurgitation, that oh, ah of the fat man, of the drunkard, of the glutton, right from the belly . . . When we had finished, he said, 'Good-bye, tomorrow at ten.' . . . Well, after three days of this, I became a little calmer. He addressed me in the familiar form. He began to tell me stories . . . The second or the third day, it got to be two o'clock in the afternoon. Toscanini never got up from the piano. He didn't smoke. He didn't take a cocktail. He didn't eat. He wasn't hungry. At a certain moment [Toscanini's wife], Signora Carla entered and said, 'But Arturo, don't you understand that Stabile has to eat something? It is two o'clock.'

"After seven days of that calvary, he accompanied me to the door of the apartment and said, '. . . I will [have La Scala] give you a contract.' Can you imagine my elation?"[7]

Stabile continued studying the role with Ferruccio Calusio, and a few times a week they performed their work for Toscanini at his home. The contract stipulated that Stabile was to be available to rehearse every day from November 1 until December 26.

## 1935 *Falstaff* at Salzburg

Halina Rodzinski, wife of conductor Artur Rodzinski, recalled having been invited by Toscanini to attend rehearsals for his 1935 Salzburg *Falstaff* production: "[Toscanini's] arm was bothering him and he cursed his decision to conduct at Salzburg . . . As soon as he began to work, Maestro forgot his pain and conducted with terrific fervor, croaking the whole score and flying into rages whenever the orchestra did not give its best . . .

"Toscanini . . . taught each singer . . . how to shape every phrase . . . where to put an accent on each word . . . [and] how to move. He would leap from the orchestra pit to the stage to demonstrate even the smallest gesture. He adored *Falstaff* and conducted it superbly with wit, life, and humor. Herbert Graf, who was the official stage director, told me that Maestro actually decided every detail of the production."[8]

After a performance of *Falstaff* at Salzburg two years later, the orchestra gave Toscanini an enthusiastic ovation. He wrote: "I wanted to do the impossible to extract the best, better than the best, of their abilities . . . [Afterwards,] many Italians came to my dressing room. I listened to a *lot* of banalities—the usual ones that everyone utters. Busch alone said nothing, but his eyes were swollen with tears."[9]

> After performances, many people visited the conductor's dressing room—among others, royalty, elite, and friends who were often not musically educated. "Banalities" here refers to the typical compliments that Toscanini was accustomed to receiving after performances, contrasted with the behavior of Fritz Busch, an internationally renowned conductor. That his colleague's eyes were full of tears and his voice speechless was a much higher compliment than were the words of the other visitors in the dressing room.

## 1950 Concert Version of *Falstaff* at NBC

I spoke to baritone Frank Guarerra and tenor Gabor Carelli together about the *Falstaff* rehearsals.

Guarerra: "We rehearsed for weeks with the orchestra, and six months prior to that with piano and the ensemble, so it was really quite well prepared."

Carelli: "*Falstaff* was in effect a festival performance. There were weeks of intense rehearsals with the Maestro, weeks before that with a coach, and out of the four weeks with the Maestro, there were two weeks only with orchestra and singers. There was a first dress rehearsal, second dress rehearsal, third dress rehearsal, and dress rehearsal, dress rehearsal! So it really came at the end to molding the musical line and the whole work, and not catching flies, as we say sometimes, when you give cues for people. That was long ago gone. But this sort of luxury cannot be allowed neither today [1977], nor in those days, except for a festival occasion like the orchestra of Maestro Toscanini performing one certain work."

## 1946 Concert Version of *La bohème* at NBC

Licia Albanese, soprano, recalled the rehearsals for *La bohème*: "First, he took me and went through Mimi's part, for two or three days. After that, he had a rehearsal with the tenor, Jan Peerce, alone. Then he put Jan Peerce and me together to do duets, and our solos, too. And then he took the baritone, Frank Valentino, alone. He rehearsed all the principals individually, then in quartets, and then finally all together, the entire cast with the chorus. This was a great way of rehearsing."

> In contrast with the one or two rehearsals most singers were accustomed to, Toscanini's work ethic was quite demanding. Insisting upon such dedicated effort from the artists who surrounded him is part of the explanation of how Toscanini raised the performance standards of symphonic and operatic music.

## 1947 Concert Version of *Otello* at NBC

Valdengo described the *Otello* rehearsals: "Often the Maestro would call me alone to his house, wanting to go over the more difficult parts of Iago, and was never satisfied. When it seemed to me that he appeared to be finished he said, 'Now do it again like an artist, not like a schoolgirl!'

"He would spend an hour on one page. I remember that in the third act of *Otello* I had to truly sweat blood before having his approval. At the passage 'Questa è una ragna, dove il tuo cuor casca, si lagna, s'impiglia e muor,' he wanted all the eighth notes in the 6/8 movement very short, and all of them precise, the way Verdi had written them. If one of them didn't come out well, he always made me repeat from the beginning. And he wanted the vocal shadings of the phrase . . . he would say—as if it were an instrumental phrase that was performed by the voice, with the same shadings."

## 1935 Salzburg *Fidelio*

Lehmann: "His *Fidelio*—impregnated with intense tragedy—was a tremendous and sensational success . . . Rehearsals with him were a perpetual shaking and quaking in anguish and pain . . . But what a compensation that *Fidelio* was!"[10]

## Nervousness

Galimir: "I felt that the orchestra itself was a little tense, not in rehearsals—in performances, but in the last years there was a general feeling of relaxed music-making at the end in the performances: 'Ah! Now it's relaxed!'"

A. Berv: "The broadcasts were tense. I know I was tense. The Maestro was very tense. I know he was, because I remember very distinctly seeing him; his face was ashen white. He was very nervous about coming out onstage."

Valdengo: "In response to Toscanini's complaint about singers who make too many gestures onstage, I told the Maestro that often the artist moves too much because he is nervous, and he responded, 'Nervousness needs to be left at home . . .' And he laughed.

"Before beginning the performance of *Aida*, the Maestro asked me, 'Are you a bit afraid, rascal?'* I responded, 'Afraid, no, but a little jittery, yes.' Lowering the tone of his voice, he continued, 'Don't you know that fear and jitteriness are sisters? This old man here, has been afraid for more than sixty years . . . but I keep it jealously hidden inside and don't let anyone see! What would happen if the orchestra understood that I was afraid? Do you know how I defend myself from fear? I become nasty . . . and, believe me, to do so takes effort . . . No one out of the huge crowd of people that come to hear me would think that after many years, one can still have fear before the audience . . . and yet, the more you go ahead, the more you make a name, the more this name is known everywhere, the bigger the fear is.'

"Before going out in front of the audience, the Maestro always sent us ahead, patting us affectionately, with a familiar gesture on the shoulder. He would stop,

---

* Valdengo was from the Piedmont region of Italy, and Toscanini gave him the nickname *baloss*, a word from the Piedmontese dialect. While there is no exact English equivalent, the closest English translations are "rogue" and "rascal."

pull himself together for a moment, and then would go out himself, determined and sure."

On the day of a concert Toscanini took a one-hour bath to overcome his nervousness while thinking of that evening's music.

Bruno Walter wrote about the "shyness I had to overcome before every rehearsal. I clearly remember how . . . on my first journey to England, I felt so great a dread of the impending orchestra rehearsal at Queen's Hall that I was tempted to telegraph a cancellation of the London concert. I was comforted by Toscanini's assurance, when many years later I casually told him of my . . . attack, that he himself had had the same inclination and had been in a similar condition before his first orchestra rehearsal at the Metropolitan Opera in New York."[11]

Toscanini's first rehearsal at the Metropolitan Opera was for Wagner's *Götterdämmerung*. Toscanini may have been concerned about the language barrier, as he was not fluent in English in 1908. He conducted the rehearsal from memory, correcting mistakes in the orchestra parts that no one before him had noticed, something he also did at his first visit to the Bayreuth Festival in 1930. (See pages 52 and 55–56 for more about this first rehearsal at the Met and his rehearsals at Bayreuth.)

Toscanini once told soprano Elisabeth Rethberg that he was nervous before every performance, and that he considered it a good incentive to do one's best.[12]

## Concentration and Self-Discipline

Harold Freeman, clarinetist: "As we used to say, we never knew that an hour and a half could last fifteen minutes. It didn't seem like any time at all—the power of concentration."

Novotny: "He was totally involved physically as well as mentally. He would be just completely wringing wet on the podium."

## Repertoire

In 1932, Toscanini responded to a questionnaire: "I love and admire all the works I conduct, symphonic or operatic, because—I conduct only those I love. My preferences in the symphonic area are for the greats: Haydn, Mozart, Beethoven. In recent years I have thoroughly studied Bruckner's monumental symphonies. I gladly leave modern works to other conductors. Among operas, I value those of Wagner and Verdi above all. It is difficult to state a preference for one of Wagner's operas. I have noticed that if I am conducting this or that Wagner opera, or playing it at the piano, whichever one it happens to be possesses my heart. And yet, every time I glance at the score of *Parsifal*, I say to myself: This is the sublime one. In Verdi's operas, I value not only the melodic richness, but also the effective and sure musical and dramatic power. When I conduct *Falstaff* at Busseto I think about the possibility of a Verdian Bayreuth, on the model of Wagner's Festspielhaus. These two masters are precisely the representatives of German and Italian national music."[13]

Vladimir Horowitz, legendary pianist: "After he stopped conducting he told me he was sorry he had not conducted more music by certain composers, Rachmaninoff, for instance. He never wanted to play his music . . . Toscanini told me, 'I was so stupid. I heard Rachmaninoff's Second Symphony. Such beautiful music!' He also said that he should have conducted more Tchaikovsky."[14]

## Knowledge

Carelli: "He made many corrections in the Ricordi edition of my *Falstaff* score. He told us they were misprints and we all corrected it. He knew exactly where the wrong printings were and what should be corrected."

Vardi: "He explained one thing about a Mozart movement, and about how he found the tempo. Let's assume that it was a minuet. So he went back and looked at all the minuets of Mozart at that tempo. He would do a lot of research before he would decide how something would go. He was not just an instinctive musician. He was a very learned one and he knew what was going on. He had the whole score imprinted in his mind. He knew exactly what was there. He never talked in abstracts."

V. Horowitz: "He and I got along all right. We constantly talked about music. Mozart was a special subject . . . He did not conduct many Mozart concertos, mostly because pianists those days played at best only two or three of them—generally the D Minor or the A Major [K. 488]. I had not played any in public. But both of us knew all of the major Mozart concertos and loved them. I own scores of the concertos with the Maestro's markings and metronome indications."[15]

In answer to Haggin's question about appoggiaturas, Toscanini demonstrated at the piano with the opening section of the *Don Pasquale* Overture. Haggin wrote, "There had to be variety in the treatment of the appoggiatura, and, [as Toscanini said,] 'this is a matter of taste, which the conductor must have.' And he cited the appoggiaturas in the aria in the second act of Gluck's *Orfeo*, which 'Bruno Walter make always the same.' The German manner of treating the appoggiatura that he considered wrong was, he said, started by Mahler."[16]

Haggin: "Toscanini once said, 'Beethoven is very exact—but even Beethoven sometimes write different'; and he cited the pizzicato note that Beethoven wrote now as an eighth-note, now as a quarter, now as a half."[17]

Yehudi Menuhin played the Beethoven Violin Concerto with Toscanini and the New York Philharmonic as a seventeen-year-old. He recalled their private rehearsals of the slow movement with Toscanini at the piano. "There are two bars marked to be played in one bow on the G-string, but I had always played them in two bows on the D-string . . . We discussed this at great length, and I agreed to play it as written. The next day, on the very afternoon of the concert, I got a handwritten message from him: 'I think that after all, you'd better take it in two bows on the D-string.' He was very conscientious, very meticulous about every detail."[18]

Igor Stravinsky, in his autobiography, wrote about Toscanini's 1926 La Scala production of *Le rossignol*: "I was struck by the deep knowledge he had of the score in its smallest details, and by his meticulous study of every work which he undertook to conduct . . . I have never encountered in a conductor of such world repute such a degree of self-effacement, conscientiousness, and artistic honesty."[19]

## Self-Improvement

Glantz: "He would always say, 'I could have improved.' Because when we came back the following year and would play a Beethoven symphony, there were new things that he had discovered in the score that the whole orchestra noted. He was never satisfied. He always thought that he could've done better. Therein lay his absolute greatness. Not like other conductors: When they got through with a concert—well this was it. He would acknowledge the applause of the people and the orchestra but he'd walk off and try to do better the next day. He was never completely happy with the result, and this is a great thing in a human being."[20]

Weber: "Up until his late years he was looking for things and improving. And he just learned his music; he knew every note. I wish the young students coming out of conservatories, and musicians that are playing in orchestras, could have had the experience that I had at that formative stage of my career, to form high standards and use that as a guide throughout my career—to constantly seek perfection. Humbly, I'm never happy with what I do. I always think I can do better. I always want to do better, and I don't give up trying to do better, and I think I got that right at the beginning. It was the high standards that were given to me by this great man."

> Aaron Copland told Haggin, regarding Toscanini's success with his sole performance of Copland's *El Salón México*, that Toscanini deprecated the performance when Copland spoke to him afterward in the green room.[21]

Coletta: "I think he enjoyed putting himself on wax for its permanency. But whenever we would rerecord something he would always refer back. He frequently listened to his own recordings, and was never pleased. Because he'd come into a recording session and say, 'I heard a broadcast I did of this piece,' and he would name the date, and say, 'But I want to do it so much better.' And hitting himself in the jaw, he'd say, '*Cattivo, cattivo*,' meaning, 'I was very poor. I was very bad in that performance, and I want to do it better now.' So he was always searching for a better performance, from himself as well as from the musicians."

A. Berv: "Toscanini was genuine. I remember when he conducted us in Beethoven's Fifth Symphony—and Lord knows, we played the Beethoven many times with him—we went through the entire first movement, and at the end of the movement he was furious with himself. He said, 'I cannot conduct this symphony. I cannot! I will never conduct this symphony again!'"

Brieff: "I remember once the opening of the Fifth Symphony of Beethoven: a very difficult opening. What came out was: Da-da-da-da-da-dum, and I was simply amazed. It was a terrible moment. We all died. And the Maestro just hung his head. He was inconsolable. He went offstage when it was over, and his son, Walter, told me he just beat himself for being 'so stupid.' Being 'so stupid'—it's a very difficult thing, that opening, but it had never happened to him, so yes, he was very hard on, and demanded a great deal of himself."

Galimir: "He always studied the work, and always found something new. And it's true . . . only [the way] he did [it] now was right, and what he did differently before was a mistake, 'stupido.' When the orchestra went to South America, on the boat they heard a shortwave broadcast of the Semiramide Overture. Toscanini was cursing: 'What stupid players! What bad conductor! Bad! Bad!' Then the announcement came: 'Arturo Toscanini and the New York Philharmonic.' A marvelous performance . . . But he said, 'Stupido! Brutto! Anch' io! [Stupid! Ugly! Myself also!]' And . . . he felt the same way when he listened to someone else. It's natural: When you are so convinced—which every musician must be—before you go on the stage you have to be convinced that what you do is the only possible way of performance—if somebody else performs in any other way you have to disagree. It's very difficult to find that something is played differently than you think, and still is good. And very rare."[22]

Vardi: "One of the funniest incidents was when we all took a trip to South America with the orchestra in 1940. Suddenly out from a big radio came a recording of Beethoven's Fourth. He heard it. Everything stopped. And he was listening, pacing up and down, and criticizing—wrong tempos, terrible balance; he was knocking it to pieces. And at the end they said, 'You have just heard Arturo Toscanini and the BBC Symphony.' He got mad at the radio. He got mad at everybody. It was one of the funniest things. He didn't know it was him!"

Bolognini: "All of a sudden we started to hear the Fourth Symphony by Beethoven. There were some places that were wonderful, and some places, *comme ci, comme ça* [so-so]. We were watching the Maestro, and could see that there were spots that he didn't like. When the announcer said, 'conducted by Arturo Toscanini,' he was so enraged that he ran out to the upper deck, and afterward, I went to see what happened to the Maestro, and until midnight he was there, thinking. He was so disappointed. He said, 'I should have never given the okay for the recording, because I am never satisfied.'"

> Albanese was moved to tears by Toscanini's humility and strict self-criticism. When she visited the maestro after the performance they gave of *La traviata* in 1946, he played her parts of the recording that had been made of it. Despite Albanese's opinion that he had led a great performance, Toscanini criticized some of his tempi, and demonstrated at the piano what he characterized as being the correct tempi. He originally had refused to allow the publication of this recording. It was only after he learned that copies of it had already proliferated on the black market that he reluctantly agreed to officially release it.[23]

Civetta: "Toscanini often listened to his recordings. Was he pleased with what he heard?"

Hugo Burghauser, bassoonist and chairman of the Vienna Philharmonic: "Oh, no! He was almost never pleased. He sometimes played recordings in his house for his guests, among them myself, and sometimes he gave a commentary. He even said, 'Look here. I got a letter from a person, reverent, and he said, "Dear Maestro, *le Maître* [the master], I want to bring your attention to this spot in your recording. I think it's muddled up." I said this man must be telling the truth. He's sincere.' Toscanini put the record on the turntable, and he said, 'Yes. I can't deny it. He is right.'"

# Rethinking

Crisara: "He was a great conductor, probably one of the greatest we ever had. But he had the kind of humility which I recall—he came into a first rehearsal one season of the Beethoven Third, the 'Eroica.' He stood in front of the orchestra, and before he started, he said, 'The last time we did this you were fine,' pointing to the orchestra.

And he put his hand on his chest and he said, 'And I was terrible. Now let's get to work and do it well.' This was the great Toscanini that could stand in front of the ninety fellows that were his employees in a sense [in the NBC Symphony] and say, 'I was bad. So we've got to get to work and make it better.'"

A. Shulman: "We were doing the slow movement of the 'Eroica,' the 'Marcia Funebre.' When we finished it, he stopped for a minute, and said, 'Gentlemen, I have been conducting this music for fifty years. I do it *male*. I do it badly. Please, may we do it once again—not for you, but for me.' Well that's a big man because very few conductors would be open enough to admit it. What it boiled down to was like you would view a great painting and every time you look at it you see something that you hadn't seen before, so he would go back to these scores, and restudy them, and suddenly say, 'Well I've been taking this too slow,' or maybe too fast, or change his concept of it completely. Because those of us who approach maturity know that the most permanent thing in life is change. Maestro knew it."

David Sarser, in addition to being a violinist in the NBC Symphony, also installed and maintained the sound equipment in Toscanini's home in New York: "I'd often tiptoe through the main hall of his home on the way out, and see him sitting in his chair under the lamp, studying his scores in absolute silence. You could hear a pin drop in the room, but I know that in his mind, he heard the performance. His whole orchestra was in the room in his mind. We'd always be quiet because he was studying the music, possibly for the next day's rehearsal. And he'd conduct with his finger, and the score was always two inches from his eyes because of his eyesight, and he heard what he was looking at. Many times I heard him say at the rehearsal the next day, 'Did not sound like last night,' meaning how he actually had heard that score in his head. 'This is the way I heard it yesterday.' He heard this at home, and he imagined it perfectly but it didn't turn out that way. Many times he'd sit there at home for an hour or two, and then all of a sudden ask for a certain performance from seven years or ten years prior to be played for him."

Brieff: "The Old Man demanded so many things from us; but what was so extraordinary was that he made the same demands upon himself. This man never stopped studying scores that he had done over and over and over again. When he would make a mistake, which didn't happen too often, he would cry, '*Sono stupido!* [I am stupid!]' in a large and loud voice. He would very often stop in rehearsal and say, 'For so many years I have done this phrase this way. But I think'—He said 'I think'; he always qualified it. He never said anything was definite—'I think maybe Beethoven meant this. Let's do it this way.'"

D. Walter: "Working with him was always very exciting. I think of the last Beethoven performances, which not only were less dramatic and more introspective, but had new details that represented new thought and analysis."[24]

Brieff: "To me it was an extraordinary experience, because he never stopped learning things even in works that he had done for so many years. And it was a great lesson for me. In other words, when we do it, we think it is the last word. It really isn't. And he was very simple about it. He made tremendous demands upon us, and it was difficult sometimes to be able to meet those demands. But at the same time, you respected him because you knew that he was as hard on himself as he was on the orchestra."

D. Walter: "He remembered not only what was in the score, but he remembered every time you had played it before, and every time he had heard it before. And one of the most startling demonstrations of his memory—although he didn't intend it as a demonstration—was the last time we did the Beethoven Seventh. He started on the podium by saying, 'I have been up all night, listening to our previous performances in my mind.' And he said, I forget the exact dates, 'In 1939, *non c'era male* [it wasn't bad].' Then he mentioned another performance that was 'a disgrace,' and he got angry. '1944 was not bad.' And we did it on tour in South America. He liked that. He hated it in 1947. And he really specified all the things that we did well, and all the things that we didn't do well, or for his taste, in all the performances we had done . . . He remembered every rehearsal and every concert, and he said, 'This time is perhaps the last time that I will play this with you, so this time we will do it well.' And he proceeded to say, 'You know that you are stupid and I am stupid, but Beethoven was not stupid, so this time we will do it as he wrote it.' He really remembered every one of the performances that we had given with all the errors, with all the good things. It was quite exciting."*

---

* David Walter's memory may not have accurately matched each date with Toscanini's evaluation of that year's performance. I included the anecdote to provide an example of Toscanini's self-reflection in preparation for a performance, not as a reliable record of his opinion of specific performances.

# Restudy

> Toscanini rehearsed from memory, but kept the score on a music stand,
> to his left, for easy reference.

Guarerra: "In the rehearsals, when he wanted to see something, he put on the pince-nez, or he'd pick up the score and put it right up to the tip of his nose and read and say, 'Yes, that's the way it is.' But the interesting thing about this is that he constantly referred to the score—constantly referred to it!"

A. Berv: "Every time he conducted Beethoven's Fifth Symphony, it was the first time. No matter what he conducted, it was always the first time. He gave every bit of energy to everything he conducted."

Philip Frank, violinist: "Despite his explosive temperament, the musicians admired him endlessly. Once, we gathered around him after a rehearsal to comment on the refreshing reading he had just given a particular symphony. It was so vital, invigorating and young that we all found new inspiration in it. This, of course, was characteristic of his interpretations. He replied that when he prepared a program and studied the score, even one he had performed many times before, he made it a practice to regard it as a new composition, which he had never seen before. In this way, he analyzed every note, every bar, every nuance and phrase, to reach the full meaning of the composer's intentions. No wonder he was unique among conductors! . . . To the end of his life, Arturo Toscanini saw himself as a student who always had more to learn. In truth, he was a great teacher and an inspiration to all we musicians who had the good fortune to work with him."[25]

Bloom recalled a visit at Toscanini's home: "I was talking to him upstairs and we were waiting for lunch to be served and he was very tired. So I said, 'Maestro, you look tired.' We had already finished our business and I said, 'I don't have to stay for lunch. Why don't you take a nap, and lie down?' He said, 'No, caro [dear]. It was just that this morning at five thirty, I couldn't sleep. I woke up and started to study the score of the symphony.' Well the symphony was the Beethoven Fifth. So I said to him, 'Maestro, how many times have you conducted this?' He said, 'Oh, many, many times.' I asked, 'Fifty, one hundred, one hundred and fifty?' He said, 'Many times, caro, many, many times.' He said, 'I am always afraid that I missed something.'

You know, this kind of dedication is pretty hard to find anymore where after literally hundreds of times conducting this work—he was then about seventy-five—to still have this same dedication that he'd get out the score and study it just in case he missed some subtlety. To me, that was a lesson in dedication."

D. Walter: "That this man, at his age, should feel that there was still something to look for and learn in a piece of music he had played so many times—this not only was moving, but inspired you to do more work yourself. It meant that although he was old in years, his mind and spirit were young."

Bachmann recalled visiting Toscanini at his summer residence on the Isolino in Lago Maggiore, Italy. Upon his arrival, Toscanini asked Bachmann to hurry up the stairs because there was something very important the octogenarian conductor wanted to show him. Once Bachmann was upstairs, Toscanini showed him the score of Brahms's Second Symphony, which was opened to a page in the second movement. Bachmann recalled Toscanini's exclamation: "For more than fifty years I've been conducting the Brahms Second Symphony, and for all these years I was a stupid idiot, blind. I didn't see one thing that I just discovered after fifty years." What he hadn't previously noticed was a small diminuendo sign in one bar of one instrument.

Rostal: "His approach, how sincere he was to music. He said, 'Who am I? The composer is important.' Always: 'È scritto, scritto [It's written].' He adhered to every little thing that was printed in the score. Sometimes, he had his doubts. After conducting for example, Beethoven's Leonore Overture for a hundred times and more, one day he said, 'I discovered that one of those slurs is not by Beethoven. No. It's . . .' And Toscanini sang the phrase with the unslurred note. So, all excited, new discovery. Two months later he got back to the old way! But he always tried to discover new things. He was very nearsighted. He'd hold the score right in front of his eyes. But no matter, his knowledge about music was still terrific."

Galimir: "And Brahms! The Third Symphony of Brahms! He struggled with it for a long time: I think he was never really happy with it. But when we played it the last time, in Carnegie Hall, he was so happy. Everybody was happy. I think he found it—he had the feeling 'That's it.' That was a wonderful performance: I think it was the greatest Third Brahms I ever heard or played; it's one of the things I won't forget."[26]

Brieff: "On two occasions, he invited me to conduct the NBC summer concerts. At one of the concerts I did the Seventh Symphony of Sibelius. I lived in Riverdale, close by to him, and I went down after I did the second concert, and what was he listening to? The recording of my performance of the Sibelius Seventh. And I said, 'Maestro, do you like it?' He said, 'Very good, but I don't know this work. I am trying to find out. I am listening to it.' He never did the Seventh of Sibelius, but he was that kind of a guy; he never stopped probing and trying to find the answers. This is what I mean by his never-ending search for perfection.

"There was one performance we did of the Brahms First, and near the end, there was an extra timpani note he added, and it's not what Brahms wrote. And I was very curious about that. I said, 'Why did you do that? Why did you put that in?' He said another person had suggested that it might be a good idea, and he said, 'You like?' I said, 'Maestro, I must confess that I didn't like it.' The next time we did that in the next town on the tour, it was taken out. Why should he ask me if I liked it or not? Because he wasn't sure himself at that point whether this was good. The man's eternal search for the truth in music is one of the things that I shall ever carry with me, and it inspired me in many ways; it gave me a tremendous goal to strive for."

Vardi: "What used to happen was: An artist would play the same piece over and over again in different places, and it would be different every time. They'd have something new to say in the piece. They would find something. When we rehearsed with Toscanini, we rehearsed Monday, then Wednesday, and whatever the days were, and changes would happen in the piece itself. We'd do a symphony with him one time, and do it again the next year, and it was a different interpretation—a little bit faster, the singing parts were a little bit different. There was a different feeling."

James Levine, conductor and host of the motion picture *Toscanini: The Maestro* by Peter Rosen, said in the film: "Apart from the beauty of individual performances, the Toscanini recordings are important for what they show us about his neverending search. If you listen to a piece in three or four different performances under his direction, you can't help but be struck by the differences in concept. They all carry his stamp; but they also show that he was constantly rethinking, questioning himself."[27]

# Preparation

James Dolan, NBC Symphony librarian: "One day a week, usually early in the week, I would visit with him, and he would go over nearly every part himself, especially if it was a new work. He would want to see the material. Many times, in an older work, where we would be having trouble with the parts, he would personally go over them . . . He would always like to . . . look over each individual part . . . He wasn't just content with the musical content of the score; he wanted to know the problems each musician was faced with as he played his music: proper turns of pages, clear notation, and cuts properly marked if there were any. He would say, 'Dolan, remember . . .'

"Before any performance of a new work, especially, or the first time he would be doing an old work from a completely new set of parts, he would usually take the parts home and edit each part.

"I have shown these to conductors who would marvel at his foresight, and how he would work with the parts. I would show them, for instance, the last stand of the second violins, and they would see all of the Maestro's annotations written in his own handwriting. Normally, one of each part is given to the librarian, and he copies all of the others, or a copyist does it. But the Maestro just loved to do it himself, and know that it was correct and that it was there.

"There were other times after stormy rehearsals, that Maestro Toscanini would call for all of the music and go over every part before he left for home. I have seen him stay in his dressing room working far into the night forgetting his dinner until all would be correct. Then he would tell me of how he had known the composer, and how the composer had encouraged him when he was a young conductor."[28]

Bachmann: "When the Maestro got up to conduct he knew exactly how your part looked out of the 104 players. He knew exactly what to expect from you. What made him more furious than anything else was if somebody was not 100 percent prepared.

"He said, 'There is nothing difficult in an orchestra except one thing. And that's one thing I don't permit for myself, and I won't permit it for anybody else—and that is if they are not 100 percent prepared. If I can come to the rehearsal over age seventy and know every part, then I can expect that that man, who has to know only one part, has to know it well. I don't have to tell him how to play because he is a good player, but I have a right to expect that he does his part 100 percent like I do my part 100 percent.' It was the easiest thing in the world to play with the Maestro if you were prepared."

A. Shulman: "He came prepared. He knew what he wanted. He knew how to re-hearse. So at the end of an hour, when we were scheduled for two and a half hours, he'd say, '*Alla casa.*' He was satisfied. 'Go home. Rest. You've done your thing.' But on the other hand, if we didn't do our job, then all hell broke loose, and let's face it—not without justification."

Posner: "He never came to a rehearsal unprepared. Some other conductors meander through it. They talk their way through, but he never did. In all the fifteen years I was with him I don't think there was one time that he wasn't prepared for a rehearsal. And if he said something, it was generally 99 percent accurate. I wouldn't say he was infallible; he admitted a mistake once in a while. But if he made a mistake, he said, 'I am stupid.' And then he'd go back and correct it."

## Shostakovich's Seventh Symphony

A. Shulman recalled Toscanini's first rehearsal for the American premiere of Shosta-kovich's Seventh Symphony: "A remarkable thing happened, which left us flab-bergasted, and which I've never forgotten . . . At our first reading of our parts he stopped us in a huge tutti and said, '*Contrafagotto* [contrabassoon], what are you playing?' And it turned out that the contrabassoon was playing a B-natural in his part instead of the B-flat in Toscanini's score. Maestro's ear was one of the three great ears I've encountered in my years of playing under conductors; the others were Monteux's and Cantelli's."[29]

Bloom: "After a little while we took this miracle of his ear for granted. It was just natural for him to be able to pick out the note that was wrong in a passage where nobody knew what was going on. Where it was really brought home to me once, and I never forgot it, was when we did the first performance of the Shostakovich Seventh Symphony in the United States. He couldn't have had that score more than two weeks before we saw the music because it had just arrived and it was all hush-hush. It was smuggled in from Russia, and so we started to rehearse this thing. There were parts of it that were very thick and muddy. I have to say turgid; they're unclear. And I remember I was sitting there and he was rehearsing a sec-tion that had cellos and the violas playing, and they were divided in each section into five parts. There were all these different stands playing different things, and he always had a score beside him, to his left, never in front of him because he couldn't see it; the score was there for reference. And at one place he said, 'Just a minute, I think that's an F-sharp in the third viola part.' And you know, really, it's just mud at that point. And he'd look at the score like that—you know, two inches from his face. He couldn't see it and by the way, that was one of his vanities—he didn't want to wear glasses. He looked at it and he said, 'Yes, it is F-sharp. They made a mistake in the part.' And to hear that, suddenly I thought to myself, I sit here every day and these minor miracles happen and I just take it for granted. I realized what this man had just done, and after that I realized how hard it would be to be a conductor like Toscanini. Boy, he had a fantastic ear, but of course he had the famous photographic memory. He'd look at a page of music and then it was indelibly imprinted in his mind."

The errors had gone undetected by Shostakovich, who had attended rehearsals and performances of the symphony in Russia.

## Memory and Ear

Bolognini: "He knew the score so well it was impossible to fool him. I remember in the Philharmonic, we were playing *fortissimo* in some piece; and he stopped and said to one player—the second clarinet or someone like that, 'Did you play this note? Because I didn't hear you.' And the man said, 'No, I didn't play it.' The Maestro had a tremendous ear."[30]

Gregor Piatigorsky played the Cello Concerto of Castelnuovo-Tedesco with Toscanini and the New York Philharmonic in 1935. At their second private rehearsal at which Toscanini played the orchestra part at the piano, the conductor remarked to Piatigorsky that he felt it was better to use the third finger in a particular passage instead of the fingering the cellist had used at the first rehearsal. Piatigorsky was amazed that the maestro heard the difference, because Toscanini had been positioned at the far end of the room, and couldn't see the actual fingering.[31]

Toscanini's first orchestral rehearsal at the Metropolitan Opera was in 1908 with *Götterdämmerung*, which he led from memory. Amazingly, he heard and corrected mistakes in the orchestra parts, which, for decades, none of the well-known German conductors had noticed. At one point he said to the cellists, "You are playing an A; the note is B-flat." The first cellist replied, "I've never played anything but an A here or elsewhere." Toscanini said, "Then it's a mistake in the part. I see you are not convinced. Would you like me to get the orchestral score?" Toscanini looked up the passage, proving he was right, whereupon the orchestra broke out into applause.[32]

## Memory

Valdengo: "When I asked him how he could remember everything he replied to me, 'You know, I see everyone's part here inside, in my head! I don't want to brag, but since the time when I played cello in the orchestra, I played many operas from memory, so that I could enable myself to follow the performance, watching the stage.'"

Shaw recalled observing Toscanini in 1954 as he prepared for *Un ballo in maschera*: "He was relearning at age eighty-seven, and recalled the whole thing from memory, and finally conducted the opera from memory. I mean he knew every aria, every recitative; he knew the words; he knew the whole thing. He could have written out the whole book."

Valdengo auditioned for Toscanini's concert version of *Otello* in 1947 by singing part of the role of Iago, after which Toscanini came onto the stage and, accompanying himself, sang the "Dream" to demonstrate how he wanted it sung. Valdengo wrote, "Toscanini sang the entire 'Dream' with eyes closed, accompanying himself from memory."

> According to Bachmann, at one point Toscanini wanted to perform the slow movement of Joachim Raff's Quartet No. 5. The score, however, could not be found. Toscanini wrote out the score from memory, including the dynamics and articulation, even though he hadn't played or seen it for many decades. Several months later, Bachmann, a collector of rare scores, found a copy. When it was compared to Toscanini's manuscript, only one error had been made!

D. Walter spoke about "the bassoon player who asked to be excused because his C-sharp key wasn't working, and Toscanini quickly reviewed the bassoon part in his mind and came up with the pronouncement that as a matter of fact there is no C-sharp in the piece; and there were other demonstrations of his memory.

"The most important aspect of his memory was that he not only knew all the notes—dynamics and written indications that were in a piece—but he knew them very deeply."

Leon Barzin, conductor and violist: "I was a member of the New York Philharmonic Quartet, and I remember being on the train. We had to play in Pittsburgh, and we were studying the score of one of the Opus 18 of Beethoven. We were just looking at it together, the four of us, when he passed by and said, 'What are you doing?' And we told him. He said, 'Will you look at page 25? Third bar, there's a mistake.' His memory had to do with everything, not only opera or symphony. It had to do with all music."

Bachmann recalled a demonstration of Toscanini's memory at the maestro's home in Riverdale, New York, one New Year's Eve: "A few people started to talk about the superb memory of Toscanini. Maestro said, 'You are making a very big mistake. That's not memory. A conductor can make a mistake but if the orchestra is good enough nobody will notice it. But I'll tell you what memory is.' And he did the following thing. He asked his son to bring down any score at all of Wagner, Beethoven, or Brahms. He asked William Steinberg to sit down at the piano and pick out anything and play a little of it, just a few bars, and stop whenever he wants to, except one thing: 'When you stop and wherever you stop, don't lift up your hands. Leave your fingers on the chord at which you've stopped.' And so Steinberg played from *Siegfried*. Maestro tipped it off that this is in the third act and so on. Toscanini said, 'Do you have your hand on the chord?' 'Yes.' And Maestro said, pointing to the pinky of the left hand, 'This is in the timpani and in the second trombone. This is here and there. This finger is in the second viola, the second violin, and the second part of the first violin. This finger is in the second oboe and second flute. And he went through all the ten fingers, describing the complete orchestration. And he said, '*This* is memory.'"

## Bayreuth

When Toscanini was invited to conduct at Bayreuth in 1930 by Siegfried
Wagner, it marked the first time a non-German-school conductor had ever
appeared there. The maestro considered Bayreuth to be a great shrine of
art and refused any compensation. However, at the first rehearsal he was
seriously dissatisfied with the quality of the orchestra and was planning on
canceling the performances. It was only after Siegfried promised to make
some personnel changes in the orchestra that the maestro agreed to stay.
Conducting as always from memory, he discovered several mistakes in the
orchestra parts of *Tristan* and *Tannhäuser* that had gone undetected for
several decades by all of the great conductors at Bayreuth.

Haggin: "[Violist Nicolas] Moldavan, who went to Bayreuth for Toscanini's performances of *Tristan* and *Tannhäuser*, told me that the German musicians there had
resented the intrusion of an Italian in this shrine of German art where hitherto only
Germans had performed—until Toscanini's first rehearsal of the orchestra, when
he reduced them to stunned silence by detecting in their playing mistake after
mistake in the orchestral parts that had for years gone undetected by the German
conductors."[33]

At a rehearsal of act 1 of *Tristan*, Toscanini asked why no one was playing the cymbal part at the end of the act. He was told that there were no
cymbal notes in the parts. The maestro insisted that the manuscript be
consulted, where, to the Germans' surprise the cymbal notes were found,
clearly notated![34]

At La Scala Toscanini was accustomed to staging the productions himself.
At the Bayreuth rehearsals of *Tannhäuser* he disapproved of the existing
staging and choreography for the Venusberg Bacchanale. He had read all
of Wagner's writings in their entirety and insisted that the Bacchanale be
staged and choreographed exactly as Wagner had specified.

Alfred Wallenstein, conductor and cellist: "During a rehearsal of *Tannhäuser*, when
[the soprano performing] Elisabeth entered for 'Dich, teure Halle' . . . the stage was

darkened. Maestro stopped and asked, 'Why is the stage so dark?' And Siegfried Wagner said, 'That's what Father wanted.' And Maestro said, 'Father wanted?! You have the writings of Father?' They had, of course, at Villa Wahnfried . . . so they went straight into the library, and he took down the particular volume he wanted, turned to the exact page, and said, 'Here! Read!' And Wagner said that for Elisabeth's entrance there should be the brightest lights possible. There were thousands of incidents like that: It might involve only a rest or a grace note; but he wouldn't be satisfied until he had seen the source material. Whatever he did he did with tremendous knowledge of the background of the music."[35]

# CHAPTER 4

# Tempo

*Everything in Toscanini's credo was essentially tempo, time. The moment you make the wrong tempo, the best idea and the most correct playing is worthless or reduced in its worth. His greatest credo was, "Make it in the right tempo," which is what Richard Wagner said and wrote.*

—**Hugo Burghauser**

Burghauser explained to Haggin: "The Salzburg *Meistersinger*, some musicians said was too fast. In reality it lasted five whole hours! But it seemed fast because it was so lively in expression . . . His *Parsifal* in Bayreuth was the longest ever. No Richard Strauss or Karl Muck or Furtwängler conducted such a *largissimo Parsifal*. He could be slow if it had to be slow."[1]

When I interviewed Burghauser, he said, "Richard Strauss was the fastest *Parsifal* conductor, and Strauss admitted it: 'I am not old enough to conduct it slow!' It was true; it was too fast. Toscanini did not conduct many things faster than other conductors."

## Composers

Sarser: "Toscanini was a contemporary of many of the composers whose works he played, and he had the opportunity of talking to them and knowing them. And I would take his word for what the tempo should be for a given work of a composer that he knew personally and whose works he did the first performances of, more than I would of somebody else who says he's too fast. He had a tendency to be very spirited, but listening very carefully to many recordings of his performances, I can't say they're too fast. When he'd conduct a score of Beethoven, he stuck to the tempo markings. He stuck to the phrasing—everything which Beethoven wanted."

Toscanini to Melchior: "What Wagner meant is very clear. Just examine the score. You will find everything there."[2]

> According to Burghauser, one of Toscanini's greatest qualities was his desire to understand the composers' original intentions for each composition he conducted, including ideas that were often lost through the years. When he conducted Brahms's First Symphony with the Vienna Philharmonic, he asked Arnold Rosé—the ensemble's concertmaster who had performed premieres of much of Brahms's chamber music under the guidance of the composer—how Brahms had wanted the finale played. The movement's Allegro is usually conducted in two, but Rosé explained that Brahms was very specific about wanting a flowing tempo, yet conducted in four to avoid any haste. Toscanini was careful to bridle and hold back, yet play in a flowing, passionate manner, which is harder to do in four than in two. He was happy to discover this desire of Brahms, and Rosé felt this was the very truth of music making, as Brahms wanted it.
>
> Rosé: "He has given me back my youth."[3]

## Some Tempos Have Become Slower

Harold C. Schonberg has pointed out that the tempos of the Brahms D Minor Piano Concerto have gradually become slower. The performances Horowitz played with both Toscanini and Bruno Walter in the 1930s average approximately forty minutes. In the 1960s, Rudolf Firkušný, Arthur Rubinstein, Van Cliburn, and John Ogdon averaged forty-five minutes. And in the 1980s, Krystian Zimerman, Daniel Barenboim, and Claudio Arrau's timings were from forty-eight to over fifty minutes.[4]

# Playability

Arthur Granick, violist: "No matter how difficult a passage was to play, one always ended up being able to play every note of it without being cut off by a lack of time, which is what happens with some conductors. You could play everything with him and have enough time to play it, and yet the music went on with good tempo. Allegro movements were never too fast to play."

Winter: "The fast movements were always at such a judicious tempo. He had such an understanding of not only the structure, but also what was possible on the instruments. In spite of the fact that people thought he took fast tempos, he never took a tempo where you couldn't play every note, and this included anything of Wagner or Strauss. You could play every note with Toscanini."

Glantz: "My first contact with Toscanini was in 1926 playing a rehearsal of Respighi's *Pines of Rome*. The opening bars depict children at play. He took it so fast that it was almost a physical impossibility to manipulate the tongue to that degree. So during the intermission I went up to him . . . and said, 'Maestro, the opening measures: They're almost impossible to execute. Would you be good enough, when you come to that spot, to slow down just a hair?' And he shook his head and said, 'Yes.' And the next time we rehearsed it, when we came to that spot, he . . . let us play a little slower. And that showed his greatness because he listened to me and respected my opinion . . . and that's how it was done from thereafter. From then on, he just looked at me, and when we recorded it, he slowed down there. I knew that that man was something, to accept criticism from the trumpet player . . . If you'd ever do that with Stokowski he'd kill you. That was our first rehearsal."[5]

Bachmann: "The first time we played the *Daphnis and Chloé* Suite by Ravel, before the rehearsal, everybody was sitting breaking his fingers because the beginning is the sixty-fourth notes, and very difficult. So when Maestro announced that he is going to do the Ravel, everybody was absolutely shivering. The legend that preceded him was so big that we were afraid that he would hear things that didn't exist, but he didn't. He was a very realistic man. He heard every error; sometimes he called us on it and at other times he didn't. Just before the first rehearsal I was summoned to Maestro's dressing room. He gave me a list: 'Eight bars before T tell the second oboe not to play ritardando. Tell him to play sforzando,' something like that. He said, 'What are they doing in there?' I said, 'Maestro, this is very difficult.' He said, 'Difficult? I don't think so'. Well we went in and we were shivering. He went through the entire first movement, and he turned around, which he very seldom did, and said to me, '*È difficile*? Is this difficult?' And I said, 'Not in this tempo, Maestro'.

"'Well,' he said, 'if a conductor doesn't feel an orchestra's capability, and he doesn't know how far he can go, then no matter who it will be—Heifetz plays a Paganini caprice, but if you will want it twice as fast he won't be able to do it. There are certain physical limitations. Now if the conductor doesn't know this, he's no conductor.'"

Burghauser: "Of another conductor's recording, Toscanini said, 'This is so fast it cannot be played correctly, and for this reason it is totally wrong. I conducted it, too, and I'd go to the very limit of playability, and if I would surpass it then it was wrong.' Whereas Walter, Furtwängler, and Weingartner did, in Schumann's symphonies, in scherzos, choose a tempo which was so fast that Toscanini never would dare to match it, because he himself was a good cellist; he must have known this cannot be played correctly or clearly, and this was his limit. No *Schlamaazel*, no Schippers, no Karajan give heed to this principle. They make it beautiful, fascinating, but wrong, technically wrong. Furtwängler was so sick; he was half-deaf, he did not hear the big stage music, and could not coordinate it. It was all topsy-turvy. People gave him the greatest ovation; he was Furtwängler. So, the people don't even hear correctly. It's a blessing not to hear correctly. For me it's a curse to hear correctly, because I don't like it if it's wrong."

# Steady

Nathan Gordon, violist and conductor: "Actually the tempos were so steady that you were always able to play all the notes, be it Wagner, Strauss, or Beethoven."

S. Shulman: "Wagner is frightfully difficult for the orchestra to play, especially string players, and passages in *Walküre* that are almost unplayable were always playable with Toscanini because the tempos were so steady that you could manage to fit in the notes. With other conductors they would be a fake."

Civetta: "Lots of people criticize his tempos as usually being too fast."

Vardi: "They were never as fast as people thought they were. With him it was just so steady that it sounded fast. He was the only conductor I could play all the notes of *Don Juan* with, and I have a fairly good technique on my viola. With some conductors, the fourth beat disappeared, and you just skipped that many notes to catch the next bar. But with him it was so steady you could play every note. I never found it hard to play with him as far as tempos are concerned. I think tempos are a question of taste. He had a lot of drive in his beat. I never thought it was too fast."

## Clarity

Weber: "He never took a tempo where the music was not clear or unplayable. I think it seemed faster than it actually was because it was so clean and transparent. It seemed fast, but in playing, everything was playable. It was never muddy. And that goes for Brahms, which sometimes gets to be a little muddy with some conductors, and particularly Wagner."

Civetta: "What about the controversial subject of his tempos?"
S. Shulman: "Everyone says how fast they are. If you take the metronome marks in the scores of Beethoven and compare them to Toscanini's recordings, you will find that they sound fast, but metronomically they are not fast; they're close to what Beethoven marked. Of course, Beethoven's markings were always very fast, but the thing that gives the impression of being so fast is the enormous clarity. There is no jumble. When he got through with a score it was so clear that the clarity itself gave a feeling of speed."

## Sense of Timing, Rhythm

A. Shulman: "Another thing Maestro had was his remarkable sense for the judicious selection of tempos. We played Strauss with conductors whose way of achieving excitement was to take virtually unplayable speeds, in which we didn't play half the notes. Despite the fact that we played fast tempos with him, it was always *tempo giusto*, a just tempo, because he had such rock-bound rhythm, that we could play more notes in difficult works than with other conductors who would take a faster tempo, and we'd slop through it. The best example I think would be *Till Eulenspiegel* of Strauss. He would take it slower than every other conductor, but it would have such iron-bound rhythm that it would create the illusion that it was infinitely faster than it was. It was a correct tempo. His rhythm was absolutely incredible. And that's what gave the excitement to the performance."

Posner: "He had a remarkable sense of timing and line. He instinctively knew what the tempos of the things were, and you felt it was right. He was so very often criticized for playing too fast, but I don't think so. His tempos were just right because you could play all the notes. Very often with other conductors—I've played with the biggest of them, Reiner, von Karajan, Bernstein, Mitropoulos—when they'd play a Wagnerian piece it was a jumble. And they would try to get so much speed and breakneck tempos just to create excitement and it's the wrong thing. The best analogy I can think of is Heifetz, who is the most fantastic technician in the world, yet he doesn't play that fast if you listen carefully. The thing that makes it so remarkable is the preciseness of the rhythm, and that's what Toscanini had, that marvelous sense of timing. It was really great."

Saul Goodman was the New York Philharmonic's timpanist for forty-six years, including ten years with Toscanini, from 1926 to 1936.
Civetta: "Out of all those qualities that you mentioned—the balance, the ear, the memory, etc.—is there one particular thing that was outstanding about him?"
Goodman: "Well, yes, his rhythm. His sensitive, accurate, powerful rhythm."
Civetta: "What pieces would you say this was most evident in?"
Goodman: "'Siegfried's Death and Funeral Music' from Wagner's *Götterdämmerung*, *Boléro*, and *Daphnis and Chloé* of Ravel."

Bloom: "In the *Midsummer Night's Dream* Scherzo, his tempo was terribly fast but it was absolutely rock. There wasn't one moment of that scherzo that didn't have intensity and rhythm in it. When you started that piece at the beginning until the end where it said 'copyright,' there was no deviation in the tempo; and he created this intensity."

# Words

Guarrera: "Toscanini had a tremendous knowledge of the score and the meaning of the words. He would say, 'If music is written in a fast tempo, this is all relative.'

In other words, if you sing so fast that you cannot be understood, then it's too fast. You'll find that whenever many conductors see the word *presto*, or something indicating fast, they go so fast because they say the composer wanted that. And that is true to only a certain extent. Toscanini said that it's all relative, and would bring out the speed with a flavor of the words. He knew just how to coach it out of you." Carelli: "That was especially important in *Falstaff*, where so many of the ensembles have so many words, and all the words are hard to understand, because there are several people singing different words simultaneously. He wanted every word very clear. You had to be able to pronounce it. If you can't, the conductor is wrong because Verdi never wanted anything which could not be sung."

## Consistency of Tempos

Bolognini spoke of Toscanini's conducting of Wagner's operas *Tannhäuser* and *Parsifal* at Bayreuth in 1931: "I remember when he conducted operas by Wagner that are so long, the difference between two performances of an opera would be only one minute."

Glantz: "I used to mark every number I used to play with the Maestro. I put down the timing of *Boléro* was thirteen and a half minutes on the dot no matter how often we'd played it or what lapse of time took place in between. He would always have the same tempos. They never varied . . . even with longer compositions. And months would go by or a season would go by and we'd play it again and the timing was exactly the same precisely, almost electronically. That was the most amazing thing. The man's judgment of tempo was never fickle or erratic like some conductors: If it felt good, they would speed up the tempo. If they were unhappy, the tempo would lag."[6]

Melchior biographer Shirlee Emmons wrote that Melchior "found security in the knowledge that there would be no deviations in rehearsal or in performance, no 'personal' interpretation of Wagner's chosen tempo . . . For him it was simpler to spend rehearsal time working hard to learn the precise tempo, and then, on stage, to have the security of that familiar and mercifully undeviating tempo."[7]

Carboni: "Other conductors, when they come to the concert, get excited and play the music faster, thinking that way it is more brilliant. But when the Old Man took a tempo at a rehearsal you knew that when you played the piece at the concert it would be that tempo."[8]

## Tempo Relationships

J. Bernstein: "Tempo is a very funny thing. I mean, if you play a little faster, or a little slower, it doesn't change the music. It depends on how everything is connected. He did the Third Symphony by Brahms, and the third movement was pretty fast. Before he died, he made all four Brahms symphonies again, and he made the same movement so much slower. It was beautiful the first time; it was beautiful this time. It depends on how it is connected. Tempo is not a thing which you can criticize if it's done beautifully and all the phrases connect with each other. So tempo doesn't disturb anything. The trouble with most of the young conductors is that they start to run without any connection. It becomes terrible. But in his case, the Brahms symphony, the third movement, was slow, much slower than the older record, and it was beautiful. And earlier it was beautiful."

Civetta: "What about some of Beethoven's slow movements?"
Galimir: "Yes, they were different. We were used to slower or faster or other tempos. When he started, you said, 'Oh my God, why so fast?' But by the end of the movement, you were convinced he was right. Somehow, it's the proportions. A tempo is not something that has to do with the metronome mark. It depends how you beat it up and down, from the beginning to the end. And one can only really say if the movement was too fast or too slow after it is over, not before."

Galimir, to Haggin: "In Europe, when we played . . . the Beethoven Seventh, we used to play the second movement very slowly. Toscanini decided it said 'allegretto' and must be allegretto; so suddenly you played it very fast; and this was a great shock, after you had played it for ten years very slowly. But after you were through with the movement the very first time, you had to say to yourself, 'Yes, I think it's right.' The sense of proportion was always correct with him."[9]

Galimir: "The second movement of the Seventh Symphony is a very long movement, and he felt the length of the movement so well that by the end, it sounded proportioned to me. I was convinced he was right. There are other possibilities:

One can also play it slower. I'm sure that Furtwängler's is much slower. There was one incident in the Seventh Symphony, in the third movement Trio, it says, '*assai meno presto* [very much less presto]'—he took it very literally, and really played it very much less presto, which up till then, we were used to playing it quite a bit slower. Again, after you played it with him, what he did was very convincing. And that's the only thing that counts: If the interpreter convinces you, then he is right."

Civetta: "Also the 'Funeral March' of the Third."

Galimir: "Fantastic!"

## Transitional Modifications

Burghauser: "After he established the basic tempo with the very first phrase, what he was most aware of, in lifelong incessant search of, and like with a divining rod hoping to find, was the right transitional modification of the tempo in what followed. In the 'Haffner' Symphony, after the first proclamation, *forte*, comes a pensive continuation, *piano*; there has to be this little modification of tempo, which you cannot fix with a metronome, but which is clearly different. Toscanini broke his head and his brain to achieve a nuance of difference which would be just enough and not too little—and convincing. When . . . he was not sure—which he expressed quite openly—or when he thought he knew, and the playback showed him it was wrong—then it was disastrous. So he played the 'Eroica,' and after the first theme and the second theme there was a transition which did not have this proportion that he wanted, this slight difference in tempo unnoticeably going into the next phase of the *plasticus*.

"And when the machine reproduced this to him he said, 'Oh, what a *stupido cretino son Io!* [stupid idiot I am].' First despair and hopelessness, then anger—he took the record and smashed it: '*Tu bestia* [You beast]—you are the witness of my insufficiency!' But, say, in ten times he missed—a near miss—once or twice, the point is that eight times he hit the bull's eye. Yet he was aware that it's always like with a tightrope walker: You can't be sure; there is no net that catches you; and you may fall to your destruction. It can be wonderful—or it can be no good at all. He was always aware of this—for any one of us—and for himself. Yet it didn't upset the work. If another conductor were afraid, he would be inhibited. Not Toscanini; and this was another thing about him: his powerful spirit."[10]

## Setting a Single Tempo for an Entire Movement

Granick: "He felt enormous strength in Mozart, and that during his short life Mozart had arrived at a very great power of expression, a new kind of expression. The Maestro interpreted his music in a very straightforward way, actually, giving great strength to the structure of the piece, and always with clarity and infinite nuance, never acceding to a custom prevalent at that time, of inflicting the conductor's own personality on the music. There were no starts and stops, no ritards and accelerandos; the music just went on. I think that with the great many moods which Mozart had and of which Toscanini was the master in his conducting, the orchestra didn't have to play in such a limited fashion and, in a way, denigrate the greatness of Mozart, as was often done at the time by not giving him the full largeness of creativity which he had.

"As to the speed of his last movements which were frequently written to be *Presto*, they were a little faster than many other conductors. Fast movements were never too fast to play, but they went apace; they didn't stop for anything. There were no personality hang-ups where a conductor had to stop. He didn't have to stop. He didn't have any of these hang-ups. He just went on and brought things to a logical climax; and you always felt with Toscanini that the music was going someplace, that something was going to happen."

Haggin described "a Schubert 'Unfinished' remarkable in the way its steady tempos created an almost super earthly quiet and calm in which both the dramatic force and the serenity of the work were achieved."[11]

Shaw: "Toscanini sought expressive quality through dynamics or texture, not through tempo, which was the constant."[12]

Haggin commented on Toscanini's interpretation of Schubert's Ninth Symphony, writing of "the esthetic beauty . . . of a movement played in a single tempo with only slight modifications that are the more effective for the steadiness from which they depart."[13]

About Toscanini's performance of the same symphony with the Philadelphia Orchestra in 1941, Haggin wrote, "In the second movement . . . he set a tempo for the opening section that he could maintain unchanged not only for the alternating section but for the catastrophe in the middle of the movement, so that the increasing urgency and tension of this passage was achieved without any acceleration, and in fact a slight broadening at the end gave shattering power to the chords with which the passage breaks off into momentary silence."[14]

# Control

Civetta: "In conducting a rhythmic piece, such as the march from the 'Pathétique' or a Rossini overture, did you find it may have become too driving?"
Koutzen: "No, for me, no. Always in control. For me it was never too driving. It was never too fast for me. It was always under control, no matter what tempo. He knew exactly what he was doing."

# Toscanini and the Metronome

Sarser: "I found if you were to clock his Beethoven against the metronome markings in the scores, they were pretty close to perfect. If they weren't, he'd do it over. He wouldn't be satisfied unless he played Beethoven at least accurately."

Haggin, discussing *Harold in Italy*: "The third movement is titled 'Serenade of a Mountaineer of the Abruzzi to His Mistress' . . . The serenade was played by Toscanini in the tempo Berlioz had prescribed with his metronome marking in the score . . . Koussevitzky's declared position was that to do what the composer directed in the score was, in effect, not to want the score to be alive. Those are his own words. And his way of bringing the English horn melody to life was to play it more slowly than Berlioz directed. But the actual result was to change what Berlioz intended as an animated serenade, into a lugubrious lament . . .

"Toscanini's additional reason for considering it necessary to obey Berlioz's metronome markings for the several movements of *Harold* is worth reporting. The wanderings of Harold are represented by the recurrence, in successive movements, of a melody of a solo viola that is first stated in the introduction of the first movement . . . And for that melody to be in the same shape and time each time it recurs in the later movements, those movements have to be played in the tempos Berlioz prescribed with his metronome markings. If one changes the tempos of the movements, as Koussevitzky did, one changes also the shape of the solo viola's melody.

"Regarding a passage in the finale, which culminates in a series of imposing proclamations by the trombones and tuba: Berlioz not only prescribed the basic tempos of the movements with his metronome markings, but marked every change of tempo he wanted, and he marked no change of tempo for those imposing proclamations in the finale. Therefore, Toscanini does not change the tempo when he gets to them . . . Koussevitzky's disciple, Leonard Bernstein, plays the passage as Koussevitzky did, slowing down the proclamations to make them even more imposing, instead of which he makes them over-emphatic, ponderous and bombastic."[15]

Halina Rodzinski recalled a visit she and her husband, Artur Rodzinski, paid to Toscanini, who began discussing a recent broadcast he had heard of Rodzinski's performance of Beethoven's Seventh Symphony. He asked Rodzinski why he had conducted a certain passage in the finale faster than Beethoven's prescribed metronome marking. To demonstrate, the maestro seated himself at the piano and began to play the passage at the speed indicated by Beethoven. As the momentum of the music's galloping rhythm intensified, Toscanini's playing accelerated and became out of sync with the metronome. H. Rodzinski: "Maestro noticed the discrepancy and stopped playing. He struck his right hand with his left. He threw an embarrassed glance at my husband (who was suppressing a smile), and as his face flushed, shouted: 'But I have blood in my veins!'"[16]

# Rubato

Moldavan: "What Toscanini taught me was that a piece of music has a frame, and you phrase and build within this frame . . . Most musicians distort: If you listen to recordings, you hear this bar is a little longer and this one a little shorter; and Toscanini showed that it wasn't necessary to take such liberties to make a piece of music beautiful. This conception of music was one of the important things in his conducting."[17]

Sarser: "He didn't like to take big liberties and distort. He was accurate and I can't see anything wrong with that. If a person has heart and feeling, and can put this across within the framework of exactly the way the music was written, they are a great artist. But if a person can't do that, sometimes they have to put a little schmaltz or a little something of their own to try to bring this music to life. Toscanini brought it to life usually playing it the way it was written."

Winter, speaking about playing with the NBC Symphony after an absence: "Being thrilled became commonplace. I had forgotten how thrilled I was, but the minute he started to conduct the *Mignon* Overture my hair stood up the same way it did the very first time I played for him. There was a clarinet cadenza at the very beginning, which he conducted exactly in tempo, no rubato, and it sounded absolutely magnificent. It was the same thrill all over again."

Civetta: "And all this was instinctive, wasn't it, or was it learned?"

Winter: "It was both. He edited himself very carefully, but the wellspring was always one of feeling, and he tried very hard to identify with the composer, to feel what the composer was looking for."

Coletta: "If one person takes a phrase and distorts it, and then the next artist takes the same phrase and wants to top the distortion of the previous performance, you have a series of enormous distortions. Then you have chaos. So I feel that you have to make great music within a beat. There has to be a little rubato somewhere along the line, but still arrive in a legitimate place, not to distort. Casals put it beautifully. He said, 'Fantasy with order.' And I think that's what Toscanini had. He didn't distort, but he had freedom within that beat."

Civetta: "A subtle rubato."

Coletta: "A subtle one, right. That's the art, the subtlety."

Anne Mischakoff Heiles: "Sometimes my father directly attributed a simile or an idea to the Maestro, for example, when he told me to play a phrase in Brahms 'like a leaf falling from the tree,' trying to suggest a natural but subtle freedom."[18]

Burghauser described a Salzburg production of *Die Meistersinger*: "The second act—was literally unheard of! The poetry of went on with Sachs and Eva! And Beckmesser! . . . and those subtle modifications of tempo!"[19]

Ernest Ansermet: "In the last years of his life Furtwängler said to me, 'I am now convinced that it is possible to give music all the required expressiveness without altering the tempo.'"[20]

Frank Miller, principal cellist of the NBC Symphony: "His treatment of the phrase was plastic and free within the bar, but each bar was exactly as long as the next; and that was its greatness—the freedom within the bar that didn't destroy the continuity of the bars. Casals in his prime did the same bending of the phrase within the bar; and his phrasing still remains very beautiful. He has more of what Toscanini had than any cellist I can remember."[21]

Katims: "There is also the belief that he played everything strictly in time, as if with a metronome. Wrong! He played with a rubato so subtle, as natural as breathing . . . Once when I was discussing a score with the Old Man, he said of a particular passage, 'This must be *assolutamente preciso* [absolutely precise]—like with a metronome. Here, I show you.' He reached over and selected the appropriate tempo on his electric metronome and began to play the passage in question. But after only a few beats of the metronome he was no longer with it. He shut it off and said, 'But you can't be a machine!' And another time, when I suggested that one of the guest conductor's playing of the 'Perfumes of the Night' movement of Debussy's *Ibéria* was dull because he played precisely what was on the printed page—nothing more, nothing less—Maestro insisted that that was what he did! I brought the score over to the piano and asked him to play that section. As he played I pointed out the slight *stringendo* made here, the *poco ritardando* he made there, his rubato in another spot, etc.—none of which was in the score. Again he protested that it wasn't possible to be a machine."[22]

Katims, to Ben Grauer: "What was fantastic about Maestro was his very tremendous, subtle sense of rubato. It was so subtle that you never were aware of the freedom he was taking. It was like breathing. *Rubato* comes from the Italian word [*rubare*], meaning 'to steal.' You steal a little bit from one note and add it to another note. You go forward, you hold back a little bit. You don't take two breaths in exactly the same way; your heartbeat doesn't beat exactly the same way twice. So when people say, 'Toscanini always played everything precisely in time,' nothing could be farther from the truth. Because what was on the printed page was just the beginning. It has to be done with amazing control, because rubato without control is musical chaos. It was done in such good taste.

"The fantastic thing about rubato I can best explain . . . by telling you a story which Maestro told me a number of times. He was doing [Verdi's Te Deum], and there was one passage in it that had him a little bit puzzled. He didn't quite know what Verdi intended. So he went to Verdi's home and played it through for him. And when he finished, Verdi said, 'But that's exactly what I wanted.' Then Maestro said: 'But you didn't put in here *accelerando, ritardando, stringendo, decrescendo.*' Verdi said, 'Of course not. Because if I did that, every damned fool would exaggerate it.' He told me this story because you have to really feel it very naturally. And if you have that instinct and good taste, you do find it. Once you have to begin to explain: Now this note has to be a little shorter, that one a little longer, now go here—it's just as if I were to ask you, 'Would you please describe the color yellow to me?'"

Ben Grauer: "It becomes dehumanized, verbalized instead of felt."
Katims: "Exactly."[23]

Burghauser recalled a rehearsal of Brahms's *Liebesliederwalzer*: "Toscanini went to the piano and said, 'I don't ask for any new ideas—only a few things, in tempo and . . . flexibility.'"[24]

Kurt Weill, composer, wrote to pianist and composer Ferruccio Busoni after hearing a performance of Toscanini's at La Scala in 1924: "Charpentier's *Louise* was performed, Toscanini conducted, and that in itself was an event that made this whole trip worth the effort. I never knew that one could play 'on' an orchestra with such freedom, with such willful rubatos . . . I will remember this evening for a long time."[25]

Civetta: "Would you say he bears a tremendous influence on today's conductors?"
Granick: "Yes, I think so—because I think most sensitive conductors who hear Toscanini realize the tremendous amount of elasticity with which he conducted, and yet conformed to the written score. Still, it was elastic. And in much of the music of the twentieth century, which has changes of tempo every other bar or so, Toscanini's rubato really made sense out of all of these changes, so that they weren't idle differences of tempo, but all converged into something that created a movement that cohered."

Ralph Hunter prepared the chorus for Toscanini's last performance of Cherubini's Requiem in 1950: "He had not done the piece in years, and he did not have a score. I had the score that was available, which had been sent from Italy for this performance. Without looking at mine, he began to play the piece, one movement after the next, in precisely the correct tempo. Each time he set a tempo he would stop and turn on his metronome, and show off a little bit to prove that he was exactly right. He altered some of the printed tempo indications in the score, preferring them either slower or faster. He went through the complete work, playing it at the piano, singing the important parts, conducting and screaming, and it was exciting. He asked me for my score. He got out his favorite red pen, and proceeded to edit my score, from page to page, not just a note above one voice, but under each voice part: *pianissimo, forte, espressivo*, whatever he wanted. He was constantly adding things. For instance, at 'Salva me,' he wrote *espressivo molto*; at the words 'Pie Jesu,' *molto legato*. He also added *poco ritenuto* and *a tempo* in places where it was not so directed by the composer. At the fugue, which was indicated at 120 for the half note, he took that at 112, and said the edition is incorrect."

> Regarding his ever-evolving interpretive style, the argument that he used less pronounced rubato in his later years, is an often misunderstood generalization. Interestingly, the enormous tempos fluctuations in his recording of the first movement of the Beethoven Ninth at age eighty-five, and the arbitrary four bars of *meno mosso* in the *Coriolan* Overture demonstrate that even in his old age he continued to play music as he felt it. Furthermore, aside from some of the published accounts describing his interpretations (see Kurt Weill's letter to Busoni on page 73), we don't know how he interpreted the majority of his repertoire in his twenties, thirties, and forties, because no recordings were made of his work in those years.

## Rethinking

Gianandrea Gavazzeni, conductor, wrote that Toscanini's performances were "always changing because he was convinced that a great composition is never merely a substance to be poured out, but rather a living organism." Gavazzeni referred to the "evolutionary quality of his operation, which was tireless, never sated, never still."[26]

Harris Goldsmith, pianist and music critic: "In general style, I find that Toscanini did tend, in later years, to become more cut-and-dried. I find that many of these performances, especially the ones conducted in recording sessions, tend to be more impersonal, more matter-of-fact, with absolutely unanimous ensemble, beautifully blended strings taking the place of subtle, little variations in tempo, and care and detail of phrasing. I think many of these later performances are great performances. I find that in occasional cases, that there was just not the same care in the shaping and the emphasizing of the music that I find in his earlier performances where there was much more chance taking; there was more variation of tempo. In fact, there is a Beethoven Fifth Symphony performance that was broadcast in 1933, where Toscanini was as rhetorical as any of his colleagues. You can hear in the development section of that performance a huge slowing down, and in the coda a tumultuous speeding up. In his later performances, everything seemed to have flattened out into an even keel. And I find that this is not just an isolated example; it is typical of many of his performances from the period."

Martin Bernstein, bass player: "It's quite clear that Toscanini was much more relaxed when he was younger, and that's just the converse of what happens to most people as they age. The [earlier] performances are still quite tense; they are very, very musical indeed; but there is ample opportunity . . . for intensification of the dramatic values of the work by subtle changes in tempo. Some of them are not even subtle. I don't mean to imply that they're gross but that they're much more easily perceived. The first movement of his 1929 recording of the Mozart 'Haffner' Symphony sounds almost like Mengelberg."[27]

J. Bernstein: "I played all Beethoven's nine symphonies with him many times. It was many times different. He was always looking for something else. I couldn't compare one performance of a symphony which was similar. He was changing all the time. And he had difficulties, because he wanted to take certain freedoms, and he felt he wasn't allowed, and this disturbed him very much. In the 'Eroica' he used to start by adding extra time in the beginning, twice after the downbeats. Then later, he eliminated this. I remember once in the Ninth Symphony we almost lost him; he started to conduct in eight, in twelve; we didn't know where he was, because he had some ideas. The orchestra went through, but he had ideas."

## Slow Music

Schonberg: "Toscanini felt that the German conductors played too slow, just as Horowitz felt that the German pianists played too slow. [Horowitz:] 'Everything adagio . . . So Toscanini reacted against that, perhaps a little too much. He wanted to show how the music should really sound . . . Now everybody is too slow. They all want to show what profound musicians they are. If you play slow, you are profound.'"[28]

## Young

Some of the musicians thought the maestro was afraid of slowing down in his old age, and therefore consistently demonstrated a youthful demeanor.

A. Shulman: "In later years certain things were played faster; and I think that he was afraid of being accused of growing old. Though, the *Tristan* Prelude did get slower and broader; and this was true also of the Prelude to *Lohengrin*: It got so broad that the violins ran out of bow."

Bloom: "I've even heard people say the older he got, the faster he'd take things to prove that he was still young. You know, that's absolutely ridiculous. The man would never do anything to prove anything except what he meant to do."

> The idea that his tempos accelerated in his old age because he wanted to prove he was still young is hard to consider valid when one thinks of his last performances of the Brahms symphonies, the *Barber of Seville* Overture, "Siegfried's Death and Funeral Music" from *Götterdämmerung*, the *Tristan* Prelude and "Liebestod," the third movement of the "Pathétique" Symphony, the finale of Mendelssohn's "Reformation" Symphony, and the *Parsifal* Prelude. And this generalization is further complicated by the fact that he spent his final years conducting in Carnegie Hall, which had different acoustics than NBC's Studio 8H* where slightly faster tempos were often taken as a natural reaction to the dryness of the room's acoustics.

## Italian Tempo Markings

D. Walter, to Civetta: "One of the things that disturbed him was our misunderstanding of Italian, the national language of music, and I am constantly amazed at the fact that the average musician will think of *andante*, *largo*, *grave*, and *adagio* as all meaning slow, whereas they have specific meanings and, importantly, different meanings."

D. Walter, to Haggin: "For example, the literal translation of *andante* is 'going,' and its meaning in music is 'with flowing movement.'"[29]

---

* Studio 8H was the home of the NBC Symphony from 1937 until the orchestra was moved to Carnegie Hall in 1950. During rehearsals the acoustics were somewhat reverberative, but at concerts—when filled to its capacity of 1,200—the acoustics became very dry. Today, the TV show *Saturday Night Live* is televised from 8H.

D. Walter, to Civetta: "*Allegro* in Italian doesn't mean fast, it means happy. So now when we say *allegro* in a piece of music, how happy is happy? He had very, very precise ideas of what was written in the score and how you should understand it. So with the combination of careful reading and watching his very meaningful gestures . . . we achieved something that very, very few orchestras ever achieved. He was a great teacher . . .

"He taught us to look carefully at the composer's indications on the printed page—to see, for example, what he wrote after *Allegro*. He would say, 'Is not *allegro*. Is *allegro ma* [but]—' or '*allegro con* [with]—' Every word meant something. In *allegro giusto* you had to pay attention to *giusto* [just, proper]; in *allegro vivace*, to the *vivace* [vivacious]. When we played an andante he would say, '*Non marcia funebre!* [Not funeral march!] Andante!'"

D. Walter, to Haggin: "I remember his stopping us once at the beginning of the second movement of Beethoven's 'Eroica': 'Is written *Marcia Funebre*. You play *funebre*; I want *marcia!*' And this exactness extended to everything else in the score—dynamics, time values, phrasing . . .

"This was the first of countless demonstrations of his respect for the composer's text. The printed score didn't tell you everything; but Toscanini believed it was what you had to start with; and he made you think of the exact meanings of the words you found there."[30]

## Slow Movements

Rostal: "Toscanini said, 'The classical andante by Mozart, Haydn, Beethoven is moving.' *Andante* means 'moving,' not 'slow.' And he conducted in a good, moving tempo, never too slow, or never as slow as other conductors, especially the European way."

Bloom: "Sure, there had to be among the orchestra members—quite a rethinking of a lot of things because we were used to doing things a certain way and suddenly this man comes along and opens their eyes by saying *andante* means 'to go,' *andiamo* [let's go]. *Andante* is not synonymous with *slow*. *Andante* is a walking speed, and so in the light of that, we would do an Andante movement of a Mozart symphony and this thing marched. It kept its calmness but it didn't die because of lack of momentum."

Winter: "What people didn't realize about Toscanini was the enormous sensitivity within these 'fast' slow movements. There was a whole world of little touches that the audience was never aware of, that we would get with the stick—never talked about, and almost always unexpected. It was shown with the stick, and we would naturally respond to it."

Civetta: "He's been criticized for his fast tempos. Did you find they were too fast?" Granick: "Well, no. In regard to slow movements, for instance, Toscanini included his audience in the performance. He felt that most slow movements were so boring because conductors took them too slow. In addition, there was a vogue of inter- polating the conductor's feelings about the music into the music, beyond what the composer asked for, and sometimes they made ritards and almost came to a dead halt, and they started again and stopped and started—all of which left the audience with a feeling of boredom. When Toscanini played a slow movement, he played it as it was written, mostly, in what he interpreted as the tempo that was asked for. When it was *andante*, he didn't want to play it *adagio*, yet many conductors did. So he played it a little faster than was the custom. I give very little credence to the crit- ics who think that way, because they praised so many really poor conductors who showed their special feelings about the music by really ruining it by slowing down and accelerating and doing everything possible to show their own natures, their own characters, their own personality, rather than what was really in the music."

D. Walter spoke about Toscanini's conducting of Beethoven's Seventh Symphony: "When I heard for the first time all the different things in Toscanini's performance I was so excited that I could hardly contain myself. I remember in particular the shock of the second movement. It is often referred to as the slow movement; and you know the usual slow tempo . . . So you can imagine the effect on me when Toscanini began the move- ment in his tempo . . . He set a tempo that conformed to the meaning of Beethoven's direction, *Allegretto*, not to the traditional preconception of 'slow movement.'"[31]

## *Die Zauberflöte*: "Ach, ich fühl's"

Haggin: "Clasping his hands as he acted Pamina's agitation, he exclaimed, 'Pamina say "I lose my Tamino! Where my Tamino!" Must be *andante*, but is always *adagio*!'"[32]

Hupka: "She is a desperate girl who is in love, and is saying that rest will only be in death. She feels that the happiness of love is all gone. She wants to kill herself. She's agitated. You don't sing in that condition of soul, where you want to commit suicide, as a slow lyric *adagio*. You sing it with passion. She is desperate."

## Acoustics

Galimir: "There was a period of tension; but at the end I thought it was very relaxed and beautiful. Of course it was also that Toscanini felt much happier in Carnegie Hall because of the sound. That 8H sound was very clean; but it was not an ingratiating sound; and when we went to Carnegie Hall the playing really started to sound. And I felt that the orchestra itself was a little tense in performances—in the earlier years, not in rehearsals . . . but there was a general feeling of relaxed music-making at the end in the performances: 'Ah! Now it's relaxed!'"[33]

Civetta: "Toscanini has been often criticized for taking very fast tempos."
Gordon: "These criticisms stem from a lack of understanding. For years we played in an acoustically dead studio, which was like a vacuum. It was almost like canned music, horrible. You'd get a hollow sound out of the orchestra. We recorded so many things in this studio from where we played most of our performances, all of which were live broadcasts that were recorded. His tempos were often on the fast side because he was subconsciously avoiding that vacuum. When we moved to Carnegie Hall, suddenly the acoustics were so superior, and the orchestra's sound came alive. The recordings we made in Carnegie Hall were not criticized as much as those from 8H."

Barzin: "I was asked why his tempos go faster. And I said you must understand that Toscanini is a man who lived in the bel canto period* and he has always produced in the hall or in the theatre where there's a reverberant bounce, and that little bounce is part of his interpretation. 8H had no bounce at all, and therefore he was trying to re-create the interpretation with the bounce without having the bounce, so he speeded up. I said all you have to do is bring him back into Carnegie Hall and I

---

* *Bel canto*, literally "beautiful singing," is the style of operas written by Rossini, Bellini, Donizetti, and their contemporaries. It is also used to describe a style of singing that stresses vocal flexibility and beautiful sound rather than dramatic declamation, though the music of the first part of the nineteenth century often has strong declamatory passages and Verdi's music is filled with bel canto passages.

predict that within an hour and a half of rehearsal, he'll be right back where he was in tempos because as soon as he's going to hear his old way of hearing the music, he's gonna go right back in the tempo he usually had—which, I must say, if you see '8H' in certain recordings, they're a little faster."

Nevertheless, despite the logic of generalizations about Toscanini, there are often exceptions that tend to weaken these generalizations.

## Following the Orchestra

Brieff: "There are some places where you just let the orchestra play by itself. And he had that trick too."

Cusumano: "In the *fortissimo* tutti sections of the scherzo of Beethoven's Ninth Symphony, he would never try to control the tempo. He knew it would be a mistake to even try."

Usually, however, Toscanini insisted the orchestra follow his tempo. On a rehearsal recording of Mozart's *Magic Flute* Overture, Toscanini is heard saying, "I cannot conduct with your tempo. I want my tempo. Maybe is wrong, but I cannot conduct with your tempo."[34]

## Accompanying

Civetta: "How did he work with soloists?"
Coletta: "They had to do it his way, including his own son-in-law, Horowitz. He ruled. 'Pull them along, pull them along.'"

Mieczysław Horszowski, pianist: "I could feel that he was following every note in my playing—not as note but as part of the line of music; and that if I had made an unexpected ritard or rubato . . . the orchestra would have been immediately with it. Sometimes playing with an orchestra . . . is like playing with an overcoat: You are not quite at ease. Playing with Maestro Toscanini, you had wings."[35]

Bachmann: "We played the Elgar *Introduction and Allegro for Strings*. During the rehearsal, the quartet (which was Mischakoff, Miller, Carlton Cooley, and myself) thought that there should be a ritardando leading back to the first tempo. And we forgot to tell Maestro about it. So at the rehearsal he went ahead and we made the ritardando. He caught on immediately, made the ritardando, and at the end I said, 'Maestro, excuse us. We didn't think of . . .' 'Why? You're the soloists. You feel it that way? Play it that way. I'll follow you. I'm accompanying you. I'm not the soloist. If I think it's not right, I will tell you so. But I won't tell you not to do it because you're convinced of it and I'm convinced of mine.'"

Barzin: "I played the solo viola part in *Don Quixote* many times with him. It was the only time I didn't feel the stick at all when I played the solo. What he did was unbelievable. He colored around you. He was so sensitive to orchestral color that if you had good taste, he never bothered you. He was terrible with musicians who didn't have good taste; but those who had taste, he wanted to play music with them. He gave them freedom. So actually I never felt the stick; it was there. He would hear my tone or what I did and he liked it, so he began playing around with all the instruments around me. And that, I think, is a great conductor. To be a fine conductor, you have to be able to play upon your instrument: The orchestra, and the human element becomes very important, and that's where Toscanini was supreme, although some musicians were scared to death of him. This memory thing scared a lot of people. But when you finished a performance you felt you had done something that probably would never happen again."

Bloom recalled that Toscanini allowed him the freedom to play oboe solo passages as he wished, including the first movement of Beethoven's Fifth Symphony and the second movement of Schubert's Ninth Symphony:

"We were doing the Schubert C Major Andante con moto movement, which starts with an oboe solo. I played it and got through about the first sixteen bars. Then there was another solo, and then he stopped and he started to say something. And there was a very wonderful gesture, the greatest compliment I ever got in my life. He stopped in the midst of saying something to me, put his hand over his mouth, and said to himself, 'Toscanini be quiet. It's not the way I would have done it but it was also good.' Now for him to admit that somebody could do something not his way but still be good, well, you can imagine, you can understand why I think that's the greatest compliment I ever got because he never gave compliments and he never bothered me after that at all."

Horowitz—who had married Toscanini's daughter, Wanda—considered Toscanini his mentor, and played a subservient role to the maestro. When Horowitz disagreed about interpretation, for example, in the Brahms Second Piano Concerto, he didn't assert himself.

Toscanini planned to conduct this concerto with Ossip Gabrilowitsch and the New York Philharmonic in 1935. However, after listening to Gabrilowitsch's performance of the piece with the National Orchestra Association, Toscanini felt that their views of the work were too different and he canceled the performance.[36]

The first concerto that Horowitz and Toscanini collaborated on was Beethoven's "Emperor" Concerto with the New York Philharmonic in 1933. Horowitz had never performed the work before. The conductor Issay Dobrowen had misinformed Horowitz about Toscanini, explaining that the maestro favored slow tempos. At their private rehearsal Horowitz began to play the first movement's Allegro rather slowly. Toscanini interrupted him and indicated his faster tempo, whereupon Horowitz joyfully shifted gears, as he shared Toscanini's choice of tempo. Their collaboration was harmonious and they performed the concerto after one rehearsal with the orchestra.[37]

Schonberg: "Horowitz always said that Toscanini was not as hard to work with as many people thought. If an artist really knew the music, there never were problems. When Horowitz played with Toscanini they almost always went straight through because even when Horowitz thought of stopping and asking for some kind of adjustment he hesitated to interpose. [Toscanini always rehearsed and performed from memory, but at rehearsals had the score on a stand to his left, for reference.] Horowitz explained, 'He had everything memorized, to the last note—but I felt a little uncomfortable. So I discussed things with him before or after rehearsals. It was not difficult. He could do anything he wanted in front of an orchestra.'"[38]

## Critics

Civetta: "What about the slow movements of symphonies?"
Krasnopolsky: "I think he made his own interpretations reasonably calm and musically valid. You can't please the whole world, especially the critics. That's why they're

called critics. They have to find something. When the critics say they're too fast or slow, it is their own opinion. But what comes out is very important.

Rostal: "He being an Italian opera conductor, some people were criticizing his Brahms. For me, it was great, the greatest revelation. There is a sort of sixth sense, and he had it, as far as tempos are concerned, as far as knowing how the melody has to come out. The way he analyzed those things, it was great, great. So I enjoyed every bit, no matter what we performed, what we did, I always learned a lot."

## Generalizations

Making generalizations about Toscanini's work is tempting, and at first they often seem valid. However for every generalization there are many exceptions to the rule, thereby weakening the generalizations. For example, Toscanini's tempos were often faster than many other conductors, yet there are numerous cases where his tempos were slower than the majority of conductors. Examples are *Parsifal*, his last few performances of the Prelude and "Liebestod" from *Tristan*, and some of the allegros in the Strauss tone poems.

Gilda Dalla Rizza, soprano, described singing "Depuis le jour" from *Louise* with Toscanini in 1924: "He took [it] . . . so slowly that I kept wondering whether my voice would give out . . . But when I performed it I realized why . . . All hell would break loose after this aria, and there was always . . . several minutes of thunderous applause. The effect of this aria was stunning, for this slow, rapturous cry of love underlined an enchanted dream on the top of Montmartre after all the confusion of the city."[39]

## Breathing

A friend of Toscanini's once remarked to him that his conducting always had a flowing motion, like the waves of the ocean, and that the music always seemed to be heading towards a destination. Toscanini responded that a doctor had once told him he had unique breathing facility, that he breathed easily, unlike many people, who breathe haltingly, in a breaking

manner. This quality was reflected in Toscanini's beat and in the characteristic flow of his rhythmic style.

## Life—Sonority

Hupka: "Another unique quality of Maestro was the movement, the pulsation,
the flow of the music, like when you throw a stone in a calm lake, and you see the
movement of the ripples. There was nothing stagnant, nothing stale. It was living."

Krasnopolsky: "He put life in the music. He especially liked to play Rossini overtures
because he created a holiday-like atmosphere! It was wonderful; he was like a child.
The tempos were really fast, but we didn't feel they were too fast. We liked it. And he
also liked Strauss waltzes. He used to wind them up so that it was a joy to play them
with him. To my understanding he made everything a masterpiece. He put life in it."

Burghauser: "The imagination that it was faster than usual was only on account of
the very liveliness of expression. He conducted with such plasticity and liveliness
that you had the impression that it was as fast as you ever heard it, and it was not
faster metronomically. He made it seem fast, through liveliness, but it was not faster.
We proved it against the metronome, and still people believe it was faster. Listen
to his recordings."

Lehmann spoke about Toscanini's interpretation of *Die Meistersinger*: "You know
how the first act can be somewhat boring, with that long scene with all the guild
members carrying on. Well, he infuses into it such vivacity and so many different
shades, marking the character of each one, that it seems almost short."[40]

Freeman: "It was life; it was portrayed. Take *Traviata*—if it was nervous music, what
are you going to do, walk ten paces a minute? No, it can't be. It's there; it's the life.
The music is there. What gives it the blood? The conductor up there in front does
it. Don't ask if it's fast or slow. Did you get the message? Did you cry? Could you
feel the happiness? Could you feel the tarantella in your feet? Or is it important
whether it's fast or whether it's slow? No; I think he would say, 'My dear, no.' It's not
the tempo. It is the blood of the music. It is what the painter tried to do with color
on a piece of canvas, which is harder to do with little black dots on a piece of paper.

Can you imagine taking little black dots on a piece of paper, and making it cry, laugh, dance, march, or be sad? Was there love? Did it portray love? Did it distract you from your everyday thoughts, and give you the message, the story and the picture of what it was? Why do you go to hear *Traviata* so many times or a symphony so many times? There's a message you get from it; there's beauty you get from it. And if it's there, don't worry about the tempo. But if it's not there then what didn't it give you? What caused it? Then maybe it was the tempo that didn't give it to you, or maybe it was a bad interpretation. But nobody complained about the interpretation; they loved the interpretation, but they thought it was fast. 'Then why did you like it if it was fast? Why did you like it if it was too slow?' In Beethoven's Third, certainly, he was criticized for slowness. But remember, the man wasn't going to work; he was going to a funeral. You knew it was a funeral. You knew it was sad. It was heavy. The sixteenth notes were heavy. The quarter notes were long; it was black; it was a casket with a body. Did you get the message that it was a funeral? That's it. Are we criticizing music or tempos? The music was there. Stokowski said, 'Conductors are disappointed musicians; critics are disappointed conductors.' So they had that problem. They said it was fast. I saw a couple of critics that wrote about it; I said, 'How did you like it?' 'Oh I loved it.' But one of them wrote that it was too fast. He loved it but it was too fast."

## CHAPTER 5

# Opera

*Don't ever get discouraged . . . don't allow yourself to be defeated!*
    —Toscanini

Opera in nineteenth-century Italy was a popular form of entertainment and a prime opportunity for socializing. The house lights were kept on during performances; and it was customary for members of the audience to move about the theatre, visiting with one another, talking, eating, and drinking. Usually the chatter died down when an important aria was sung; and then the attention was on vocal displays, and climactic high notes—both written and interpolated. After the opera, a full-length ballet was performed!

There were no orchestra pits. The orchestra was placed on the floor between the front row and the stage. Before beginning his first season as artistic director at the Teatro Regio in Turin in 1895, Toscanini insisted on the construction of an orchestra pit.

Orchestras and casts were assembled at an opera house for a few months at a time for a minimum number of rehearsals. Singers basically stood and sang without any serious thought to acting and staging. The scenery was comprised of generic painted backdrops. By the time Toscanini began his artistic directorship in Turin in 1895, he had acquired a good deal of opera-conducting experience. He began to insist on conditions that gave priority to the highest artistic standards in the preparation and performance of the operas he conducted. Toscanini meticulously rehearsed and personally supervised every aspect of operatic production, including set, costume, and lighting design, staging, and choreography.

He revolutionized audiences' behavior at opera performances by instituting several reforms: refusing to allow latecomers to enter the theatre until the end of a scene, requiring women to remove their hats so as not to obstruct the view of the persons seated behind them, banning encores, and doing away with the tradition of performing a ballet after a full-length opera on the same evening. The maestro insisted on the construction of orchestra pits in Turin and at La Scala, that the curtain open horizontally from the center instead of rising vertically, and that the house lights be lowered during performances.

Fred Zimmermann, New York Philharmonic bass player: "In some things Toscanini was ahead of his time. I mean the early days when he was a young man conducting in Italian opera houses where the audience was accustomed to get arias repeated, and he defied the audience and refused to repeat the aria and walked out. From the beginning he was different from the others—a man of great musical integrity and great courage."[1]

Throughout his career, Toscanini performed with virtually every major opera singer. Of these, many have been interviewed on radio and film, and have produced auto-biographies, or memoirs about themselves—but few have focused extensively on Toscanini's influence on their career beyond various anecdotes. Giuseppe Valdengo (1914–2007) is the only singer who wrote a book about his association with Tosca-nini: *Scusi, conosce Toscanini?* (Excuse Me, Do You Know Toscanini?).

There was a luxury of rehearsal time for each of the concert versions of the three operas Valdengo sang with Toscanini. He had private rehearsals with Toscanini at the piano, piano rehearsals with other cast members conducted by the maestro, and several rehearsals with orchestra. Afterward, the maestro would sometimes tell anecdotes and reminisce. Valdengo was no stranger to Toscanini's studio at NBC. Here he had the opportunity for additional interaction, and he visited the maestro at home for private coachings and consultations. Toscanini also threw parties, large and small, which provided more occasions for Valdengo to be with him in social situations.

The maestro was fond of chatting with his friends on the phone after midnight, and enjoyed gossiping! Valdengo would call the conductor after midnight, when

Toscanini had retired to his bedroom. Valdengo made audio recordings of some of these phone calls. He also kept diaries that he utilized to cite specific dates to convey some of what he shared about Toscanini in his book.

Toscanini valued Valdengo's musicianship and vocal abilities; Valdengo perceived and appreciated Toscanini's wisdom, and made the most of the maestro's vast experience. Considering the various opportunities he had to rehearse and converse with Toscanini, and in light of his highly emotional tribute to the maestro made shortly before his own death, I trust Valdengo's unique and thorough account.

Each of the quotations in this chapter attributed to Valdengo and every quotation here attributed directly to Toscanini are translations of Valdengo's text, and therefore references to Valdengo's original text in *Scusi, conosce Toscanini?* are omitted from this chapter's endnotes.

## Passion for Opera

Valdengo recalled what Toscanini said about Guido Cantelli, the young conductor whose work Toscanini most admired and promoted: "I want for Cantelli to conduct opera and learn to admire Verdi and our melodrama. Everyone conducts concerts more or less well, but opera is difficult." To Cantelli, Toscanini said, "You will always like conducting concerts, but you will progress and will dream of conducting opera. Of course, the difficulties, the annoyances and the fatigue you encounter will be greater, both because of the singers who will stumble over trying to find the interpretive style that you want, and because of the acting, the gestures, and the staging. And let's not talk about the possible arguments with the producers and the deplorable whims of the audience. But, believe me, when you will have succeeded in overcoming these difficulties, oh! Then it is *complete* happiness that comes to flood your soul."

When Valdengo asked Toscanini whether he preferred to conduct concerts or operas, the conductor responded, "Opera has always been my passion; I always tried to find intelligent singers, conscientious and willing to follow me; and I rejected hams, who I could never endure. To tell the truth, I have always shaped the singers myself."

# Puccini

Puccini spoke about Toscanini to Arthur Abell, music critic and author of several books on music: "No other conductor gets out of my scores what he does. It was Toscanini who conducted the premiere of *La bohème* in Turin. He was then only twenty-nine years old. His interpretation was more than a great reproduction—it was a veritable re-creation. I sat there enthralled. Toscanini and I often disagree; we have violent quarrels and call each other all kinds of vile names, but we always become reconciled again, because we have a genuine respect for each other as musicians. I am nine years older than he is, but in many ways, he is musically much more advanced than I am. He is a genius! Under his magic baton, my scores, and those of Wagner and Verdi, become illumined and the manner in which he translates that luminosity into sound baffles description.

"Moreover, Toscanini conducts everything from memory. His phenomenal memory is the despair of all other conductors. When I heard him lead the orchestra and singers through the four acts of *La bohème* at that Turin premiere without a note in front of him, I felt like shouting what Nicodemus said to Jesus: 'Rabbi, we know that thou art a teacher come from God; for no man can do these miracles thou doest except God be with him.' Toscanini's interpretations are, in fact, miracles, and his unrivalled memory is a cosmic manifestation. Toscanini is close to God when conducting."[2]

# Rehearsals for the Twenty-fifth Anniversary of *Manon Lescaut* at La Scala

Arrigo Tassinari, principal flutist at La Scala, described a rehearsal of the second act of *Manon Lescaut*, which begins with a flute solo: "After three or four bars he stopped me and shouted, 'No! Tassinari! More freely!' Of course I could play more freely, but I also had to keep in tempo. So . . . I leaned a little on the first note of each *gruppetto*. 'No, no, no!' shouted Toscanini. 'On the stage, there's a woman putting powder on her face; I want to have the impression of seeing the dust from that powder!' But how was I supposed to . . . get face-powder out of a flute? . . . How he did that *Manon*—it was like opening a bottle of champagne! . . . Every now and then, when Toscanini stopped, Puccini would come over and embrace him. 'I didn't know I had written such a beautiful opera' . . . Puccini always told Toscanini to do as he pleased, even to make changes."[3]

Filippo Ghignatti, English horn player and oboist: "I recall what Puccini told the maestro at the rehearsal of his *Manon* . . . It was the twenty-fifth anniversary of that opera. Toscanini called Puccini from the podium and told him to look over some harmonies he wrote in the score in a certain spot which showed emptiness, and see what he thought of it, or better still, listen to them. Puccini's answer was, 'I don't have to. If you put those notes there, it's because they are needed.' Toscanini replied, 'But you wrote this opera, not me, and you must see if you would like the correction I've written.' 'The opera, yes, but you are a better musician than I, and I take any correction from you.' Toscanini asked the orchestra to play those penciled notes and Puccini listened very attentively and then said, '*Benissimo!* I will call Casa Ricordi [Puccini's publisher] and tell them to insert that in all the scores.' I was seated second to the conductor, and Puccini was leaning over the barrier that divides the orchestra from the public. He was standing just over my head. That is how I heard the conversation."[4]

> For Toscanini to change what Puccini had written, and for the composer
> to accept the conductor's changes without the need to first hear the revi-
> sions, was remarkable.

Puccini: "Dear Arturo, You have given me the greatest satisfaction of my life! *Manon*, as you interpret it is superior to what I thought it to be in those distant days. You have brought this music of mine to life with incomparable poetry, *souplesse* [supple-ness] and passionate temperament . . . I am happy above all because you have been capable of understanding my young, passionate spirit of thirty years ago! Thanks, from the bottom of my heart!"[5]

# Singers

Valdengo asked Toscanini about the artists he best remembered among those who had performed with him, to which Toscanini replied, "I have had so many good ones, that I couldn't say. I always cherished Pertile, la Toti dal Monte, Galeffi, Stabile, Pasero. With artists one needs to know what to do. You are strange people, and it's important to know how to stroke you the right way, as with velvet." Valdengo said, "And taking me by the arm, he laughed heartily.

"I asked him what he thought of the voice of Caruso, and he replied, 'The voice of Caruso was warm, rich with color, and full of pathos. Caruso practiced every phrase a lot, every passage. Just think, in the morning, before the performance, he sang the whole opera that he had to perform in the evening. Caruso had a terrible throat and, looking at it, you would never imagine that a voice so soft and warm could ever emerge from it.

"'Speaking of this, I would like to tell you about this strange incident. It was the opening of the 1913–1914 season at the Metropolitan in New York, and *La Gioconda* was about to be performed, with Caruso. A little before the curtain rose, I went, as was my habit, to visit the artist in his dressing room. When I was close to the door, I heard the voice of the house doctor, who exclaimed, "But, Commendatore, there's no way you can sing with a throat in that condition." And I heard Caruso saying, "Doctor, just brush my throat with a tincture of iodine and glycerin, and don't worry, all will go well!" I went in. Seeing me, the doctor said, "Maestro, just look at this throat and you be the judge of whether he can sing in this state." I walked closer, and the doctor shined a light in Caruso's throat. You would not believe it, dear rascal! Even I, who know next to nothing about throats, was absolutely horrified. Just think, the soft palate was so large and so inflamed that it covered the entire opening to the throat—so disturbing! I said, "But Enrico, you can't sing like this." Without answering he looked at me, and then turned to the doctor, "Doc, just brush it and then you'll hear." On his insistence, the doctor brushed his throat. I went to my dressing room really worried. This was the beginning of the Metropolitan season, and I have to say, dear rascal, that after seeing Caruso's throat in that state, I went down to the orchestra pit in high agitation, consigning my soul to God. My face must have registered my shock, because I saw the musicians staring at me. I began conducting with my heart in my mouth, waiting for Caruso to enter, and when I saw him in front of me, a cold shudder snaked along my spine, I was so afraid of a disaster. Well, when he opened his mouth and enunciated the first verses, "Assassini! quel crin venerando rispettate," the voice came out in ringing tones more beautiful and louder than ever: brilliant pearls poured from his mouth! After the "Cielo e mar" aria there was a brief intermission. The audience had gone crazy: They wanted an encore no matter what. I assure you that I had never heard Caruso sing so wonderfully well. From the podium I blew him a kiss . . . and you know that it takes a lot to please me . . . What a voice, what a voice, dear rascal! Called to the front of the stage to endless applause, Caruso looked at me and winked mischievously. After the act I ran onto the stage to embrace him.'"

Toscanini said that to hear Tamagno in *Guillaume Tell* was "a delightful thing: Musically, he left a little to be desired, because singing as he did by ear, when he went off track, it was difficult to put him back, but when he opened the valves in the high register his voice was unleashed like a chorus of silver trumpets. When Tamagno came to the cadenza of the aria 'O muto asil del pianto' ('Asile héréditaire'),* that C-natural of Tamagno nailed me, enraptured, to the podium . . .

"And to say that I am never fond of tenor fermatas, but that C, on which Tamagno made a fermata, believe me, was truly worth the entire performance." Valdengo continued, "The Maestro was irritated because the recordings that circulated did not do justice to the voice of that phenomenon."

Valdengo: "The Maestro enjoyed discovering beautiful voices. One day, talking about the soprano Renata Tebaldi, he said, 'Tebaldi's voice is heavenly, dear rascal; it is one of those voices that enter into the soul, that go directly to the heart. It is a pure, clear, luminous voice. When Tebaldi sings, all is serene, the sun shines; it seems that the very scent of spring is released from her.'"

Valdengo: "For the role of Fenton in *Falstaff*, a very good-natured character that illuminates the opera with charming grace, [Toscanini] had wanted above all a beautiful, fresh, young, and spontaneous voice. He had heard a broadcast of *Faust* from the Metropolitan in which the protagonist was the tenor Giuseppe Di Stefano. He said to me enthusiastically, 'That C in the *romanza* is truly perfect, both in the sound produced and in its diminuendo, and I must admit that this is one of the most beautiful voices that I have ever heard . . .' Di Stefano was unavailable for the engagement, but the following year he did sing Verdi's Requiem with Toscanini."

Valdengo asked, "Who do you think were the most exceptional vocalists?" The maestro responded, "The most exceptional vocalists that I heard were Francesco Tamagno, Luisa Tetrazzini, Titta Ruffo, and Enrico Caruso. Many others had beautiful voices, but they couldn't be considered particularly exceptional."

---

\* Toscanini's opera performances in Italy were all sung in Italian translation, as was then customary.

## Singers' Repertoire

Toscanini, discussing Valdengo's voice teacher Michele Accorinti: "You had the great fortune to meet someone who knew immediately how to classify the kind of voice you have, because very often it happens that teachers make mistakes. So there have been young people who have studied for a long time as baritones, while later, and in many cases too late, it was discovered that they were tenors, or vice versa. How many beautiful voices were ruined due to the wrong classification!"

Valdengo: "The Maestro asserted that unfortunately the idea of exact qualifications for singers has been lost, possibly even from a lack of voices. 'The contralto, the real dramatic tenor, the basso profondo have almost disappeared from circulation,' he repeated to me often. 'And in this way one hears lyric tenors that sing dramatic operas and sopranos who become celebrities in mezzo-soprano roles, while thickening the tone.'

"I asked the Maestro what he thought of the legendary nineteenth century soprano, Adelina Patti, who succeeded in singing *Norma* and *Barbiere*. He said, 'Look, dear Valdengo, it's true that la Patti sang *Norma* and *Barbiere*, but her voice was not adapted to everything, even if she was defined as a phenomenon; nature, at a certain moment, rebels and puts its foot down. She sang everything, but I don't believe that she was perfect in all parts.'

"One afternoon, arriving at rehearsal early, I entered the Maestro's studio while he was playing the aria from *La sonnambula*, 'Ah! non credea mirarti' . . . 'What beautiful music!' I cried out. And he continued to play, and then said, 'You know, rascal, after a week of Wagner rehearsals, a little Bellini puts everything in place!' The night before, the Maestro had conducted an all-Wagner concert at NBC."

> Wagner was one of Toscanini's favorite composers. However, he refreshed himself by playing Bellini's music at the piano after a week of immersion in the complexities of Wagner's music.

## Recitals

Valdengo: "In 1952 when I got back to New York, I called the Maestro, who immediately invited me to visit him. That year the Maestro reviewed the most important operas in my repertoire with me . . . I submitted the new programs for my recitals for his review and comments and he suggested that I insert some new pieces. I asked him if it was a good idea to add some modern compositions. Toscanini advised me to add Ravel's *Don Quichotte à Dulcinée* to my program.

"The Maestro regretted that in Italy, piano and voice recitals were not appreciated: 'I don't know how people have the courage to listen for an evening to an entire concert of piano music. No matter how lovely it is, after two and a half hours even a saint would tire out. Wouldn't it be better to listen to a singer as well? It would be much more varied.' I reminded him that even a baritone or a bass for an entire evening can become boring . . . He responded, 'You can vary the program, maybe inserting some violin pieces.'"

Recalling one of Toscanini's New Year's Eve parties, Valdengo wrote, "I remember that he had me sing Ravel's 'Chanson à boire' and then the *stornelli* [folk songs] that I would improvise about the more famous persons in New York's musical scene."

## Flexibility in Performance

In rehearsal Toscanini insisted on his tempos; yet in performance he could be the most flexible accompanist and, in a crucial moment, save the performance from potential disaster.

In casting the role of the Queen of the Night for the 1937 Salzburg production of *Die Zauberflöte*, Toscanini wanted a soprano who had reliable high Fs and a powerful, fresh voice. He chose Julie Osvath, a young singer from Budapest, whose experience until then was mainly in operetta. During the first performance, which was broadcast live, she began singing in an unpredictable manner during the coloratura section of the first act aria. Haggin was at the performance and reported, "When suddenly Osvath began to lag behind the orchestra in a long coloratura phrase, Toscanini kept going until the end of the phrase, where he stopped to wait for her to reach that point, and then resumed conducting in her slower tempo, amazing me with the way he stayed with her, and led the orchestra, in every change of her erratic course."[6]

Winthrop Sargeant, violinist and music critic, recalled performing the Bacchanale from *Tannhäuser* with Toscanini as a member of the New

York Philharmonic. In the concert version, the offstage chorus part is transcribed for four violinists and is usually played by the first two stands of the first violin section. Toscanini, wanting to maintain the offstage effect, assigned the parts to the last two stands. These violinists weren't accustomed to playing exposed solo parts; at the performance they became nervous and their bows became unsteady. Suddenly, Toscanini pulled out his handkerchief and began coughing violently into it. This had the effect of immediately taking the pressure off the four violinists. They played the passage flawlessly as they shifted their attention to the ailing maestro. This wonderful trick, which Toscanini employed in similar emergencies, was one he may have learned during his many years in the opera house, to calm a nervous singer on the stage.[7]

## Staged vs. Concert Version

Albanese: "On the stage he couldn't be so fast like that, he said to us. Because the stage is a distance from the conductor, and until the sounds come, and we react, it requires the tempo to be a little slower."

## Singers and Rubato

Civetta: "His performance of opera has been criticized for being so ruled over and so literal to the score—"
Guarrera: "Not true!"
Civetta: "—that it didn't breathe, that there wasn't enough rubato."
Guarrera: "This is a greatly debatable gray area. What is liberty in music? What is rubato? When you say that this is interpretation, then you're doing it with a certain intent. When you take and exaggerate this, it becomes sloppy and it's called provincial or bad musicianship when someone wants to hold a phrase or a high note too long. That's obviously wrong; that is no longer interpretation. Let whoever says that he was dogmatic in his tempos listen to *Bohème*, *Aida*, or even *Falstaff*, which Verdi wanted almost metronomically correct. There are places where he would allow you to breathe and stretch, but all within a given framework of the bar or group of bars."

## Holding High Notes

During rehearsals for *Otello*, Toscanini told Valdengo, "Verdi . . . always implored me, 'Toscanini, don't let the baritone hold notes in the "Dream"; at most, just a little hesitation in the two passages with the F-naturals.'"

> After his concert-version performance of *Un ballo in maschera* in 1954, Toscanini told baritone Robert Merrill that he heard him take a good breath before one of the E-flats and let him hold the note.[8]

## Tradition and Style of Cadenzas

In response to Valdengo's inquiry about an interpolated high note in *La traviata*, Toscanini wrote to him, "My dear Valdengo, I believe that the *puntatura* that is often done in the Violetta-Germont duet in the second act of *La traviata* is as old as the opera itself. I have always heard it and always allowed it; in fact, allow me to say something heretical. I prefer this *puntatura* to the original notes written by the Maestro. Only it would be necessary for the artist to sing that magnificent piece with paternal emotion and not to shout it, as is generally done . . .

"About that much debated G-flat in *La traviata*, I'd like you to observe once again that traditions aren't established on a whim, but are variations on the work of the composer, derived from the conductors' thoughts and not concocted by chance.

"Tradition, dear rascal, derived from and matured in the minds of the composer, and the first conductors and performers, can't be changed by some slapdash person whose head is flooded with badly thought-out, speculative plans, meant to satisfy the ends of propaganda."

Valdengo: "I sang *L'elisir d'amore* at the Metropolitan with Bidú Sayão, Ferruccio Tagliavini, and Salvatore Baccaloni, conducted by Giuseppe Antonicelli. I knew that Toscanini had listened to the radio broadcast of the opera and I tried to do my best so as not to have that great friend have to give me notes. It was my habit to finish the first act aria with a high F-natural. The following Monday I went over to Toscanini's and he immediately addressed me: 'What filth that F is at the end of the *romanza*! . . . You ruined everything and it seemed like the finale of *Un ballo in maschera* . . . I should also mention your friend Tagliavini for that cadenza in the finale of the first act *romanza*, "Quanto è bella, quanto è cara." He sang it well, but that cadenza from *Trovatore* really doesn't belong . . . ! Next time, pay attention to what Donizetti wrote; he is much more noble than that. You singers, if you don't add something, you're never satisfied.'"

> Operatic performance traditions developed during the first years of a
> work's performances, often under the supervision of the composer. These
> traditions evolved within the framework of the work's style, which is de-
> rived from the era in which it was written, the composer's compositional
> traits, and the individual mood of each work. Here, Toscanini implored
> Valdengo to adhere to the opera's style during his cadenza, chastising him
> and Tagliavini for using the styles of *Un ballo in maschera* and *Il trovatore*
> for their cadenzas in *L'elisir d'amore*.

## Transposition

Valdengo: "To my question about the transposition of compositions—that is the performance of a piece of music in a different key than that in which it is originally written—the Maestro responded, 'To tell you the truth, it is a problem that has always been in my heart, because I consider it better to lower the key of a *romanza* or of a passage, instead of having an artist sacrifice the whole evening because of a note or a certain passage. I conducted *Aida* many times, and I always noticed that the woman remains nervous until that blessed C in the Nile scene.

"'The transposition of a composition has never bothered me. In fact, dear rascal, it is only noticed by those few who follow the theatre by profession. The audience has its foibles, and woe if one breaks the news that its favorite sang a certain aria in a lower key than what is written . . . it will immediately expect less from the artist. I cite you the example of Pertile, whom I wanted to sing *Il trovatore* at La Scala. Pertile was reluctant and I understood that it was entirely because of that famous C in the "Pira." To relieve him from embarrassment I said to him, "You can sing the 'Pira' in any key that you want." And that is the way it was resolved.

"'Even in *Aida* I always considered it advisable to end the famous tenor aria "Celeste Aida" with four B-flats on the staff instead of with the high B-flat. And this is because a tenor is always worried about finishing the *romanza* with a high B-flat, while, instead is much more comfortable with having the high note brought down an octave, because the high B-flat is then no longer a final note that one must finish under the compression of the breath, but becomes a passing note. Besides, these notes were originally written by Verdi, who knew the difficulties of the voice very well.'"*

When Lotte Lehmann was near the end of her operatic career, she had difficulty with high notes in the first act aria of *Fidelio* at the 1934 Salzburg Festival. Erich Leinsdorf wrote, "Toscanini . . . wanted to spare her anxiety and attempted to provide relief. First he proposed to transpose the entire piece [down a half-tone], and I was assigned to read through it with the orchestra in a special rehearsal on the day of the second repeat performance . . . After performing the aria transposed, the Maestro felt, as we all did, that the recitative had suffered in the lower key, particularly Leonora's phrase 'so leuchtet mir ein Farbenbogen,' which came off poorly in B major . . . To remedy this and still help Lotte, Toscanini then devised a clever transitory harmony that left the entire recitative in the original key and yet transposed the aria into E-flat.

"While the whole enterprise was open to legitimate criticism, I found it a document for Toscanini's approach to a complex masterwork . . . He was a pragmatist and not a stickler for the printed dot on the *i*. And it showed that he went to great lengths to accommodate an artist whom he admired and appreciated."[9]

## Word Changes

Valdengo wrote, "After an *Otello* rehearsal, Toscanini had assembled the artists in a circle and advised, 'If anyone has difficulties with some passage, don't be uneasy; tell me, and we will try to remediate the problem.' I remember that Virginio Assandri, the interpreter of Cassio, came forward, saying to the Maestro that he was finding it difficult to pronounce the vowel *u* in the phrase 'che nube tessuta'; that A-natural on the vowel *u* wasn't coming out well. Toscanini remained immobile for some moments, thinking, then responded to Assandri, 'Instead of saying "che

---

* Verdi composed an alternative ending for "Celeste Aida," whereby instead of the high B-flat being held for two bars, it is held for one and a half, after which the words "vicino al sol" are repeated on the B-flat, an octave lower, during the orchestra's E-flat major chord and resolution to the B-flat major chord. This allows the aria to end as Verdi wrote, *pianissimo morendo*.

nube tessuta," try to say "che nube tramata" and you will see that it will come out very well: Verdi himself wouldn't be against it!' Assandri tried, and on the *a* vowel allowed us to hear a magnificent and brilliant A-natural.

"[Toscanini explained,] 'Why ruin a phrase because of a vowel or because of a note? One needs to try and adjust everything and resolve the situation at any cost.' Apropos of this he cited the phrase in the tenor's aria from *Faust,* 'Salve dimora casta e pura [Salut! Demeure chaste et pure]' and said, 'For many tenors it is better to say, "che la fanciulla a me rivela"; and for others it is better instead "che a me rivela la fanciulla"; there is really nothing wrong with that . . . The important thing is to succeed in emitting a beautiful C, assured and enjoyable to the ear. Not all throats are made in the same manner.'"

## Education of Young Singers

Valdengo: "I asked the Maestro what his thoughts were on the study of bel canto, and how young students should embark on this art."

Toscanini: "It's a long story. First of all, the students must not, at least in the first year, be initiated in the study of music . . . The knowledge of music in the first years, instead of helping, harms them. It seems an absurdity, but that's the way it is. And that's because, with a knowledge of music, the youth create preconceptions. They know, for example, when a particular note is high and they think about it too much. It is the teacher that must guide the youth and only the teacher should recognize which notes are which. In the Italian conservatories the study of musical performance should be approached in more depth, and that of, let's say, music history should be somewhat lighter. It's enough to receive a sprinkling of music history because artists will have plenty of time to study it during the course of a career. What would be most valuable is the study of bel canto under, it is understood, the guidance of an experienced singer and not (and unfortunately this frequently happens) with teachers that can be excellent musicians, but ignorant of vocal technique; second, solfeggio (begun only after vocal studies) and then a lot of music for performance, acting, and a bit of piano.

"After two years of vocalization studies, the student may begin the study of sight singing; but, for me, the first thing that he must know—I never get tired of repeating it—is a deep knowledge of how to breathe. The breath is the basis for everything. The way in which many teachers give instruction on how to use the soft palate, the uvula, the diaphragm, and so on, are all tales that serve to create a mentality of fear in the student. If he wants to, he'll have more time later to know how to produce the tone and how the organs in the throat are made. You, when you sing, do you think of the uvula, the soft palate, or what do you think about?"

Valdengo: "'Maestro, when I sing I think about breathing and of the expression of the words and of nothing else.' He looked at me and said, 'This is the way one must do it; if you think too much, you'll never get around to singing well.'"

# Breath Support

When Toscanini discovered that Valdengo had been an oboist, he exclaimed, "Oh! You played the oboe! Then you must have a good understanding of breath, because, to sing, one needs to breathe just like when one plays the oboe; let's only hope that you are not crazy like all the oboists that I have known."

Before their concert version of *Falstaff* in 1950, Toscanini cautioned Valdengo, "Whatever happens, always watch me, sing calmly, on the breath: The breath fixes everything when it is taken well and calmly. Also do some staging because in this way the expression comes out better."

# Diligence and Perseverance

Valdengo wrote, "To demonstrate how one could obtain everything with diligence and perseverance, the Maestro cited the case of the bass Nazzareno De Angelis, who had succeeded in achieving the marvelous *mezze voce* in singing Rossini's *Mosè* like a light tenor."

Toscanini: "See if you can find the recording of *Mosè* recorded by De Angelis, as it will help you with the study of breathing."

Valdengo: "I acquired the recording and I was amazed at the way he performed those stupendous pages. I told this to the Maestro, who retorted, 'That result is the fruit of immense preparation. Only with practice can one overcome the difficulties. Just think: The tenor Fernando De Lucia secured a pianist with the patience of Job in order to practice certain passages an incredible number of times, which he studied and polished inexhaustibly to attain perfection. Listen, if you can find it, to "Addio, Mignon" recorded by De Lucia. Those sobs seem real, whereas they are nothing other than the result of infinite hours of practice. You listen and let me know what you think.'"

## Covered vs. Open Sound

Valdengo: "During the lessons, the Maestro often digressed, giving me precious advice. One day I was singing a phrase and, I don't know why, but during the passage I produced an open note. The Maestro immediately stopped playing, looked at me, astonished, and said, 'What an ugly note, rascal! My God, how ugly! . . . Why is it that you sang that note open?' I excused myself, and he promptly said, 'There is no excuse, my dear. But you must never open an E-natural, an F, at any cost. Let them say maybe that the sound is more covered [*chiuso*], but don't you ever open it.'"

Toscanini spoke to Valdengo about Antonio Cotogni's voice: "In that voice one didn't hear the transition between the registers; the voice was all equal. Hearing it, it seemed that everything was natural, while, instead, the poor Cotogni had practiced years and years to acquire that perfection."

## Singing Lightly

Toscanini: "Young singers, at the outset of their careers, must alternate between the practice of perfecting many vocal exercises, a lot of Monteverdi, and a lot of music by late seventeenth- and early eighteenth-century composers, because only in this manner can one perfect the voice, keeping it nimble and fresh. This is particularly helpful for heavy voices that have the need to vocalize, more than others. Moreover, never overtire the voice, but always perform lighter arias. This is a medicine that will be of help for an entire lifetime. Unfortunately, many times, singers are made to sing operas that are too heavy to support a voice and then, in two or three years, you see youth who seemed that they would astound the world, finishing with zero."

Valdengo: "Toscanini found that many youth, today, after a limited period of study, already believe they are accomplished singers. They want to sing right away in big theatres, tempted by the illusion of earnings; they debut with inadequate preparation, and the result is that they disappear from circulation after a few years."

Toscanini: "The success of a singer is conditioned by continuous, unceasing study, by a high level of sacrifice, and, even—let's come out and say it—by a strong sense of humility. Given all this, a singer should never try to overreach his own capacity in order to arrive at goals prematurely.

"These are the [essential] conditions sine qua non to be able to seal one's success, then, in well-known operas. But it takes years and years! To think that in my time, a soprano dared to sing *La traviata* only after ten years of a career, when, that is, the voice was completely conditioned. A baritone wouldn't risk singing *Rigoletto*, *Trovatore*, *Barbiere*, unless he had arrived at full maturity and, that is, at full mastery of his vocal organs.

"It is essential that the artist, at the beginning of his career, do a good apprenticeship in secondary roles in a great theatre. The contact with artists of proven experience can serve as a very effective example; not counting that the advice from those people can represent true treasures."

## Vocalizing with *Ernani*

Valdengo: "One day before rehearsal, Toscanini said, 'You know, yesterday I was thinking, and I want to suggest to you something that [Mattia] Battistini always used to do to keep his voice fluid and his breath controlled. Every day, Battistini vocalized, repeating the phrase from *Ernani*: "Da quel dì che t'ho veduta bella come un primo amore." Remember, Valdengo, that this phrase is like a study of bel canto, maybe better, and when you succeed in singing it with ease, your voice will be so malleable that any phrase in the baritone repertoire will seem like nothing.' I implored the Maestro to explain to me how this could be: 'You see, this phrase is almost all written on the *passaggio* of the baritone voice, and to do it perfectly there needs to be no discernible break between the medium register and the high register. Battistini, who did not have a very dark voice, and in fact tended toward being a dramatic tenor, always performed this phrase as a voice exercise, singing only vowels in place of the words.'"

Valdengo: "I sang that difficult phrase every day for my whole career and I have to say that there is no better medicine for the baritone voice. If some young baritone reads this, sing this phrase and you will see the great benefits: unity of registers, smoothness, and great control of breath. The phrase in *Rigoletto*, 'Veglia o donna questo fior,' will no longer be difficult, after having studied and restudied that of *Ernani*.

"The Maestro told me that he heard a recording of the baritone Enrico Molinari who, like Battistini, sang that divine page of music in a marvelous way."

Toscanini: "If you hear that recording, you will have an irresistible urge to practice and do increasingly better. Dear rascal, I will never forget the *Lucia* at La Scala with Toti dal Monte, Aureliano Pertile, and Enrico Molinari. What a magnificent trio and what artists of rare class."

## Vocalizing at the Piano

Valdengo: "I had gotten the confidence to sit at the piano and vocalize before the rehearsals in the maestro's studio at NBC. One day when I saw him coming, I jumped to my feet . . .

"Toscanini responded, 'Practice, practice. However, I think that to vocalize the way you do, seated and accompanying yourself, is not good because the brain must always think about too many things, and so you don't really do any one thing right. Play the chord, then leap to your feet and sing the phrase you want with your voice, and think only of this without any distractions. A small distraction is enough to cause a note to come out badly. The brain controls everything and the voice, without it, will achieve nothing.'"

## Scotti and De Luca

Valdengo: "I wanted to know the Maestro's opinion about the fact that some singers, who at the beginning seem shut off from a theatrical career due to insufficient voice, go on to have brilliant careers. Others with good voices, who seem to have a future, fade away like meteors in the theatrical firmament."

Toscanini: "Actually I knew singers with limited voices who had first-class careers and others who, though in possession of exceptional voices, didn't know how to take advantage of the precious gift lavished upon them by Mother Nature, and crashed to the ground. It's just that the brain, my dear, is the essential part of a singer and, unfortunately, many singers are missing this essential attribute."

Valdengo: "He mentioned as an example Antonio Scotti, whose voice was unexceptional, and whose portrayal of Scarpia succeeded nevertheless in achieving marvelous effects."

Toscanini: "It seems absurd, my dear rascal, yet I saw Scotti capably hold his own against Claudia Muzio and Caruso and receive greater acclaim than that paid to Titta Ruffo.

"Another who knew how to work with his brain was De Luca. He succeeded in rendering the letter scene in *Butterfly* so alive, for example, and so much did he feel the part of Sharpless, that the audience, captivated, would concentrate all its attention on that character and at the end of the duet with Butterfly, which really doesn't have vocal effects, would burst out with interminable applause. And while you can say that it's anything but easy to wear modern clothes onstage, neverthe- less De Luca in that part knew how to rise to the importance of the protagonist."

## Conserving the Voice

Toscanini: "The singer must always find the voice there, right at the flower of the lips, and not force it out. He must have all the notes ready when he wants them. It must be he who is the master of his voice and not the voice who controls him. A good voice is given to few privileged ones and one needs to know how to conserve it with moderation and proportion.

"Remember, never give all of your voice if the phrase doesn't demand it. The better you know how to pace yourself, the longer you'll last. Remember, again, en- cores during an opera are the ruination of the voice. Never do encores. First of all, it's anti-artistic; second, all it does is tire the vocal organs; third, if the encore goes badly . . . you are done for: They will say that you can not stand the test, that you are finished, and many other pleasant words that will embitter your life. Satisfy the audience, but make sure they go home with the desire to hear you again.

"Speaking of which, now would be a good time to speak about Titta Ruffo who had a beautiful voice, healthy, relaxed, and powerful, but thanks to using theatrical effects he ruined himself, and at age fifty, maybe sooner, he was finished. Titta Ruffo always sang at full throttle, never sparing himself, giving two or three encores. In the Prologue to *Pagliacci* when he arrived at the scream, 'Andiam, incominciate,' on the high G, he achieved an effect that grabbed the audience in a big way, but in the long run, it did nothing but wear out his vocal cords. But I'll tell you more: Not content with holding the high G, he reattacked on the *a* vowel in 'incominciate . . . andiam incominciaaaaaate,' giving great jabs to the curtain. Continuing on this ruinous course, he was finished early . . . it was a great pity!

"On the contrary, there was De Luca, an intelligent singer, who knew very well how to pace himself vocally. De Luca always sang with perfect, calculated mastery of himself and of his voice, and still sings! One could say that while Titta Ruffo spent the capital of his voice, De Luca used only the interest of his voice. And there was no comparison in timbre between Titta's voice and that of De Luca: That of Titta was powerful, especially in the high register; the higher he went the more beautiful it became. De Luca, on the other hand, had a short extension, in a register almost always open, but De Luca used it with great astuteness, knowing how to measure it out appropriately.

"In *Rigoletto* De Luca obtained marvelous effects, singing almost everything *mezza voce* and this way, my dear rascal, when he let out a loud note, it seemed something out of the ordinary, when in effect it was nothing but knowing how to pace himself."

Valdengo: "The Maestro told me that in his life he never met an artist smarter than De Luca."

Toscanini: "Listen: You know that in *Rigoletto*, after the famous quartet in the last act, a big applause always burst out. De Luca, after the quartet, had to begin the recitative 'M'odi! ritorna a casa, oro prendi, un destriero, una veste viril che t'apprestai e per Verona parti, sarovvi io pur doman' . . . and because he found it difficult to sing the first phrases, that are a bit low, when the applause faded, he broke out loudly with the phrase 'e per Verona parti, sarovvi io pur doman!' And this way he skillfully resolved the problem!"

## "Do Not Push the Voice!"

Valdengo: "The Maestro very much liked the voice of Cloë Elmo, who interpreted the role of Quickly [in Toscanini's performance of *Falstaff* in 1950]. 'Elmo has a very beautiful voice but I would like to advise her not to sing *Trovatore* too often . . . Azucena is a dramatic part and it's easy to heighten the character's dramatic quality, to risk everything, including damage to the vocal cords, especially in Elmo's case, exuberant as she is both in voice and temperament.'

"One day Ramón Vinay and I were rehearsing the duet between Otello and Iago from the second act of *Otello*: When we finished, the Maestro got up from the piano and went to sit on the sofa. We were waiting anxiously for his judgment.

After some moments he said, 'It wasn't bad, but you shout too much . . . for good-ness sake don't do what Caruso and Titta Ruffo did in their recording of this duet. Two magnificent voices, without a doubt, but it seems that instead of interpreting their parts, they want at all costs to compete as to who can sing louder . . . Many artists, when they are singing in duet with a colleague, think of making the voice bigger, believing that if they only scream, the sound arrives louder in the audi-torium. They are mistaken. When for example, a tenor-baritone duet is sung, if the baritone, who has a heavier voice, wants his voice to be heard more, he must attempt to imitate the tenor.

"'Nature will always get even with a reckless person who tries to exceed the lim-its that she places on him. Why try to make the voice bigger than that which you have? Better to be smaller but of beautiful quality. To amplify the voice you must push your breathing, which results in roughness on the vocal cords, removing the sweetness and the beautiful color of the tone.

"'Toti dal Monte didn't have a big voice; in fact, it was very small; but you could hear it projected to all points in the theatre, making it seem as though she was right there. It was the vibrations [*vibrazioni*] that enabled that voice, which did not have much volume, to reach everywhere . . . Also Tito Schipa and Alessandro Bonci didn't have big voices, but they were so well placed and full of beautiful vibrations that they filled the whole theatre.

"'Then there are certain voices that in a room, appear so powerful that one must plug the ears, and in the theatre, contrarily, don't succeed in surpassing the wall of sound produced by the orchestra.'"

Valdengo: "He told me the name of a bass that he heard in a room that had made such an impression that he immediately engaged him for La Scala. 'But what a disap-pointment when I heard him in the theatre with the orchestra . . . It seemed like he was singing backstage. I couldn't hear him anymore! Even in this instance Mother Nature has her say, and for this reason the youth who are initiated in the study of voice must all be heard in the theatre to avoid future disappointments.'"

## Singing Full Voice at Rehearsals

Valdengo recalled that when the full cast began *Falstaff* rehearsals in 1950, the maestro wanted everyone to always sing at full voice.

Valdengo: "He affirmed that rehearsals must be sung at full voice the way one sings in the theatre; if not, it is better not to rehearse at all. If, at times, I watered down my part, he would immediately say, 'Yes, yes, it's okay . . . but do it again, *forte*. The singer who is singing *sotto voce* at the rehearsals so as not to become tired is simply acquiring a bad habit, and doesn't achieve the right atmosphere, ruining everything that has been done before. It's better not to sing and to go for a long walk . . .'

"He recalled that Caruso, at the rehearsals, always sang at full voice or at half voice, as the part demanded, and he didn't spare himself."

Toscanini: "Of course, at that time, I must add, the rehearsals, especially at the Metropolitan, were better distributed and one didn't do piecework the way we have to now."

To save their voices for the performance, singers sometimes rehearse in a half voice or quietly sing an octave lower. While Toscanini insisted that singers sing at full voice during rehearsals, as in performance, he reminded them to never push the voice beyond its natural capacity. Toscanini cautioned them not to destroy their sound through the harshness that results from pushing the voice to excessive volume.

## *La forza del destino*

Valdengo: "I often used to go to Riverdale to ask him for advice on the operas that I had to sing. He always affectionately lavished on me that precious wisdom acquired from innate genius and his very long experience. He gave me advice on the operas I had to study, about the characters, about the interpretation, about everything.

"I entreated him, 'Maestro, when you have a moment of time, wouldn't you like to go over *La forza del destino*?' 'Whenever you want,' he replied. The next day I arrived in Riverdale with the score. He listened to me, and lavished precious advice upon me. I remember that, among other things, he said, 'The first baritone aria, "Son Pereda, son ricco d'onore," you must sing simply, without burdening the voice; if not, it becomes heavy. Besides, if you it sing lightly, it will cost less effort.'"

# Drama and Text

Lehmann: "It amazed me to find how a pure musician like him works from the dramatic text. A vividly acted performance was as important to him as a complete realization of the music . . . Nothing escapes that keen, relentless eye."[10]

> During rehearsals of *Falstaff* at La Scala in 1921, Toscanini asked the singers to speak their parts with piano accompaniment, to clarify whether they understood the characters they were portraying.[11] And at *Otello* rehearsals Toscanini read passages from Shakespeare's original text to the singers.[12]

Gilda dalla Rizza, soprano, recalled rehearsing for the 1923 La Scala production of *La traviata*: "I remember that at a rehearsal of the second act, he repeatedly told me that I wasn't putting everything possible into the famous 'Dite alla giovine.' I tried and tried again but I wasn't able to express all the emotion that Toscanini demanded. At one point—who knows why?—I threw myself into it with all my will, all my soul, all my heart, and burst into real tears. 'That's it, that's it!' he shouted from the podium. '*Traviata* needs emotion!' Toscanini gave everything of himself when he conducted; and when I sang, he would be singing with me to make me feel the expression."[13]

Toti dal Monte, soprano, discussed Toscanini's 1922 La Scala production of *Rigoletto*: "He urged me in particular to sing 'Quanto affetto! quali cure . . .' more smoothly. I came to the famous 'Caro nome.' I was very worried, and tried to do my best. Toscanini stopped and said, 'Listen, dear, technically you sing this *romanza* perfectly, but holy God!—it needs more than that. First of all, Verdi's women express love in the same way . . . They all have the same sort of "heartbeat." And yet there are differences. Why do you think Verdi wrote this "Caro nome" in such a staccato style? For laughs? No, no, no. Verdi used this technique of short pauses between the syllables of the first words to indicate Gilda's anxiety, the trembling of a girl experiencing love for the first time and she feels almost breathless, at the thought of the man she loves, who has inebriated her with many beautiful words.'"[14]

Describing rehearsals for the 1923 La Scala production of *Lucia*, dal Monte continued, "In the duet with the tenor, 'Verranno a te sull'aure,' Toscanini stopped. 'Dear Toti,' he said, 'you sing this phrase well, but there isn't enough air in your voice. There must be more color, more sweetness, more expression . . . It is necessary that you bring forth all the warmth of your soul in this passage, to express the drama of these two who meet at night. You do not give it here. I do not feel it. It is all too cold . . .'[15] 'This is a woman who meets her lover at night secretly. You're only concerned with singing *piano*. Forget the *piano*, it's not *piano*; the heart must be in this phrase!'"[16]

Bachmann: "He was fighting not to have the great soprano, Luisa Tetrazzini, sing Mimi in *La bohème*. It wasn't that he didn't like her voice. He thought she was marvelous, and yet he fought tooth and nail that she shouldn't take the part, because he thought that dramatically, it would be ludicrous, funny, and just ridiculous to see a huge person, very well endowed in all parts of her body, lying in bed or on a sofa and dying of tuberculosis."

## Stage Direction

Toscanini often functioned as the stage director of the operas he conducted, demonstrating his vision to the dancers, actors, and singers.

Dalla Rizza recalled that Toscanini supervised each of the staging rehearsals for the 1923 *La traviata* production at La Scala.[17]

Dal Monte remembered the La Scala production of *Lucia* in 1923: "The *Lucia* rehearsals were detailed and enervating . . . There were thirteen staging rehearsals for the curse scene alone."[18]

Giovanni Martinelli, tenor, described Toscanini's production of *Il trovatore* at the Metropolitan in 1914: "Toscanini was determined to present *Trovatore* as Verdi would have wanted it. The result was a veritable revolution in thought on the opera. He staged the opera himself, since he wanted to be certain that at every point the stage action would not interfere with his direction. We had a minimum of fifty rehearsals of two hours and more. Think of it . . . The first of these rehearsals was to set the chorus and the bass, Ferrando . . . for the 'Abbietta zingara' in act 1. This scene takes about five minutes to sing. Toscanini took more than two hours to arrange the singer and chorus, placing and moving them as he wanted."[19]

Sachs quoted journalist Giulio Ciampelli, who observed a staging rehearsal for the La Scala production of *Die Meistersinger* in 1922. He described Toscanini "literally running and jumping all over the stage, first to this group, then to that one, demonstrating positioning, gestures, clapping his hands to keep the piano and the massive forces together, shouting and singing."[20]

Bachmann: "I was invited to attend a rehearsal of *Die Meistersinger* in Salzburg. At the end of the second act there is a big fight, a big to-do, a big commotion, with hundreds of people milling about on the stage. Wagner's direction was that by the time everybody is off the stage you can hear from far away the night watchman who sings an announcement that it is eleven o'clock at night. But he couldn't do it because by the time he came in there was still a bunch of stragglers. So they tried again and again and again. But they just couldn't clear the stage in time. Finally the Maestro said to the stage director, Dr. Herbert Graff, 'Can I do something, now?' 'Yes, Maestro.' 'You watch me. I'll do this tenore; I'll do this soprano; I'll do this alto, basso.'" Directing the artists from the orchestra, Toscanini gestured to indicate where, when, and how the performers should move. Bachmann continued, "Every person was off the stage, the orchestra was playing, and you could see and hear the night watchman come from far away. This is greatness of understanding."

Toscanini: "Just think that, at La Scala, sometimes I came to tell the prima ballerina that some of her steps were wrong and that I would have done it in a different way. Climbing onto the stage, I showed her how she had to do it and the ballerina always said I was right!"

For Toscanini's concert version performance of *Falstaff* in 1950, he wanted the cast to incorporate some staging into the performance. Valdengo recalled, "In the duet with mezzo-soprano Cloë Elmo, in the second act, the Maestro required colors that were truly stupendous. I remember that he made me repeat the phrase 'Lo so, continua' and the other 'Stregoneria non c'è, ma un certo qual mio fascino personal.' He wanted that we again do a little staging, to be able to enter deeper into the character and to color the phrases as intensely as possible the way he wanted.

"As usual, in the duet between Falstaff and Ford, the Maestro sang Ford's part, passage by passage, having me again do a bit of staging: He couldn't conceive that someone could interpret a part of Falstaff's size without making some appropriate movements."

For his La Scala production of *Pelléas et Mélisande*, Toscanini had the stagehands wrap their shoes in cloth to eliminate any possibility of their footsteps' being heard in the theatre.

# Period

Toscanini: "I understand, and I have to admit, that with the coming of film, television and of many other modern devilries, even the theatre needs to somehow modernize itself. But everything has a limit! Can you imagine Gounod's *Faust* transferred with complete nonchalance from the Middle Ages to the middle of the 1800s, without perceiving that in that time it was ridiculous to speak about love potions, magic, and devils? You know it well! And yet that is what happened at the Metropolitan! They brought a devil with a big top hat out on the stage. The only thing missing was that at a certain moment, maybe he should have pulled out a rabbit or a white dove, and the scene would have been truly complete!"

# Wigs

Toscanini: "Certain characters have been refined with lighter wigs and with other modified contraptions, and up to here I agree . . . but then abuse immediately takes over! For example, I have noticed that tenors no longer wear wigs while performing their respective characters. It's not their fault, but that of their directors who let them become lax, and this is something they should absolutely not do. I ask myself, for example, how one can conceive Edgardo in *Lucia*, a sixteenth-century character, who comes out with a new haircut, nicely tapered from top to bottom, and parted on the side! Always wear your wig, dear rascal, and don't ever be tempted by these stupid fads of modernism. The wig immediately changes the appearance of your face and gives the proper character to the role you will interpret. Without the wig, remember, you will always be Valdengo! The audience that goes to the theatre to attend a performance that takes place in a specific period, wants to have the illusion of reliving that period through the performance, and has every right not to be disappointed by foolishness."

# Costumes

Toscanini: "Once I happened to see a Manon dressed in the last act with impeccable elegance. Evidently they didn't read the directions written in the opera, where it says, 'Manon and Des Grieux are from the lower classes and are poorly dressed.'

"The same thing happened with *Linda di Chamounix*: You see her spring out in the last act in a farcelike ballroom costume, with modern high-heeled shoes. But in the libretto she arrives in Paris after a two-hundred-league trip, somewhat the worse for wear.

"When I conducted *Pagliacci* in Milan, in the opera season that began on September 18 until November 28, 1915, to benefit theatre artists in difficulty because of the war, Caruso, Stracciari, and Montesanto sang. This last one wanted to try a foolish innovation singing the Prologue in tails, the way he had done a few months before in San Francisco. Leoncavallo wrote me a somber letter, begging me to absolutely not permit Montesanto to sing the Prologue in tails. It was a perfectly useless letter, because you can well imagine, dear rascal if I, of all people, would have really permitted him such craziness!"

Valdengo: "The Maestro maintained that postures, mime, makeup, and costumes in a performance should also be taken care of in minute detail."
Toscanini: "It's certainly not an easy thing to sing and act at the same time in the most correct manner, nevertheless with practice and perseverance one can become accomplished in these things."

# Acting and Characterization

Valdengo: "He couldn't bear those artists who make too many gestures with their arms on stage. He told me about a tenor in Parma, who, in the aria from *Carmen* had the habit of sawing his hands now to the right and now to the left. Someone in the audience yelled at him, 'Hey, tenor, are you measuring cloth, or what?'

"Still on the subject of moving too much onstage, he told me that the great Caruso, a little because of his personality, a little, perhaps, because no one taught him, in the finale of the last act of *Carmen*, seemed restless and nervous on stage, agitated, and didn't succeed in winning over the audience as he would have if his gestures had been more controlled."

Toscanini: "While conducting *Carmen* I noticed this deficiency and I suggested to him, 'Enrico, if you want to obtain a great result in the last act, as soon as you are seen by the audience when you enter onstage, stop, with the attitude of someone who is already finished. Let your arms down by the sides; have a far away dreamy look, and remain like this until after the phrase "Minacciarti non vo, t'imploro . . . [Je ne menace pas! j'implore . . . je supplie!]."' At the next performance, Caruso followed this advice and the result was so dramatic that it was truly frightening. Before that tragic immobility the audience froze.

"There are artists that move too much. Others, instead, stay too still; others never know where to put their hands; others roll their eyes around, like china dolls. These defects can be corrected through study and intelligence, but, as in all things in this world, it is necessary to act from the beginning with timeliness, and not wait to remediate them when one has already advanced on one's career. The more a habit is entrenched, the more difficult it is to get rid of it.

"In my career I have rarely found artists completely versed in musical performance as a natural part of their character. One of these was undoubtedly De Luca, who knew how to carry himself in all situations. If you had seen him in *Rigoletto* . . . He was marvelous, and in the first act, he did these somersaults that perfectly illustrated the idea of a court jester. De Luca was a great artist, intelligent and highly capable of endearing himself to the audience.

"Another complete artist is Vinay, truly superb and unsurpassed in playing parts in which force and violence triumph. No artist, at this time, can compete with him in the interpretation of *Otello*!

"Remember also that if you are interpreting violent or vulgar characters, you must never make these characteristics overly strong; it annoys the audience. There are artists who make Tonio in *Pagliacci* into a brute. It's necessary to remember that even he is a man with a heart and soul. If you interpret him with this quality of humanity, you will gain a better response from the audience.

"And yet, believe me, almost all the singers that I trained, not excluding many with big names, made me work very hard to obtain from them the performances that I so inescapably demanded, right up to the point that the characters they took on seemed alive and animated in the way that was dreamed of and wanted by their creators."

# Prompters

Valdengo wrote: "Having remarked to the Maestro that at the City Center [New York] there was no prompter, he said, 'I wouldn't want to attract the rage of all the prompters, but honestly, I tell you that I would do away with prompters, and I think that at City Center they have done very well to eliminate them. First of all, it is unaesthetic. Does it seem appealing to your eye to see that huge box, sometimes so big it makes you think of a coffin, stuck right there in the middle of the stage, with that ridiculous little mirror on the side? Second, I am convinced that to do without it is a very good thing. Believe me, when one practices with due commitment, is well prepared musically and the conductor knows his craft, the prompter is completely superfluous. Did you perhaps need it in the *Otello*, in *Aida*, and recently in the *Falstaff* that we did together at NBC? Everything proceeded very well without any need of a prompter and why is this? Because I made you rehearse, I coached you at the piano the way one should; I also gave you a tongue-lashing in moments when I saw it was necessary.'"

# Diction

Valdengo: "Toscanini was meticulous about the pronunciation of words, which he wanted clear and distinct. He was capable of having me repeat the same word twenty, thirty times. He became irritated when I, out of force of habit, didn't pronounce the *r* consonant well."

Toscanini: "See, for example, if when you say the word *guerra* [war], you deliver the *r* consonant too softly, without its customary incisiveness, the word loses its exact expression, while if you emphasize the *r,* the word becomes more virile, more vibrant, and one hears the exact meaning."

> In Valdengo's native region of Piedmont, the letter *r* is not rolled on the tongue. This kind of pronunciation is called *erre molle* or soft *r*. In the word *guerra*, the *r* is a double consonant, which in the Italian pronunciation is emphasized by rolling the *r*.

Giulia Tess, soprano, remembered Toscanini listening to her rehearsals for *Salome* sung in Italian at La Scala (with Ettore Panizza conducting) in the 1920s: "I shall always recall vividly how Toscanini insisted on my pronouncing the word *terribile* in a special way—*terrrriiiibiiiile*—and how right he was—for it had a bloodcurdling effect."[21]

Valdengo: "When the first orchestral rehearsal for *Aida* was over, we went to say hello to the Maestro in his dressing room. He was savoring his usual milk and rum. He greeted us with affectionate cordiality, but before we left, he turned to Richard Tucker and Eva Gustavson and said, 'After this rehearsal, you two will not be eating for a few days, because you devoured so many consonants that you will suffer from monstrous indigestion . . . and that's not saying much!'"

Burghauser: "Toscanini was in fact a poor linguist. Though he knew of course by heart the words of all the Wagner works, he wasn't able to pronounce one German word correctly . . . Yet when a Hungarian chorus from Budapest sang with us . . . Beethoven's Ninth Symphony in German, and began to sing not *Freude! Freude!* but, being Hungarian, pronounced it *Freide! Freide!*, Toscanini at once interrupted and shouted, 'Not *Freide!* It is *Freude!*' So, although he was himself not able to speak fast correctly another language, he was aware of every wrong nuance in pronunciation, diction . . ."[22]

Alexander Kipnis, bass: "I sang for the first time with Toscanini in Bayreuth in 1930 . . . I had a rehearsal with him as soon as I arrived . . . I sang the entire monologue of King Marke from *Tristan*. Toscanini walked back and forth in the room; he didn't interrupt—he just listened; and once in a while he made a gesture as if he were going to conduct. When I finished he didn't say a word, but only grabbed me by my hand and took me down to where Siegfried Wagner was sitting in the Festspielhaus, and said, 'Why don't all the singers sing like that? Your father wrote "Muss es sein"; but on your stage they sing "Mussssss es sein" with six s's.' He was objecting to the fact that the singers gave more importance and emphasis to pronouncing the word than to singing the music."[23]

## Otello

Valdengo recalled his first coaching session for *Otello* with Toscanini: "The Maestro said, 'Let's rehearse the first recitative. You know, Verdi's recitatives are what make the opera.' He himself sang the chorus part, 'Si calma la bufera' and I began, 'Roderigo,

ebben, che pensi?' I don't remember how many times the Maestro made me repeat
that recitative. He sang every phrase for me, explaining its significance to me in
terms of expression, whether *piano* or *forte*, whether light or dark. He instructed
me to never disregard the text, which especially in *Otello* has the same importance
as the music. 'More intention,' he used to say; 'pay attention to the eighth notes and
to the sixteenth notes, but don't merely do sight singing exercises.'

"He had never wanted to hear me sing the 'Credo' and one day I said, 'Maestro,
we have had many lessons but I have never studied the "Credo" with you.' Toscanini
reflected for a moment and then said, 'You see, dear, the "Credo" is a piece already
made, joined there to give the baritone an aria, but it is the recitatives that count,
especially in Verdi's operas. It is from the recitative that one knows a singer, my
dear friend. Everyone, more or less, sings an aria, but in the recitative you run the
risk of a pratfall! Let me hear a little of the recitative from *Forza del destino*, "Invano
Alvaro ti celasti al mondo," and I will tell you right away how you sing the opera.'

"I sang it, and when I finished he said, 'You see, Valdengo, you sing it with a
beautiful voice, with a definite flair, but it's missing inflection. Listen for a moment.'
He sang it and with such expression I was truly enchanted."
Toscanini: "You see, there are characters that are already created, that is to say,
they have been clearly defined since their inception, so well, that is, to be easily
interpreted. For example: Rigoletto, Otello, Boris Godunov, Don Basilio, Boito's
Mefistofele and others. Among these characters I heard artists of all kinds who, even
with mediocre voices, were able to hold their own. Naturally the costumes and the
make-up also contribute to making these roles more easily rendered.

"There exist, however, characters that need to be created, that is characters in
which one must throw in all of one's spirit and his intelligence in order to portray
them, in the sense that one must not merely interpret them simply the way they
show up in the libretto and in the score, but must truly absorb and feel them as a
part of one's self, the way he who created them felt and wanted them.

"Certain characters are very difficult to interpret. Now, Iago belongs precisely to
this second category. You yourself have experienced just how laborious the development of Iago was, in his movements and in the special body language intended
to display his perversity. Developing the character of Falstaff was less complex
and involved, in terms of staging, even though it also presented a certain degree
of difficulty.

"Iago is the personification of evil, and the weaver of a diabolical plot which he
guides onward, little by little, until the dramatic conclusion. He must, therefore,

continuously operate on a level of refined wickedness; he should, I would say, walk with an almost feline gait; he should move his hands in a certain way and should always be aware of himself and of the villainous ends to which he is committed. If there is a moment in which the artist is distracted and forgets that he is Iago, the audience will immediately feel that the character is missing.

"Only in the 'Credo' does Iago have a moment of self-truth and opens his heart, revealing his true self. Then he goes back to being slimy, cold, and scheming. He never waves his arms around. Rarely does he have a vehement gesture. In him all is cold and calculated, and when Otello, destroyed by a fit of jealousy, falls faint, that is when Iago must rise triumphantly like Satan and feel that he is the master of all, just because the evil that he develops has finally caught up to his intent. These things that I've told you, dear Valdengo, you must always keep in mind in the way you interpret this remarkable character."

Valdengo continued, "One day, after having had me sing the first two acts, the Maestro again took time to illustrate Iago's part for me. He got up from the piano to show me how Iago must walk, how he must gesture, and what the mask of his face must be.

"I remember that the Maestro wanted a *pianissimo* at the phrase 'Ed io rimango di sua Moresca l'alfiere.' On the 'Ed io,' which is a D-natural, he wanted a *piano*, but filled with evil intention, expressed between the teeth, the way one ponders something angrily. So many times I would repeat that downbeat the way he wanted it, very clearly, like a rap of the tongue on the oboe reed. Even the trill on the word *alfiere* became the subject of long study. The Maestro wanted a trill, yes, but even that had to be evil, vulgar.

"There were days when I no longer knew to which saint I should implore and what to do to satisfy him. He was thinking of having me perform a passage in a certain way, but then, hearing it, he would change it, questioning me: 'Tell me what you think too . . . if you want to sing this piece . . . if the throat responds to you.'

"Sometimes he had me change the color of those famous 'Vigilate' that Iago expresses in the second act, addressing Otello. I remember I practiced for days and days for the way to bring out those blessed E's, that must be in the forefront with respect to the chorus, but not *forte*. One day I had to confess to him, 'Dear Maestro, I cannot succeed in finding the color that you want.' He replied, 'Practice and you'll see that one fine day nature will allow you to find it without you noticing it; everything matures little by little.' The Maestro wanted it *piano*, but so that on the note E the 'Vigilate' didn't sound like 'Vigilote.'

"He said, 'I want it to have a beyond-the-grave effect, satanic and penetrating deeply into the soul of Otello, so much that it completely deranges him.' Finally, after much practice, I succeeded in pleasing him. He was so happy that he embraced me, saying, 'Valdengo, we've found them, they exist, remember, always do them like this. This is what Verdi wanted from Victor Maurel [the first Iago], exactly like this!'

"Every time I arrived at those notes, I felt my blood chill in the veins, because I was afraid of not doing it the way he wanted it, and after the passage, he would look at me and would smile saying, 'Remember how much we practiced those few notes?'

"I sometimes practiced just one passage for hours. One day, not succeeding in pleasing him, I said, 'Maestro, I'm afraid of not being able to please you.' He responded, 'I never again want to hear you say, "I can't do it," because with willpower one can attain everything one wants, and that's all there is to it!'"

## Intonation Tip

Valdengo: "Toscanini recounted to me that in *Otello*, the baritone Maurel ran into some difficulty and couldn't succeed in singing the passage before the 'Dream,' 'che per poco alla certezza vi conduce,' in tune. In the orchestra there is an A-natural in the horn and the baritone must sing a C-natural. The Maestro recounted that 'Maurel always went flat on that note and every time he got to that passage Verdi would crinkle his nose.' I said that I must also be careful of singing the C in tune. He responded, 'Since you are a musician, it's somewhat easier. You only have to think of the G-sharp that precedes the C-natural as if it were an A-flat, and the game is done.' I tried it and from that moment I didn't worry any more about that note."

Toscanini to Valdengo: "Remember all the things I told you and treasure them. And when you get home, read Iago's part once more, thinking about the comments I made to you. Sometimes, to ponder over it without singing does a lot of good."

## Smaller Operatic Roles, or *Comprimari*

In opera, the smaller roles are called *comprimari* (singular: *comprimario*). Toscanini insisted on not relaxing the highest standards when casting secondary roles.

Valdengo: "Toscanini recalled the world premiere of Verdi's *Otello* in 1887, in which he was second cellist: 'That night was really a triumph, from the "Esultate!" of Otello to the duet with Desdemona and likewise with the second and third acts. The audience only registered disapproval in the last act when it came to Emilia's phrases on the high G-naturals, in the phrase "Otello uccise Desdemona!" Fortunately they were just a few notes, however it was a critical moment because the audience had already begun to grumble. The audience is strange. It is a lion and can be quick to destroy a masterpiece because of a trifle.'

"Toscanini said that the performers of secondary roles form the infrastructure of an opera and need to be carefully chosen. 'Many times in *Carmen* you hear [the artist singing] Morales flatten at the phrase "l'angel sen vola [l'oiseau s'envole]." Those E-flats are very dangerous. The intonation is everything. It should be sung *piano* and with sweetness, whereas, almost always, it is shouted in order to remain in tune.

"'The disadvantage of the *comprimario* is that in relation to the main artist, his part is almost always short and there is no way to recover from a mishap, while that of the main artist is long, and even if he misfires at some point, afterwards he always has a way to remedy it.

"'I always remember the night of the premiere of *Otello*, and therefore I am always concerned with having the best *comprimari*. When, after some years, I conducted *Otello* at La Scala, the first thing I was concerned with was Emilia. Even for the version that we are preparing I chose, as you see, Nan Merriman, who has an effortless voice that isn't likely to play strange tricks.

"'Puccini himself, when he was staging *La bohème*, was interested, first of all, in two artists: It seems strange, but these artists were Musetta and Schaunard; for *Manon* he wanted to feel at ease about the characters of Edmondo, the lamplighter, and the dance teacher; for *Butterfly*, that of Goro.'"

## Recording of *Otello*

Toscanini's 1947 concert version of *Otello* was recorded live and published.

Valdengo: "Toscanini informed me that the recording of *Otello* had just been released in America. He heard it, and found it to be excellent, even if some parts ended up a bit flawed. In the main it was a worthy achievement."

Toscanini: "Think about it, a chorus comprised entirely of strangers, and nevertheless they sang so well! The orchestra played famously as well, and you know how many difficulties there are in the score of *Otello*. Even the solo for the contrabasses was in tune; I am really happy. As for you singers, you carried your performances with distinction, and my conscience is also wonderfully at ease with Verdi because I did everything that I could. Perfection doesn't exist, unfortunately, but I repeat, you all did very well.

"I must also say that I don't remember having heard the 'Ave Maria' and the 'Willow Song' sung better. Nelli was very good in her rendition. That music seems easy, instead it is difficult: Those D-naturals are dreadful. Already at the first 'Salce,' Verdi put three *p*'s, as if he couldn't stress the *pianissimo* enough times. Many sopranos stub their musical toes on that one. You and Vinay also did very well. I know just what it means to face an audience . . . and during a concert it's even more difficult." Valdengo: "He complimented me on the drinking song, saying, 'You, dear rascal, you really satisfied me: Those descending chromatic scales were perfect as was the "Dream" and that other piece where, if you remember well, I drove you crazy!—the staccato piece in 6/8: "Questa è una ragna . . .""""

## *Aida*

Valdengo wrote about his audition for the role of Amonasro in the NBC concert version of *Aida* in 1949: "Toscanini began playing the bars before the entrance of the prisoners in the second act. I began and sang as well as I could. Between rushing to get to the audition and my agitation, I don't even know how my voice could have come out. As I sang, the Maestro's face became darker and darker, but I dragged forward with the sole hope of being able to finish quickly . . . When I got to the phrase 'Rivedrai le foreste imbalsamate,' Toscanini had had enough and he stopped. He remained for a very long time looking at me, peering at me in a strange and ominous way, almost as if he wanted to throw me out the door, then he shouted, 'You are ruined! What did you do with your beautiful voice, your breathing, your *mezza voce*, your diction that was so clear? You lost everything!' With those hard words Toscanini had destroyed me and I stood immobile, petrified, not knowing what to say. He continued, 'Your head got swollen from singing at the Metropolitan. Great. Good going. Now you'll have to pay for it.' Knowing him well, I knew that in those predicaments it was better not to respond and to simply take it. I tried to get away, but he already guessed my move, ran to the door, and locked it, saying, 'You know, it's not over yet; I can set you straight. Do you know what I'm going to do? I'm going to accept you for *Aida*. I'll sign you on, then I'll tear up your contract in protest. At that point you'll go around with shame stamped on your brow . . . Tell me, with whom did you sing *Aida*? . . . But don't you know that the phrase "Ma tu Re, tu signore possente" has to be sung *mezza voce*? Don't you know that? Don't you know that the recitative before the duet with the woman should not be screamed, but should be sung paternally? . . . Shame, shame!"'

Valdengo then studied the part with the baritone Giuseppe Danise. He described his next rehearsal with Toscanini: "I sang the entire part the way Danise had coached me on it and Toscanini didn't interrupt me. When I finished he said, 'Would it have taken a lot for you to have sung it for me that way the last time you came? You would have avoided angering me and receiving that tongue-lashing! Don't you think that it's more beautiful to hear the phrase "Ma tu Re, tu signore possente" . . . sung *mezza voce* instead of hearing it shouted the way everyone does and the way you did last week?!' 'Yes, Maestro, you're right.' 'Right, right, but you didn't do it correctly and angered me.'

"Finally, one day I was able to satisfy him. And he said, 'The orchestra at this point plays very softly and, if you look at the score, you will see that Verdi has put four *p*'s, that is more than *pianissimo*. Therefore it is important that the baritone does not yell, rather to sing with the maximum gentleness, the way, in fact, you did just now.'

"Another time I had arrived at the words of Amonasro, 'Se l'amor della patria è delitto, siam rei tutti, siam pronti a morir!' In the heat of singing and in trying to give it the most emphasis, I went flat on the word *patria*. The Maestro stopped me and said, 'Not so much enthusiasm on the word *patria*.' Looking at him, I read a bitter expression in his eyes.

"Although the part of Amonasro is not as long and complicated as that of Iago in *Otello*, the Maestro was still able to make it into a great part. There was not a passage of which he was not deeply aware of the color, the timbre, the expression. He often said to me: 'Remember, rascal, that Verdi saw Amonasro more as a father than as a soldier. All the phrases, except the words "Non sei mia figlia! Dei Faraoni tu sei la schiava!" must be sung with gentleness.'

"Another day at the phrase 'Suo padre,' I held the D-natural too long and at full voice. The Maestro stopped immediately: 'If the Ethiopians had a hammy king like you, they would have been scared, they would have all run away, and you would have been left alone to play at being the king.'

"One day the Maestro had me sing the entire part. The other soloists did the same. Our throats were so used to it that that music became almost second nature."

# Balance

Valdengo: "Among the things Toscanini suggested to me and that I find notated in my diary on March 22, 1949, is some advice about how a singer must position himself on stage to be better heard by the audience. Here are the exact words of the Maestro: 'Remember, dear rascal, when you are onstage, to always stay on the side of the strings. Your voice will more easily pass through the barrier of the strings than that of the winds who are on the other side. And when you sing, turn your gaze toward the audience. Many times the singing of an artist is lost because of the terrible habit they have of singing toward the wings.'

"Referring to the 'Credo' in *Otello*, 'Always seek to finish on your right side so that the audience will hear you well and don't listen to the stage directors, because unfortunately, they don't know these things. Only in this way will you succeed in having your voice heard where Verdi, to obtain a beautiful effect, has written a full orchestral *fortissimo*.

"'Even the F-sharp at the end of the baritone's first aria in *Andrea Chénier* will be better heard if you do it this way. Otherwise with all that ruckus of trumpets, trombones, etc., one needs ten baritones singing together to be heard.'"

# World Premiere of *I pagliacci*

Valdengo: "Toscanini explained that actually Leoncavallo had written *I pagliacci* to be performed in one act. That, however, only really happened on the first night; he himself had advised Leoncavallo to divide it in two acts."
Toscanini: "That first night, to change the scenery, I had to repeat a few times those few bars that close Canio's arioso. I have to tell you that we were awful . . . and so I insisted that Leoncavallo introduce an intermezzo. Leoncavallo was a good man, but lazy beyond words and didn't want to have anything to do with it. To get him to write that intermezzo I had to threaten him saying that I would no longer conduct his opera. And to facilitate the task, I suggested that he compose an intermezzo with the theme from the finale of the Prologue. That's how he did it and the second performance was a success.

"Acts that are too long tire the audience, especially the Latin audience. For the Germans it's different, and Wagner's operas are the proof. From the first reading of the score, I said that *Pagliacci* in one act is too heavy."

## *Madama Butterfly*

Toscanini: "The same thing was proven with *Butterfly* at La Scala. At the premiere it was performed in two acts and it was a grave failure, a failure that I had predicted to some friends. I was truly astonished that Puccini as much as Illica and Giacosa had failed to understand that it was a very big mistake to perform *Butterfly* in two very long, interminable acts. I didn't want to interfere and give suggestions to those three men of the theatre of such undisputed worth, but as soon as it was possible I advised Puccini to divide the opera into three acts, cutting also a lot of lengthy parts that were not important in the first act, and adding a *romanza* for the tenor in the third act. This is the way it was done, and the opera triumphed all over the world."

## Critics and Audiences

Toscanini: "In general critics are very fast to criticize and many times, unfortunately, without that objectivity and serenity that would be necessary. The critic, before grasping his pen to offer his observations, must consider the difficulty that the performer meets and it should be a requirement that he himself has had to pass through some difficult experiences. If it were so, I assure you that things would really change!

"It really should be taken into consideration that in an artist's career there are many factors that can momentarily impair the style, and above all, the health of the artist. Sometimes almost nothing, a slight ailment, or an unpleasant circumstance is enough to cause difficulty. Whoever sets about being a critic must hold all these things present and not criticize for the sake of criticizing! I knew a highly quoted critic who, however—incredible to say—was entirely influenced by his wife. If a certain artist didn't succeed in pleasing the lady, it was the worse for him . . . he was destroyed by the husband's pen! The critic must be calm, understanding, disengaged, humane, and not, as all too often happens, destructive.

"Even the audience sometimes allows itself to get carried away in a direction that is altogether unjustified. When I was a young boy in my native Parma, I heard people from the audience say, 'Tonight, it's *Rigoletto*. Let's go boo the tenor!' They went to the performance with this intention already in mind—think about it, dear rascal!"

## Importance of Endings

Valdengo: "The Maestro said that the finale of an opera is very important, especially for the general public. He used the example of a celebrated tenor who often was out of tune, but on the other hand knew how to finish well and everyone immediately forgot the confused notes he made earlier."

Toscanini: "In *Trovatore* you can work wonders singing 'Il balen del suo sorriso,' a feat that requires an uncommon capability, but if, in the long run, you do not finish well, you are done for!"

## Spontaneity

Toscanini: "Remember, art must come from the heart, it must be spontaneous: If you think about it, simplicity and naturalness are inexorably lost."

Valdengo: "He insisted on every single phrase until it came out naturally in a way that gave the listener the impression that the artist was being spontaneous, that he was creating it in that very moment, just as he did every day."

Toscanini: "Above all one needs to be natural. The instrumentalist who is spontaneous has an advantage over the others. One needs to practice a lot, but then it's necessary to release oneself from practice and study to allow the heart and the feeling to prevail."

## *Falstaff*

Toscanini said, while discussing *Falstaff* with Haggin: "Ah, for me is *most* beautiful opera!"[24]

Toscanini, explaining to Valdengo: "After the world premiere of *Falstaff*, the audience was surprised, disoriented by the new style that revealed a side of Verdi previously unknown. The audience still had in recent memory that milestone of the comic genre, Rossini's *Il barbiere di Siviglia*. *Falstaff* was a comic opera so profoundly different from those traditions that it upset all expectations. There is, in fact, a world of difference between Rossini's *Il barbiere* and Verdi's *Falstaff*.

"This explains, accordingly, how it came about that at the premiere at La Scala, a certain sense of uneasiness was created, and though its success was considerable, it wasn't even remotely comparable to the triumph of *Otello*. Subsequently *Falstaff* had, in the major national theatres and abroad, the great success that it merited. For me, *Falstaff* is the greatest Verdian masterpiece, undoubtedly destined to acquire, in time, more and more merit and prestige.

"I believe it will take years and years before the general public understands this masterpiece, but eventually when they really know it, they will run to hear it like they do now for *Rigoletto* and *La traviata*. If *Il trovatore* is the highest expression of melodrama understood as the expression of the country's distinctive character, *Falstaff* is the highest manifestation of Verdi's maturity.

"I remember that even at La Scala, it took all my courage to bring in *Falstaff*.[*] I imposed this opera upon La Scala even though many wrinkled their nose, and not satisfied, I repeated it in the subsequent years. It has been years that I have wanted to conduct this masterpiece again in America. It reaches the same heights, let me say it, as Beethoven's music. Of course it needs to be performed to perfection, but this perfection, dear rascal, is only found by rehearsing.

"It's not an easy opera at all, neither for the soloists nor for the conductors, and it should be carried out by everybody with the greatest commitment so that it can shine in all its marvelous glory.

"The role of Ford is a vocally difficult and complex part. The aria 'È sogno o realtà' is sensitive because it's decisive for the success of the finale."

Augusta Oltrabella, soprano, auditioned for Toscanini in 1935 for the role of Nannetta in *Falstaff*, and recalled his comments: "I don't like a light Nannetta. I want one whose voice has body and yet still can negotiate the agilities of the final aria . . . it is one of the most difficult Verdi ever wrote . . . not only because of the way it is written, but because it is atmospheric. It must smell of lilies and violets . . . Study the words very carefully, for it is all a hymn to poetry and nature . . . I want the last phrase, '*Le fate hanno per cifre i fior*' [Fairies have flowers for signatures] very, very

---

[*] Here, Toscanini referred to his first season as music director of La Scala, in 1899; he had been conducting *Falstaff* in various Italian theatres since 1894.

ethereal . . . every word must come out way in front . . .Tell your coach I want more metronome in the approach."[25]

Toscanini explained to Valdengo: "Falstaff is not an ordinary role that one can sing with a more or less good voice. In *Falstaff*, the text is very important. The part must be performed by an artist that besides having a voice adapted to this role, has perfect Italian diction, and most importantly, is also a good musician.

"I told you I wanted to teach you *Falstaff* and I will teach it to you. I want to leave behind a young man who knows how to sing and interpret that opera the way I desire and the way Verdi wanted, the way I already did with Stabile."

At Valdengo's first coaching session on *Falstaff*, Toscanini said, "Mind you, what you sing is not yet *Falstaff*; you can do it well, but you must rehearse and not take it all lightly the way you have the unfortunate habit of doing."

Valdengo: "I was listening and thinking, 'He doesn't know that I don't sleep at night because of this big fatso Falstaff and I torture my brain to find a way of doing it all well.'

"I sang the first act of *Falstaff* every day because Toscanini wanted me to absorb as much as possible, and that I identify myself with the 'fat glutton' as though it were second nature.

"The Maestro was very fond of the monologue in the first act because of the variety of color that the words demand. At some lessons the Maestro had me first recite the monologue, phrase by phrase, then had me sing it. I remember that I couldn't succeed in delivering the phrase 'Può l'onore riempirvi la pancia' the way he wanted it. He wanted the word *riempirvi* to take on an oiliness, 'making one think,' he said, 'of sauces, of a throat stuffed with food.'

"Danise taught me to enunciate the word *ladri* with more clarity, pronouncing it instead *laderi*, because the addition of the vowel *e* allows the word to be heard more sharply, while at the same time the *e* is not especially noticeable. The two consonants *dr* so close together take away a lot of the resonance from the word. Toscanini, who had a fine ear, noticed this and complimented me.

"Toscanini adopted all the colors of the musical palette. In the phrase in which Falstaff sings, 'Ber del vin dolce e sbottonarsi al sole' [To drink some sweet wine and unbutton oneself in the sun], he wanted the flavor of the wine to come across. He would say, 'You who are Piedmontese—and in Piedmont you have great wine—when you sing this phrase think of *nebbiolo* [a type of Piedmontese red wine], taste it in the mouth as though it is passing voluptuously over the taste buds. When you pronounce the word *dolce*, the flavor should well forth; one must feel the "sweetness" of the wine. Think of the enjoyment of the drinker at the moment in which the wine fills his mouth.' 'Yes, Maestro,' I would say, and would change the inflection of the phrase. But he'd say, 'Dear rascal, I want the wine to be sweeter yet,' and he would make me repeat it until at a certain moment, satisfied, he'd repeat, 'There, we've arrived: This is *nebbiolo*, bravo!'

"At the phrase 'e sbottonarsi al sole,' oh dear, that *sole* [sun] was never luminous enough for the Maestro! He'd say, 'I want it as bright as it is in Italy during the most splendid days of spring. I want a beautiful radiant sun in a blue sky . . . Be brave, use your imagination and make me a beautiful sun the way I want it.' Ah! How many times he had me repeat that 'sbottonarsi al sole'! There was always a little haze around my sun for him, but eventually I succeeded in doing it, as he wanted it. 'Like this it's bright,' he said, his eyes brilliant with happiness, 'Bravo, always do it this way!'"

## Characterization of Falstaff

Valdengo: "The Maestro illustrated the character of Falstaff to me down to the finest details. He insisted upon an interpretation permeated with as much realism and verismo as possible, as long as neither the dramatic nor the comic ideals were compromised. He used to say, 'Falstaff is not the buffoon that many artists think of and interpret him as being. The situations in which he finds himself are funny. He is convinced all women like him, otherwise he would not fall for a second prank, like that of the woods and fairies. Is that clear?' 'Yes, Maestro,' I responded, and he became even more fervent in pointing out all the characteristics of that unusual character." Toscanini: "His singing must be loose, never hysterical, even when he is in a rage. Fat people are in general always phlegmatic and good-natured; they never give way to making violent gestures. Even when Falstaff orders the servants to leave him alone with Quickly, he does it without yelling and deigning to glance at them. Servants come and go easily; therefore they should feel one's indifference. Remember, also, that your breathing must be on track with the music, of course, because if you run out of breath, goodbye to the bel canto line! Even Verdi was of the opinion that the role of Falstaff allows a certain freedom of interpretation in order to deliver the highest degree of spontaneity. But certainly not—let's be clear—those banal bouts of laughter inconsiderately added by some of your colleagues. The music contains the comic quality, and there is no need to add to it.

"As you will have noticed in practicing the score, this curious character dominates the opera. In contrast, however, with the rude and vulgar sensuality of the protagonist, it is the love story of Nannetta and Fenton—so pure, clean and serene—that leaves an impression on the audience and transports them to a peaceful, highly poetic atmosphere."

Toscanini: "The performance of [the world] premiere of *Falstaff* awarded a true triumph to Victor Maurel, the unparalleled protagonist, perfect in demeanor, controlled in phraseology and on stage. The audience paid him tribute with interminable applause; and every evening he had to repeat the aria 'Quand'ero paggio' as much as three times."

Valdengo: "The Maestro confided that he didn't know what he would have given to have a beautiful voice to sing that part the way he felt it in his heart. 'What is more beautiful, dear rascal, than to have a beautiful voice and to be able to sing?'

"One day he wanted to sing 'Quand'ero paggio' for me, the only piece that he still had not taught me. He said, 'Listen to how I would sing this masterpiece if I were a baritone.' And he sang, accompanying himself, keeping his eyes shut. When he was finished he said to me, 'How beautiful, right? How one feels that it was written in a flash. Now you sing it the way you feel it.' I sang it and when I finished he said, 'Mine was beautiful, but yours is also beautiful and do you know why? Because in performing it you didn't copy mine. Make sure you always sing it like that.'"

When Toscanini worked with singers whose artistry he admired, he respected their interpretations and didn't always impose his own views.

Valdengo: "The *Falstaff* rehearsals continued and every one of us made every effort to satisfy Toscanini. The reader perhaps cannot make sense of the reason for so many rehearsals; nevertheless they were necessary to make that performance as perfect as possible. I cite as an example the famous fugue of the last act. I had studied and re-studied it so much that even without the reference of the melody in the other voices, I could sing through it continuously.

"One day, the Maestro wanted to make sure, and had me sing it with my back turned to the piano. He said, 'One must never trust singers who are also musicians, because it's enough for them to see the piano keyboard from afar to remember the moment to come in.' He was right. For me it was enough to glimpse the Maestro's hands to know exactly when to come in. That day I sang the entire fugue without a mistake. I couldn't err because I had committed all the rests to memory. When I finished, the Maestro said to me, 'Tell the truth: You count the rests . . .' I responded, 'Yes.' He continued, 'That way you will never make an error in the fugue, it is the surest system. Use this system and you will always save yourself. Also in the trio of *Manon Lescaut*, if you don't count the rests, you will immediately be ruined. In that trio, dear rascal, the baritone is the foundation of everything, and if he is wrong, there is no way to put things right again.'"

Valdengo: "If Toscanini demanded very much for *Otello*, for *Falstaff* he was downright impossible to satisfy. He was always looking for something to perfect: either a word overly emphasized in a certain way, or a note to lengthen or shorten. In short, grueling work. Every once in a while he'd say, 'I'm really happy with you, you've put your head in order.' His encouragement was to continue to practice, practice to always come closer to perfection! He would repeat, 'Don't ever get discouraged . . . don't allow yourself to be defeated!'"

# CHAPTER 6

# Musical Architecture

*He was possessed enough of this arching sound dream . . . that he had enough psychic energy to carry people along with him.*
   —**Robert Shaw**

Katims: "When he began to conduct a work, he seemed to have a total concept of the music—in the case of a symphony from the beginning of the first movement to the end of the final movement. The propulsive element in his conducting was naturally conducive to the unfolding of the music to its inevitable conclusion. For him each composition was very much like the topography of a landscape with its valleys, foothills, small mountains and a high peak or two—the high point of a piece of music toward which he shaped his performance. There was an increasing intensity toward a certain point, then a relaxation away from it—like breathing in and out. He did this instinctively, and as a result the music seemed literally to breathe. He gave it the logic of speech. There was his instinctive sense of theatre. Timing was of the essence. I always marveled at the natural way he would delay a beat ever so slightly in order to heighten the dramatic effect."[1]

D. Walter spoke about the third movement of Beethoven's Ninth Symphony: "It's a theme and variations, and it's a very slow-moving melody. A theme can be slow and boring, or it can be slow and exciting if there is within it something kinetic with motion and energy. I remember having done the Ninth with two other conductors just before that time. In both cases I was terribly bored by the slow movement, although I knew and loved the Ninth, because it didn't seem to go anyplace, to hold my interest. And on occasion you'd find somebody had dozed off in the audience. But with Toscanini the movement seemed to flow constantly, so that at every point you wanted to know what comes next. And the variations seemed truly, structurally, variations. And they weren't just a continuation, but they reminded you of where they came from, and the whole thing was, for me, very exciting."

## Proportions, Climaxes, and Crescendos

Galimir: "The climaxes were always perfect. This was because of another wonderful thing—the proportion. His sense of proportion was really incredible."

Granick: "He just went on and brought things to a logical climax; and you always felt with Toscanini that the music was going someplace, that something was going to happen."

Galimir: "The sense of proportion was always correct with him; and this made the Rossini overtures so wonderful. I've never heard in a Rossini overture the crescendos drawn to that point—when it got loud, louder, always louder, and you thought it couldn't anymore, but it *still* got louder, until the moment when it was supposed to be the loudest! And the same in the Wagner. In everything—it was immaterial what—the way the proportions were made was fantastic; this was one of his best qualities."[2]

Moldavan: "Nobody could build up a crescendo as he did—by holding you back—holding you—holding you. Other conductors don't know how to do that: They run away with you; and when it comes to the *forte* they haven't anything left. He knew how to build it up gradually."[3]

## Convincing

Civetta: "What were Toscanini's performances of Brahms like?"
Burghauser: "Unheard of, totally surprising. Brahms has a characteristic reputation of being a north German, which means cold, brittle, aloof, full of neo-Bach

contrapuntal flavor and not much expression, and never sentimental. Toscanini made it singing, like a bel canto soprano, which was unheard-of, with which he captivated the whole audience . . . A third of the players had known Brahms personally, who was a conductor in Vienna also, and so we do know how Brahms wanted his music played. And this Italian is the very fulfillment of what we know of Brahms, which neither Walter nor even Furtwängler had ever done before in Vienna. Furtwängler made a wonderful Brahms, but dripping from sentimentality and feeling and arbitrary tempo-changing, which Toscanini found totally out of-style.

"Toscanini surprised everybody, and the greatest surprise was that it was with greatest enthusiasm accepted instead of rejected. This is not the Brahms we knew, of Furtwängler, Walter and Weingartner and Schalk—it was different, and he convinced them of its authenticity."

Burghauser described Toscanini's performances of Brahms's Third Symphony in Vienna: "What an effect it made! What I call *musikalische Plastik*—truly three-dimensional in plastic reality—this was what Toscanini gave us with this symphony—as he did with the Schubert C Major, which also we had never experienced. This Brahms was new, unheard of; yet it fitted into the tradition: It was only taken out of the everyday routine—noble routine, since Brahms is always noble, and yet smoothed down at the corners, at the edges; whereas Toscanini made it sharp and fresh again. And with the Fourth Symphony—the first movement, and the passacaglia, Bach-like, severe, ascetic: People said, 'How wonderful to hear once in your life an Italianized Fourth Symphony. It's not our Nordic Brahms; but it's a nice Brahms.' And there was no debate."[4]

Civetta: "What did you really learn from him?"
Shaw: "It's easier to compare George Szell's approach to his approach. Szell seemed to be able to build out of the microcosm, caring for every little balance and everything in one measure, building up the piece block by block. And Toscanini went over it like a Valkyrie running through the sky, or like sunshine sweeping across the plain, so that you always had a sense of not dwelling on the moment which was passing, but of the destination. Two things are essential: The first, that the composer left a complete thing, and if possible, the conductor should get out of the way of it, and the way to get out was to follow every direction. And the second, was that he was possessed enough of this arching sound dream, from this instant until whenever it stopped, that he had enough psychic energy to carry people along with him. He

was possessed enough by the music so that both audiences and performers had to go along with it."

Shaw, to Haggin: "While in terms of inner pulse the tempo might be enormously fast, he retained clearly before him the point toward which he was heading; and this made it possible for musicians to articulate and singers to follow him—even in his fast tempos. There was every reason to believe that the two fugues in the Credo of the Missa Solemnis simply couldn't be sung by human voices in his recorded tempos—but they were!"[5]

# CHAPTER 7

# Balance

*Is dirty—we wash!*
   —Toscanini[1]

## Clarity

William Primrose, violist: "I believe the greatest influence the maestro exerted on me and on the orchestra as a whole was his insistence on clarity. Every note had to sound."[2]

Winter: "He liked music played so you could take it down by dictation. He hated messy playing."

Weber: "He was so clear and exact. He liked everything crystal clear, his Beethoven, Brahms, and Wagner, particularly. I never heard Wagner the way he did it."

Bachmann: "The Maestro had a curious point of view about playing altogether, not shared by any other conductor up to that time. Since then it has been accepted everywhere. He was looking for the principal first, second, viola, and cello that were chamber musicians. He wanted quartet players because he wanted to incorporate

the intimacy of the quartet with the magnitude of the symphony, in which we succeeded absolutely par excellence."

Bridget Paolucci: "How did he achieve such clarity of the musical line in his
conducting?"
Hupka: "It is an extraordinary phenomenon. I always looked at it like a spider web
that would glitter in the sun: You saw every little thread of this magnificent texture,
yet you had the entire spider web. It was an extraordinary image that he must have
had on his mind to really get every detail, all these little inner voices that were in
the score which he wanted heard."[3]

S. Shulman: "I never heard *La mer* done the way he did it, with clarity."

Bloom: "When he would do *La mer* it was really a revelation the way this music just
came out, and it was all as it was written. I don't mean literally written. Debussy was
very much a meticulous composer. All you have to do is look at his manuscript. At
Eastman they have some manuscripts of the sketch for the *La mer* and, boy, just
the way it was written you can tell he was a meticulous man. Everything had its
place and when he played this thing—he got all the power out of it with none of
the so-called overlay impressionist things you get from so many conductors. I'll
never forget the way he did *The Afternoon of a Faun*. It was just so beautiful. It was
languorous when it was supposed to be languorous, but not overdone. One of the
members of our NBC Orchestra, who for many years was a member of the New
York Philharmonic, after the concert said, 'I never knew that this music was this
kind of music. I never liked it before because I felt it was somebody smearing big
colors on a big canvas, and Debussy is not that way at all.' He was sort of a Mozart
of his time. He was very clean."

Civetta: "How did he achieve the balancing of the orchestra?"
Weber: "He would make us play individually and in groups: 'Play alone.' 'Play
together.'"

Vardi: "Some of the rehearsals were absolutely phenomenal. During a rehearsal of
*Till Eulenspiegel* of Strauss, he rehearsed just the brass and percussion. It was just
marvelous to sit there and hear just that part of the orchestra. Then he'd clarify some
rhythmical things, and all of a sudden it was like a jigsaw puzzle was resolved. And

there it was, just the way the score was; you heard it. Sometimes it came off at the concert like that. Those moments were great."

A. Shulman: "The air was so remarkable for balancing. He'd have the strings take a rest, and he'd work the brass and winds in a Strauss tone poem. And to me, here I was, going to class. I was being paid to learn, to live it, to analyze it and balance it and hear it live, played by virtuoso musicians, led by a genius of a conductor. Here I was, a budding composer, and this was my class in orchestration and textural balances. He had such an incredible ear for balancing a chord: 'Too much bassoon, too little clarinet, a little bit more, you're a little bit sharp, this and that.' Soon the thing fell into place, and when it did it just jelled. You're taking the parts of a jigsaw puzzle and you're putting them in, and making the whole picture of it."

Weber: "Up until his late years he was looking for things and improving. He had an ear for sound. He had an ear for intonation. His intonation was absolutely impeccable. I don't think there was or ever will be a conductor who could balance an orchestra as well. He just learned his music. He knew every note. And when it came to intonation, in Wagner particularly, in *Götterdämmerung*, his sense of balance was absolutely perfect. He was the only one that made Wagner brass sound balanced. And he spent a lot of time on it. Also, I recall the opening chords of the *Midsummer Night's Dream* Overture. He spent quite a bit of time tuning that and balancing it to get the proper effect. And *Romeo and Juliet* by Tchaikovsky. This is the Toscanini legend we're always seeking and talking about."

Bachmann: "There was one thing that nobody had better. That is balance, which is the secret of all great orchestras. His sense of balance was unfailing. But ninety or ninety-five out of a hundred conductors say: 'No. Somehow or other this is not the color I want. You play *sforzando*, you play *piano*, you play this, the second oboe that. Try it. That's better, but it's still not what I want.' This did not exist with the Maestro. He didn't say, 'That's not what I want.' He said, 'You play too loud. You play not loud enough. You play this. You play how. Now try it.' And we tried it and that was *it*. He knew what he wanted to hear in his inner ear. He didn't have to try again and again and again."

Coletta: "If he had a harmony part running in thirds with the leading voice, I remember vividly that he wanted the lower voice to be equal in power to the upper

voice, which is obvious, that the supportive harmony should be as strong. So balances were always clear. You didn't just get a feeling of top melody and a little murky
accompanying harmony or interval of voices or secondary material. You heard them
all very clearly. He made sure that they balanced out."

Freeman, recalling rehearsals of *The Moldau*: "The first oboe plays a third above the
second oboe. Usually something is done about it; the oboe players put something
in the oboe so the second oboe player can get softer. And Toscanini was bearing
down on the two oboe players. He wanted it softer. But the first oboe player has to
be compassionate. He has to know the second oboist can only go so far on a note
like that or else there'll be nothing; and he tries to give a little more so the other
one has more control to hold it because it's a chord. If you can just hit it and walk
away from it, it would be fine; but it has to be sustained. It has to be in tune. It has
to sound good. So Toscanini stopped, threw his hands up in the air, and looked up
toward the sky at God, and said, 'I had the same problem in Rome, the same problem in Paris, the same problem in London, the same problem when I conducted
in Germany, and thank God I don't go back there any more. When I came to this
country I was in a boat many, many days. Then they started crossing in six days.
They invented an airplane, comes across in a matter of hours. They've invented all
kinds of fantastic things. But no one ever did anything for the poor second oboe
player with that one lousy little note.'"

Haggin: "In this constant study of the printed score, [he] was concerned always
with texture—i.e., with this bassoon part or that viola part buried in the tutti that
must be made clearly audible in the performance."[4]

Galimir: "With Toscanini there was never a possibility that you had to fight the
trumpets to come through—which very often happens. This, again, made it so
pleasant to play: You did not have to force."[5]

> Manoug Parikian stated that during the rehearsals for the all-Brahms
> cycle with the Philharmonia in 1952, Toscanini rehearsed the Brahms
> Third, especially the first movement, much more than the other three
> symphonies. He was particularly concerned with the balance—that each
> part be clearly heard. He felt that Toscanini was most passionate about
> clarity and intensity.[6]

Goodman: "He had a great sense of balance. He yelled occasionally if he was irritated at the balance in the orchestra. I might have been playing too loud. The first time we played the Beethoven Ninth Symphony was the first year I was with the New York Philharmonic. [Goodman was nineteen.] We were rehearsing the Scherzo that has the famous timpani phrase—the octaves—and I heard him keep saying, '*Timpano, timpano, timpano*,' which in Italian means one timpani. *Timpano* is singular. *Timpani* is plural. Well, he was saying, '*Timpano, timpano, timpano, timpano*.' And I kept playing louder and louder and louder. I thought he wanted me to play louder. And finally he stopped the orchestra. He said, '*Timpano*, why you play so loud?' 'Maestro, you say, "*Timpano, timpano, timpano*."' He said, 'I don't mean that for you. I mean that for the orchestra, for the rhythm!'"

> The rhythm of this passage is identical to the rhythm of the word *timpano* when it is spoken. Toscanini was repeating the word to demonstrate the exact rhythm that he wanted the orchestra to execute while playing the passage.

Ira Hirschmann, friend of Toscanini, described a rehearsal of *Tod und Verklärung* with the New York Philharmonic at which Toscanini went out into the hall to listen to the balance: "Toscanini asks Mr. Lange, the assistant conductor, to lead them in the last pages of the Strauss tone poem. He paces up and down the aisles, walking through the rows of empty seats from one side of the hall to the other, his arms moving back and forth with the music, his expression changing from benign serenity to displeasure when certain passages displease him."[7]

Weber: "He was mostly happy on tour. There were short rehearsals. We tested the hall. One time, I heard him clap—walk on the stage and clap his hands to hear the echo or rebound of sound."

Hirschmann discussed Schubert's "Unfinished" Symphony: "[Toscanini] told me that . . . he hesitated to approach this Schubert masterpiece. He said that it had always seemed beyond his reach, spiritually . . . He said, 'I am very nervous about this.' Imagine this great man who had conducted so many thousands of concerts . . . He said, 'I'm afraid of this piece. This is a great . . . elusive piece. I can't quite get a hold of it, and I'm worried about it. I want you to go up to the balcony and listen carefully to the woodwinds in the second movement. Tell me if you think they come off. We will discuss it afterward.' And he was in a nervous sweat about this. Of course it was angelic. It was golden. I'll never, never forget it. And I went back afterward and he looked up at me and said, 'How was it?' as if he'd have to question anyone . . . He asked me for every detail . . . And I said, 'The woodwinds came right over the top.' He said, 'You know, I worried about this. I had sleepless nights.' He poured out his feelings about the cavalier approach of most conductors to this piece of music, which for him, challenged his utmost capacity to penetrate and perform. 'No other conductor hesitates to play this Schubert . . . which to me is like a mountaintop that I cannot quite reach.'

"And he mentioned some other conductors' names. He said, 'To this fellow, or that fellow playing this would be nothing. He could knock it off. To me this is a task that I consider to be one of the most difficult things that I could've undertaken.' This modesty this humility, which he demonstrated toward the music and the musicians, reminded me of Schnabel, who said, 'I hope to improve every day.' And this man was like that. There's only a few giants of that kind that have that humility. He had humility."[8]

## Preparation and Ear

Brieff: "His ear was as perceptive at that late age as it was when he was younger. He could balance things just by looking at you."

Bachmann: "His ear, naturally, was as superb as it was dangerous, because he heard everything even if he couldn't see everything."

Guarrera: "The man was almost blind, but we felt that he could see not right at us but through us! His ear—he had radar, you know!"

A. Shulman: "Once, Mani Vardi played the first three or four performances with Frank Black and the NBC Symphony of a work I had written. And I sent the Maestro a score. And two or three days after the broadcast, Remo Bolognini came to me and said, 'Maestro wants to see you up in his dressing room.' So I went upstairs, and Maestro patted me on the shoulder and said, 'Very intelligent orchestration, Shulman, but tell me, what happened to the bass tuba at the end?' And I said, 'Maestro, the texture was too heavy, so I took it out.' It just showed that he was interested, he had looked at the score, he had studied it, and he had ears like a hawk. I think that in all the years I was in orchestras, the greatest sets of ears that I came across were Toscanini's, Pierre Monteux's, and Guido Cantelli's. The rest had good ears, and some of them were absolutely tin eared, but these were incredible ears."

## Orchestra Size

Haggin, writing about a letter he received from Toscanini in 1941: "He went on to say he had a weakness for Beethoven's Septet, which he had played the preceding season with ten violins, ten violas, eight cellos, and four basses . . . He had, he said, heard many performances of the piece in its original form by distinguished musicians; but the right balance [of seven instruments] had never been attained."[9]

M. Bernstein: "For Toscanini's 1929 recording of Mozart's 'Haffner' Symphony with the New York Philharmonic, he excluded four of the ten double bass players in the Philharmonic because there's only a small number of wind instruments. Ten bass players, ten cellists, and ten viola players are called for to balance the sonorities of a Wagner or a Richard Strauss. In Mozart, in Haydn, and in fact, in most of Beethoven, the wind instruments of the orchestra are few in number. For example, there are only two horns in the so-called 'classical' symphony instead of the four that are routine later on, or the six or eight that appear in Wagner and Strauss. It's merely a matter of preserving balance."[10]

## Doubling and Retouching

Regarding the alterations of scores, it is true that, overall, Toscanini was a purist who tried very hard to stick to what composer wrote. However, there are innumerable occasions when he retouched orchestration. In some works he changed the harmony, in opera he changed the words and made transpositions, and so on. Toscanini was certainly not unique in the practice of altering scores. His contemporaries also made orchestrational alterations with the intention to improve passages that were not very well orchestrated. This practice resulted from years of practical experience as conductors. For example, Weingartner published an entire book of his recommendations of his retouching of the Beethoven symphonies (*On the Performance of Beethoven's Symphonies*). Mahler liberally retouched the orchestration of Beethoven's Ninth Symphony, rescoring its orchestration to include eight horns and even a tuba part.

The point is that Toscanini was born in 1867, and that altering scores was a standard practice of his time and was not unique to him. The intent, however, was always one of perceived necessity, usually to attain a better balance of the texture, rather than a subjective preference for how a passage could be rescored.

Weber: "In some of the Beethoven symphonies, he doubled the woodwinds. Instead of using one first and one second, he would use two firsts and two seconds in the oboes, flutes, clarinets, and bassoons, because with a large string section, you had to balance it with more woodwinds. Not in all Beethoven symphonies—in the Ninth, in the Sixth, not in the Fourth, Second, nor in the First, but the 'Eroica,' definitely."

Bloom: "He was a great, great conductor of Beethoven. He worked at it very hard. There was this myth that he never changed anything—that he never changed any instrumentation—which I would say is basically true. He would work very, very hard to overcome some of the composers' mistakes and try to do just what the composers had written but still make it sound the way it should sound, because composers are fallible just like anybody else. They make mistakes. In Beethoven, there was one place where there is a line in the flute that is terribly important, but it turns out very often that the line is lost and I remember that I found a little piece of music paper on my stand with about two bars on it for me to play along with the flute. As far as I know, that, and a place in Sibelius's Second Symphony where he augmented something are about the only times that I have actually seen him change anything. But he would struggle and struggle and struggle not to change it, and then finally say, 'Well okay, it had to be done.'"

Galimir spoke about "the little orchestrational retouching that he did in Beethoven symphonies, because as we know in Beethoven symphonies, the Ninth Symphony, for example, has a lot of problems. Many conductors used to change the orchestration a little, not to the point where you violate the text, but just to make it sound. That's as far as he went: only in the utmost cases where he thought it must be done. I have never heard of any other freedom where he just changed something because he didn't like it. He always tried to find the composer's point of view, and then thought to interpret that point of view. An interpreter has to interpret. That's the sole function an interpreter has. Hence, where the line is drawn to say, this is up to here interpretation, and from here on is change—that's a very difficult line to draw."

> Toscanini suggested that Horowitz make some alterations in the Beethoven sonatas, particularly the last ones, to improve upon them pianistically. The maestro reasoned that it was common for conductors to make subtle changes in the orchestration of Beethoven's symphonies, and that no one ever seemed to perceive them. Horowitz refrained from making the changes because he was concerned about a potential backlash of criticism.[11]

When Haggin visited Toscanini, the conductor pointed out to him an orchestrational alteration in Smetana's *Die Moldau*. Toscanini said, "I put trumpet at the end because is not clear only with trombones."[12]

Haggin: "When [his son] Walter put on the record of a broadcast of *Die Moldau*, Toscanini stood not just listening but conducting the performance in every detail; and at the end he directed my attention to the trumpets' strengthening of the melodic line. From this I learned that although Toscanini adhered strictly to the composer's text he didn't hesitate to correct what seemed to him a miscalculation in orchestration that kept something from being heard clearly. It was surprising to learn later of the many such changes in *La mer*."[13]

Civetta: "Do you recall any changes in orchestration?"

Howard Carassy, an NBC Symphony librarian: "The American premiere of the Shostakovich Seventh Symphony was one thing. There were about fifteen minutes, which the announcer used to introduce the symphony and the conditions under which it had been composed. And during that fifteen minutes I was out onstage marking a few little things in the woodwinds. They were already onstage. I found out about it a few minutes before airtime. Fortunately, I finished before the announcer did. I think he did some flute and oboe doubling, a little bit in places; it wasn't extensive."

Civetta: "How about 'The Star-Spangled Banner'?"

Carassy: "He doubtless did do something about it. The parts that we had always used were the ones that had been used for years and years by the director of the

Marine Band. I think he made a regular orchestration. 'The Stars and Stripes,' he fixed up. It has one trombone, and he wanted three."

Goodman shared Toscanini's thoughts on the practice of altering timpani parts: "The reason composers of the nineteenth century didn't bother changing the pitch was that the mechanical-type timpani necessary for those changes didn't exist. If they started a piece in F and B-flat, it remained in F and B-flat unless there was a long period of time to change to another pitch. Don't forget that when these pieces were written, people got used to listening to the wrong notes. I remember once playing the overture from the *Midsummer Night's Dream* with Toscanini. In the transitional section the key goes to F-sharp major, but the timpani part is still using B-natural and E-natural, which are wrong notes. So I changed the note once and Toscanini stopped and said, 'Don't change the note. I want it to sound as Mendelssohn heard it, with the wrong note.'"[14]

Weber, speaking about *La bohème*: "On the stage, the Maestro came to me and pointed to an insert in the music that he had written himself, and there were a series of arpeggios. This is rather humorous: He said, 'I doubled the arpeggios in the harp. Puccini didn't know how to orchestrate. I had to teach him everything!' Of course, they were great friends, and Puccini was a tremendous orchestrator, but he wanted those arpeggios to come through, so he had it doubled by the second clarinet."

Winter recalled playing *El Salón México* with Toscanini: "Aaron Copland told me that in studying the score, Toscanini questioned a little bit of the orchestration—I think he doubled a trombone. Copland was not as highly esteemed as he is today [1977], but he said Toscanini treated him as if he were Beethoven: 'Try it your way, try it my way, and you decide which way you like better and that's the way we will do it.' And Copland said he liked Toscanini's way better and that's the way it's done now."

Robert Shaw recalled the first time he had prepared the chorus for Toscanini's performance of Beethoven's Ninth Symphony: "I had gone to ask him some questions about changes of tempos in the middle. Then I asked him about a passage where the altos dip so low, and I asked him if I could use tenor voices, and he said, 'Will it allow the music to be heard?' and I said, 'Maestro, I think it is the only way it can be heard.' And he said, 'By all means, then do it; cross the voices.'"

Albanese recalled Toscanini's alteration of the score at the end of the first-act cadenza of *La traviata*: "I did the part of the tenor and the tenor did the part of the soprano. I said, 'Maestro, can you do this?' And Toscanini replied, 'We always did, even when Verdi or any composer was alive. We used to change.'"

Weber: "A very funny thing happened one time in *Till Eulenspiegel*, where I played E-flat clarinet. After we played several performances, at a subsequent rehearsal in Carnegie Hall, he asked for me to come into his room. He showed me the score, and said, 'You know, this note I never hear in the orchestra. I don't hear it.' I said, 'Maestro, I know what you're talking about.' It's the last ascending passage of the E-flat clarinet. After that there's the long arpeggio going up to the top, and I assume Strauss meant *Till Eulenspiegel* is going to heaven. But this last screech before being hanged, there's one more note. It's an A-flat concert. And it's inaudible because it's an octave too low in the part. And I remember my old teacher, who was with the New York Philharmonic at that time, Simeon Bellison, warning me, 'Some conductor is going to ask you to play it an octave higher. When I played it with Strauss conducting many years ago, he had it played an octave higher, although it's not marked in the part.' Toscanini discovered that that note was inaudible, and said, 'I don't hear it. Do something.' I said, 'I know just what you want.' At the rehearsal he immediately went to a little bit before that passage. We played it, and I played the note an octave higher, a high F on the E-flat clarinet. And he waved his arms with happiness! 'Ah, at last, at last!' And everybody recognized it."

Goldsmith: "There are many places in the Beethoven symphonies, especially in the later recordings, where there are extra timpani details—in *Death and Transfiguration*—in *La mer* he apparently had Debussy's full sanction. What makes his changes and emendations a little bit more bearable is that in contrast to Stokowski, who would just change the orchestration to create a momentary sensational effect, Toscanini's emendations were made to further a point that the composer was really striving for in the music. It's just a matter of taste, and I really feel that while people will never really agree on what's good taste and bad taste, I feel that Toscanini's changes were the work of a much more tasteful musician than the majority of his colleagues."

# Dynamics

Novotny: "You had to watch your dynamic marks at all times. If you had a *pp* written, you made sure you played it. Whether or not you felt that was a very important passage or not, the *pp* had to be respected. There were many times when as far as loud *forte* playing was concerned, you actually could not give the Maestro enough."

Leinsdorf: "According to Toscanini, who knew and worked under Verdi, the composer always wanted his *piano* phrases sung by the instruments in a natural cantabile sound."[15] Leinsdorf continued: "In a rehearsal for *Otello* with the NBC Symphony Orchestra, Toscanini demanded a full bodied *piano* from the strings in a passage marked *ppp* by Verdi . . . He explained that the Italian orchestras for whom Verdi scored his works played everything in an unvarying *mezzo forte*, which forced the composer to write extremes for *forte* and *piano* in order to obtain nuances of any kind."[16]

D. Walter: "He would say a *piano* in Verdi is not like a *piano* in Beethoven: You see four *p*'s in Verdi, and you play one; you see four *f*'s in Verdi, and you play one. He taught us, 'You know, from Verdi I learned *piano*. It means *naturale* [naturally], play *naturale* . . . Pizzicati [plucked notes], play *naturale* . . . After a great *fortissimo*, never play *pianissimo*. Also, if you have three *p*'s, play *mezzo forte*.' And he had a sense for the different styles of music of different periods."

> Toscanini repeatedly instructed the orchestra to play *piano* markings in Verdi with a natural, singing quality, and not to play them very softly. Verdi supervised the rehearsals for the world premiere of *Otello*; Toscanini was the second cellist. In the first act love duet there is a passage scored for a quartet of solo cellos marked *pianissimo*. The first cellist was quite famous and critics often mentioned him in their reviews. He never played *piano*. Toscanini had played the *pianissimo* as the composer had written. At the rehearsal break, to obtain the proper balance Verdi asked Toscanini to play a little louder, at a natural volume level rather than asking the first cellist to play softer. From this encounter, Toscanini concluded that the *pianissimo* in Italian music was never intended to be as soft as it is in German music.[17]

Mischakoff learned from Toscanini how to interpret dynamic markings, applying the conductor's insight into his chamber music rehearsals and lessons. Mischakoff's daughter, Anne Mischakoff Heiles, wrote: "In quartets or lessons a protest to my father might elicit a similar tirade against following a marking too literally at the expense of musicality. The context was the ultimate arbiter of the dynamic level or articulation."[18]

# Small Theatre

Toscanini was very attracted to the intimacy of a small theatre, and for many years, spoke glowingly of his experiences conducting at Busseto, the town of Verdi's birth. In his old age he wanted very much to conduct *Falstaff* at La Piccola Scala.

# Acoustics

A. Berv: "When I came to NBC, Studio 8H was just like a blotter. It was so dead. It was just awful, especially after coming from the great sounding Academy of Music in Philadelphia, where everything sounded so perfect and so marvelous; you could hear all the players, every instrument. If I had to play a passage with the oboe or the clarinet or the bassoon, it blended. I could sense just how much to blend, while at studio 8H it was so difficult. If I had to play a passage with my brother Jack [who was seated next to me], it was so difficult to hear him. He could hear me but I couldn't hear him very well. I remember distinctly how Maestro Toscanini would scream and scream and scream because he couldn't hear this instrument and couldn't hear that instrument."

Haggin: "The men of the orchestra told me they hated Studio 8H because they couldn't hear each other . . . But Toscanini, they said, liked Studio 8H because standing on the podium *he* could hear everything very clearly. In addition, I was told, he felt that just as Carnegie Hall was the [New York] Philharmonic's place, 8H was *his* place, and I remember hearing about recording sessions scheduled for Carnegie Hall which at the last minute he insisted on transferring to 8H."[19] Haggin continued, "Inevitably the question arises: What did Toscanini think and say about the sound of the orchestra in Studio 8H? The only reliable report I ever had about this was that standing close to the orchestra he liked hearing every instrument so clearly . . .

"Which brings us to the question: What did Toscanini think and say about this dry and flat sound produced by the NBC recordings of the broadcasts? I never heard him comment on it; but I did hear his comments on other recordings [derived from recording sessions], and I would guess that he felt about the ones of the NBC broadcasts as he did about those others: If he heard every instrument he should hear, played as it should be played, he was satisfied; and dryness or harshness of string sound apparently didn't trouble him when it came out of a loud-speaker."[20]

## *Oberon* Overture

Samuel Antek, conductor and violinist, described how Toscanini rehearsed the passage in Carl Maria von Weber's *Oberon* Overture that occurs two bars before letter I. Toscanini insisted that the two sixteenth pickup notes played by the first violins be clearly heard. The preceding chord played by the woodwinds and strings was partially covering these two notes.

The maestro asked the violinists to remove Weber's *diminuendo* marking and play very loudly. They repeated the passage, playing these two notes louder and accenting them, both with their left hands and their bows. But the notes were still not clearly audible. Toscanini then questioned the bowing the concertmaster, Mischakoff, was using. Singing the passage several times to demonstrate the brilliance, force, and passion he was expecting, the maestro asked the concertmaster to change the bowing, whereupon Mischakoff decided to use two bow strokes instead of one. This was better but Toscanini wanted the notes to be still clearer. Mischakoff then proposed a third bowing, which the orchestra tried. This required more effort on the part of the violinists and the result was that the two notes sounded clearer, better articulated, and more forceful. Toscanini acknowledged that it was better, but still wanted the first two notes to be a little stronger and more accented. He explained the importance of the separation between the long note and these two sixteenth notes. Mischakoff then played a bowing that was quite different from the others. It called for retaking the bow in two down-bows at both the long *sforzando* note and again at the first of the two sixteenth notes. Toscanini liked it, found the clarity much improved, and asked the orchestra to try it. This necessitated that the players take more time between the long note and the first sixteenth note. It required more physical effort and skill and resulted in those sixteenth notes sounding even stronger and more vibrant. Finally Toscanini was very happy with this bowing.

Antek wrote that the orchestra had played this passage hundreds of times through the years, yet none of the other conductors insisted on its importance. For the orchestra, the passage had suddenly taken on a newly discovered quality, and the musicians were appreciative of Toscanini's insistence that they think out of the box and strive together to clearly realize in sound what Weber had written.[21]

# CHAPTER 8

# Baton Technique

*He was not a glamour puss. There weren't any fancy gestures about Toscanini—no theatrics*
*at all. Yet everything was conducive to great performance. It was a real mystery.*
   —**Harry Berv**

## Inexplicable

Weber spoke about *Pictures at an Exhibition*: "At 'The Great Gate of Kiev,' there are
tremendous scales, and in order to increase the sound, he did some augmentation
in the winds. We did *Pictures at an Exhibition* with Cantelli a year earlier, and he
used the same score and parts. Toscanini was in the audience. Maestro sat out in
the audience, without any expression, listening. And it was an experience to play
for Cantelli, knowing that the Old Man was out there listening. A lot of times we
seemed to be watching him more than Cantelli. Of course, Cantelli was a tremendous
talent; we recorded it with Cantelli, and he made it sound magnificent. Well the
next year the Maestro came back, and he put on *Pictures*, and as great as 'The Great
Gate at Kiev' sounded with Cantelli, somehow, the Maestro made it sound a little
bigger, using the same parts, in the same hall. It was something he had that other
conductors don't seem to have or been able to achieve, and I've played with 'most all
the great conductors of the past and present. Some things he just did magnificently."

## Immediate Response

Granick: "The fact that the response was so immediate, more immediate than normal, and that we all responded in the same way meant that his beat was extremely clear and expressive."
Civetta: "Was it flamboyant?"
Granick: "No. It was never flamboyant, but neither was it hidden. It adequately expressed the great intensity that was in some music, as at other times, it was able to express the most delicate things about music."

## Beautiful Beat

Civetta: "What about his conducting technique?"
S. Shulman: "The most beautiful technique I've ever seen, and I've worked with ten or twelve of the great conductors. It was a florid beat and aesthetically as beautiful as anything I've ever seen in my life. I've never seen a ballerina look more beautiful."

Galimir: "It really was a beautiful thing to watch him. He had a very expressive beat. I've seen conductors with more facility in the beat; but the expressiveness of his beat was incredible: you really could see everything he wanted in that beat: the staccato, the legato, the *espressivo*—everything was in it. You really had only to look at him, not at the music."

## Age

Krasnopolsky: "Age didn't mean anything to him. When he used to walk on stage, he walked like an old man: quiet, soft. But as soon as he stood on the podium and took the baton, forget about age. He was like a child. He forgot completely that he was an old man because when he stood there we felt the intensity and inspiration; it was great. He became a giant, forgetting age, his problems and those of the world. I played with other conductors. I played with Bruno Walter, Monteux—great conductors on their own, but nobody compared with Toscanini."

# Standing

Civetta: "Did he use a stool at rehearsals?"

J. Bernstein: "No. He wouldn't do it. In every intermission he would never sit down. He was standing all the time. If you tried to help him put on a coat, he got mad. He wanted to be young."

Granick: "Toward the end of his tenure at NBC, he had fallen off a chair and hurt his leg. His leg was numb for almost two, perhaps three years. And sometimes when conducting, he felt as though he was standing on one leg. This made him nervous and sometimes was the cause of him forgetting something in the music, which he had never done previously. But when he was asked why he doesn't conduct sitting down, he said if he had to do that he would give up conducting, because conducting came through the body and could only be done when he presented the figure of the music himself, a figure which coincided with the music, which couldn't be done sitting down. He said sitting down was perhaps for those more Germanic conductors who sat down, and talked through the whole rehearsal, where musicians used a pencil more frequently than they used a bow—which actually was necessary because he included in the Germanic school many conductors who weren't Germans but who didn't have very much technique as conductors, and the orchestra would never know what they were doing if they hadn't actually written down in the orchestra's own language almost everything to indicate what the conductor had said at rehearsal; otherwise nobody would be playing the same way."

# Didn't Talk

Freeman: "He always had the feeling of what he wanted and portrayed it outwardly with not too much talking."

Granick: "There was no one else that I know who, without using words, was able to convey as immediately on the spot as Toscanini what was being demanded by the music."

Bachmann: "He said to a very famous conductor once, 'Tell me, why are you talking so much to the orchestra? The people who know what you are talking about intellectually know it as well as you do. The people who don't understand what you say—you could talk for two hours; they wouldn't know. There will always be a player who wouldn't know what you are talking about. But he will know what you are talking about if he looks at your stick and you show him you want legato, you want staccato, you want *spiccato*, you want this, you want so. He'll understand it; but you'll have to show it to him.'"

Vardi: "Conducting is using an instrument. The orchestra's an instrument. Your hands and your motions, your body, the way you look at the orchestra, the way you act to them, your vibes to the orchestra is the music, and they will respond to you. You don't have to say anything to them. And that's what a great conductor should have, that the minute he starts a piece of music, from the first beat, immediately you have the feeling of that whole piece of music. In other words, it unfolds, the whole music does, and you become part of it. You're like part of the picture. And most conductors don't do that. Most conductors are intellectual, and they beat, and 'there's gonna be four, and watch me here.' When I play the viola, I don't tell my viola what to do. Or, a pianist doesn't tell his piano what to do. You do it. And if you have the right technique, the response is there, and that's one of the greatest things that I think Toscanini had over almost everybody. It was all in his stick; everything was there. I wish the conductors of today would learn that."

## Phrasing

Moldavan: "You produced every note clean; the phrasing was up to him. And he did the phrasing of detail . . . with his stick. When he did this or did that with it we knew what it meant: he didn't have to say anything. He did it all with his stick. Other conductors use their tongue."[1]

Granick: "The others didn't have the technique—technique being talent. There was nobody either before or afterward who was enough of an actual conductor, so that all the complexities of music were resolved during the rehearsal, and that whose actual conducting coincided so perfectly as Toscanini's with what was demanded by the music, because Toscanini's idea really was what was demanded in the music itself. It wasn't what *he* demanded. He was just a voice urging us on, but the music made its own demands. I remember that a very famous choral conductor took a few years off to learn the technique of conducting an orchestra. He was very much loved by Toscanini, who said, 'He is making a big mistake. You cannot learn from anybody how to be a conductor. You can only study the music and conduct, but you cannot learn from anybody.'"

## Didn't Dance

Paolucci: "At concerts he really wasn't a flamboyant conductor."
Hupka: "No. He was very sparing in his gestures compared to conductors who go in for a lot of acrobatics."

S. Shulman: "It wasn't the cozy Fritz Reiner technique, but on the other hand it was not the Leonard Bernstein technique. Toscanini was a conductor, not a ballet dancer."

Freeman: "He was not a showoff; he was very much to the point. Sometimes his conducting was very much in front of him, with his hands either pleading or like a little prayer, depending on the mood of the music, or happy. It was all there in front of you, and he could get it out of you."

Brieff: "He planted his two feet a foot wide apart, and rarely moved them. The only movement you got was from his body. Occasionally he'd bend down to emphasize something, but once he set his two feet down, he rarely moved them. The Maestro very seldom moved. He was almost like a stick up there."

Civetta: "Was his conducting choreographic at all?"
A. Berv: "No, no. Toscanini never jumped around, never did anything of the kind. He just stood there and conducted, and we had our eyes glued on him constantly."

Winter: "There was his incredible purity of motive—no showing off of technique or anything; he seemed to be quite unconscious of his technical virtuosity."

H. Berv: "There was never a wasted movement. In fact, what went on, from the conductor's glance and the stick to the orchestra, this was something really worthwhile."

Guarrera: "A great many conductors conduct with animated antics. This is their way of having the face behind the head, in other words for the audience. And I remember Toscanini referred to a young Italian conductor, saying, '*Si, è molto bravo, ma dirige come una ballerina*' (Yes, he's very good, but he conducts like a dancer). In other words he was making too many motions. Superfluous motions are just that, and I think they hinder rather than help."

Carelli, in discussion with Guarrera: "Your experience and mine took us to certain moments when even very great conductors cued us in certain ways that we had to agree at the beginning of the performance, 'For goodness sake, don't look at the conductor because you'll get confused.'"

D. Walter: "Toscanini's conducting movements didn't give you all entrance cues, but only the ones that were musically important; which meant that at times you had to count measures attentively to know when to come in."

Krasnopolsky: "Toscanini said, 'It's easy to wave the stick, but that's not conducting. It's not music.' His technique was very simple. The musicians understood him without the least exaggeration. He had no exaggerated mannerisms, just standard movements. He didn't throw up his hands like some conductors. He didn't dance. He didn't wiggle. He didn't bend down or up. Very simple.

"It was easy to play with Toscanini. His beat was clean and simple. He never made a gesture to impress either the musicians or the audience. He had great confidence in his musicians and therefore was never busy throwing his hands in every direction as many of them do, until you stop looking at them and just listen to the music."

Bloom: "He used to say, '*Cantare*, sing, sing, sing.' He wasn't very articulate in describing these things. It was up to us to use our intelligence and our instincts to understand what he was trying to say. He did it with his stick, which was not this graceful, beautiful ballet dancing that we see from conductors today, but every movement of that stick meant something, and he had a wonderful face. Recently, I watched a telecast of the New York Philharmonic with Bernstein doing the Tchaikovsky Fourth. And to me it was one of the most obscene things I have ever seen in my life. You know, 'Ah! Ah!'—the suffering. You see, if someone had done that in Toscanini's day, we would have laughed him off the stage. I see conductors, and to me it's ludicrous what they are doing as conductors. They are not making music.

They are acting. They are dancing. They are not making the music because they don't have the same dedication and simple approach. Now, when Toscanini conducted, he had a beautiful face. The intense concentration on that man's face was something that could transport you to watch it. He wasn't making grimaces and he wasn't exhorting with these great movements of his arms. He beat rather simply, but every movement, suave, it all meant something. When he put his baton this way, you couldn't play flaccidly. There was intensity in the baton. His tremendous concentration—it was almost like he was suffering for the music to be born."

Sarser: "His baton technique was very easy to understand. When you're so close to something so great, many times you take it for granted. He expressed what he wanted. He expressed what was in the score. If it was quiet, his beat was quiet. If it was large, he would make a wider movement. But his approach was always to bring from us what was written on the page, not to make a show."

## Clarity

Brieff: "His technique was so clean and so clear."

Krasnopolsky: "His conducting was very simple, very easy to understand, and we never had any trouble. There was no question, never any doubt of what he wanted, whether it was his downbeat or upbeat; it was very clear."

S. Shulman: "If you made a mistake with Toscanini, it was never his beat. It was always your fault and you knew it. He didn't have to bawl you out because you were bawling yourself out before he ever got a chance to. His technique was so clear that if you really made a mistake, you were an idiot."

J. Bernstein: "It was very easy to play with him. The technique was fantastic; that's why the orchestra played like one man, because you could hardly miss. It was always so correct. Ah, beautiful, this was the best. I always say: He had a bow arm like Heifetz had for the fiddle. It was the best technique that existed. I never saw such a technique with anybody else."

Civetta: "Is it possible to describe his baton technique?"

Gordon: "It was the most flowing, the most definite, and the most caring baton technique of any conductor. All you had to do was look at him to know exactly how he wanted a passage played, and that went for the inner voices as well as the main melodic line. His left hand was completely independent from the right, and told you everything he wanted. You just took a look at his baton and you knew when to come in. When you study what he did in a phrase, you know how to read music correctly. He was my greatest teacher. You got more of an insight into the music than with other conductors."

Miller: "His beat was the most beautiful. It was small and clear—the way he would place the 2 and 3. It was unique with one exception: Guido Cantelli, who was of that wonderful Italian school: no wrist. Like a string player."

Brieff: "He led, and he made darn sure that he led it, and everybody knew. And you never got lost with this man! He knew his scores so well, and the clarity of his beat was unbelievable. There was no problem so far as him telling you what he needed. But also his eyes, although he could hardly see, he knew where everybody was stationed. He was never flamboyant in his gestures.

"As far as technique is concerned, this was one of the greatest masters of the baton. Never has a baton spoken as eloquently as the Maestro's. It was unbelievable the way it sang and the way it exhorted people, the way it threw thunderbolts; and the lightning flashes that came afterwards were very, very exciting. There was never a moment in all the years I played under him that I did not thrill and learn. Oh Lord, did I learn! And hence, as the Maestro said, 'Conductors are born. They're not made.'"

Poliakine: "Because of his operatic experience he had a very good beat, tremendous—and it's rare even among great conductors. You know, Bruno Walter didn't have the greatest technique. Mitropoulos, Furtwängler: They were bad, really bad as far as orchestral technique, baton technique."[2]

Hupka: "The Maestro had such a gift that to play under him was easier than to play under any other conductor. His beat was so magnificent that an orchestra playing a piece for the first time, even orchestras that had not played previously under the Maestro, would fall right in line with his beat. It was very hard to get out of step."[3]

A. Berv: "Stokowski's style of conducting was very, very free compared with Toscanini, whose style was very exacting. His beats were absolutely perfect, where you'd see the third beat and you knew where the third beat was, first beat, second beat, whatever it was, you would always see the beat. When Toscanini guest conducted the Philadelphia Orchestra many of the men felt they were going back to school, because we were so used to Stokowski's free way of conducting. In fact, if you didn't know the compositions very well you'd have plenty of trouble trying to follow Stokowski's style of conducting."

## "Never Stop the Beat!"

Hunter: "He gave me a lesson in conducting at a rehearsal break: He told me the beat should never stop. It should always flow. I was very young, and I had a lot to learn, and he did give me that wonderful advice."

Herbert Grossman, conductor, responding to a question about whether Toscanini discussed music during social occasions, recalled: "Oh, all the time! As a matter of fact, no meal was sacred, because . . . I was very young, and I remember we were eating, and nothing had been said for perhaps a half an hour, and then all of a sudden—I was sitting at his left—a left hand with a grip of steel came out, grabbed my right hand, spoon and all, picked it up and said without any preamble. 'Herbert, don't forget: Never stop the beat. Never stop the beat.' And [he was] making circular motions with my arm. Or, in the middle, even though I'd have a bite of steak three-quarters of the way to my mouth, his hand would come out and grab me, lead me from the table, into the room with the piano, and begin to play—again, without any introduction. He said, 'Don't stop the beat.' Don't have pauses in between, because the musicians can't feel the space in between. And I think this was typical of what actually happened with everything he conducted, there was never any feeling of 'stop.' There was always this feeling of inevitability, from the beginning to the end."[4]

## Subdivisions of the Beat

Miller: "Toscanini rarely subdivided. It was marvelous the way he conducted a slow four. It was the most beautiful beat."

Gordon: "He would sometimes do a subdivision in a very subtle way."

Weber: "His stick was so clear, his subdivisions were clear—if he wanted a tempo to slow up from four, he could go into eight without any deviation or trouble. His downbeats were very exact, absolutely clear. He was the only conductor who could start the 'Eroica' without any preparation. It was just clear."

## *Parsifal*

Bloom: "The prelude to act 1 of *Parsifal* starts out very slow. It's syncopated and usually conductors would beat in eight to keep the orchestra together but he refused to do that. He insisted on doing it in a slow four, and by his doing it in a slow four you could feel the energy in the beat. The whole orchestra just had to be together, and he had to do it that way because he got a feeling in four, which was quite different than any of the others that would do it in eight. Everybody was under this intensity of rhythm because we had to be together and I'll never forget the beginning of that prelude. It was unbelievable."

A. Shulman: "I remember sitting one year with Ernst Silberstein, who subsequently became the principal cellist of the Cleveland Orchestra. We did a dress rehearsal of an all Wagner program. We did the prelude to *Parsifal*. When we finished he said, 'Thank you, see you at the concert tonight.' And Silberstein and I sat there three or four minutes. Now that can seem like a long time when you're there in dead silence—stand partners who were so moved by the magnificence of the man's concept, that we just couldn't pack our instruments away, and head for home, and rest before the concert. It was an incredible experience."

## *Oberon* Overture

A. Berv: "The opening horn solo is only three little notes; but the notes were very difficult to perform correctly for the Maestro. He'd give me the wonderful downbeat, and it just seemed like he'd lift up his arm and come right down immediately without an attack, just like he'd give to a singer, so the sound would come out and it was just perfect. His beat was beautiful."

## Economy of Gesture

Civetta: "What about his mannerisms on the podium, his choreography, what types of gestures?"

Vardi: "Very natural. No, no, he never put on a show. His beat was very precise. It was very clear, and he never did any motion that did not have any meaning to it. He had one of the finest ways of expressing himself through his beat—always clear; his intentions were always clear. He had a very natural technique. He didn't have a virtuoso technique like Monteux and Reiner; they had these beautiful virtuosic beats. Toscanini's whole belief was that the stick was an extension of his arm, which is good. I think that's the way it should be. There was music in the beat. I never noticed any extracurricular motion. He was my greatest teacher; I learned more from him about many things in music than I did from anyone else. By playing with him I got paid for taking lessons."

## Pain

D. Walter: "I remember there were times when he had arthritic pains in his arm, but he'd ignore them and, if necessary put his baton in his left hand instead of his right. He just proceeded to do what he had to do; and physically he managed to take very good care of himself. He was really a very healthy young man despite his advanced years."

## Humility

Krasnopolsky: "He said, 'The stick doesn't play; it is you, you that play.' That is why the Maestro did not like conductors who lacked humility. It was very hard for me to play with any other conductor, no matter how great was his popularity, and I played with all the 'greats.'"

## Description

Weber: "I was always impressed with his baton technique. He would use the right hand with the baton for tempos and phrasing, and the left hand for balance. What he

did with his hands was strictly for the music and the musicians. It was communication. Every motion had a meaning. I look back to those days as some of the greatest moments of my life in music. And it's difficult, because as you get older, and if you keep playing, you're meeting all kinds of conductors, and you can't help but make comparisons and say, how clear was Toscanini's beat, and so exact his wrist motion."
Civetta: "Did he use his wrists a lot?"
Weber: "Oh, very slightly, very slightly, and he used his left hand, too. And he often had his pinky stretched out from the rest of the fingers of his right hand."

Vardi: "I always used to think, when he came down with his downbeat, God help anybody if they were under it; he'd break their head. Really, it was one of the strongest downbeats."

M. Bernstein remembered Toscanini's "making gestures with his fingers over his heart implying playing with feeling."[5]

Rostal: "With this hand, when he wanted a nice cantilena to be singing, he always said, 'Cantare, cantare', and he was vibrating like on a cello or a violin, to show expressiveness from your heart."

## On the Beat

Toscanini expected that the orchestra begin to play in sync with his baton when it arrived at the bottom of the downbeat, in the same way that sound is immediately produced when a string player's bow touches the string—without a delayed reaction.

Weber: "Koussevitzky had a strange beat—he would give a downbeat, and the orchestra would start just a fraction of a second later. And a lot of German conductors had that same technique. Koussevitzky had it refined so that everything seemed to come delayed, but in time. His beat was ahead. And how does that happen? How does the orchestra come in, exactly at the same moment, after the attack? The worst one was Szell. I prefer Toscanini, the direct beat, and coming in on the beat, not after the beat."

# Facial Expressions

Civetta: "What were his conducting technique and gestures like?"

Rostal: "Hardly any movement at all. With the smallest movement as possible. But when he wanted that orchestra to come out, then he moved more and more, and the orchestra responded. That was the proper way to do it. He conducted not only with his hands, but with his face and his body. Suggestive power was all there. It was fantastic. Or, when it was some of those nonchalant movements, he conducted very easily, and was holding his lapel. It was all things which very few conductors have. When the orchestra was very loud in certain scenes in Wagner, or *La mer* by Debussy, he had the peculiarity of opening his mouth wide. At first I couldn't understand why. Then I found out why: There is too much noise around, and you open your mouth to relieve your eardrums, so they are not affected by it. And therefore he could hear to the last moment very well. He was eighty-seven years old at his last concert."

Novotny: "As he was conducting, he would conduct with his eyes, his facial expression. His complexion sometimes would get red when he wanted a real *forte*."

Krasnopolsky: "The musicians learned to watch his face, his expressions. If he was calm, it was *piano*. If he was red in the face, it meant we gave the best, the highest, the strongest."

Freeman: "If it was sad it was an extremely serious look. If it was happy, there would be a little bit, on the corners of his mouth, a little smile."

# Eyes

Krasnopolsky: "Often he was carried away and started singing and closing his eyes."

Weber: "A lot of indications were given through his facial expressions, his eyes; he would look at you or look in your direction."

Winter: "He never took you by surprise. When you had an entrance, you would see his eyes dart over in your direction a couple bars before, and then when he gave you the cue, you were all set. In four years I was never caught off guard by him. Never."

Galimir: "He always looked at the players; and with all his nearsightedness, I think he saw everything that went on. And what a fantastic look."[6]

M. Bernstein: "As a bassist, I was at one extreme end of the stage, and I had a friend, a second violinist, who sat at the exact opposite side. I saw him after a concert and said to him, 'You know something funny? The Old Man never took his eyes off me all evening.' The violinist said, 'What are you talking about? He kept looking at *me* all evening!' It was an almost hypnotic effect that Toscanini had on the players."[7]

## Mysterious

Koutzen: "As for his conducting technique, the actual physical motions, nobody could imitate it. Usually it was not a regular four-beat. His beat was basically circular. And people in the audience would say, 'How can you follow that beat?' For some reason it was the easiest beat in the world to follow. He conducted in circles and phrases, and it was so clear to us that you couldn't mistake it. I almost never remember him doing a square beat. Everything was in phrases and in circles and in body motion. But whatever it was, you couldn't say, 'This is the way Toscanini does it.' Somebody could not analyze it or teach it to you. It would be absolutely impossible, and it will never be recaptured, just like the varnish on a Stradivarius—no chemist can find out what he had in that varnish. Nobody will ever be able to analyze the beat of Toscanini."

Civetta: "What about his influence on today's conductors?"
Weber: "Cantelli and De Sabata had that same distinct clearness; it was the same Italian school. That one protégé of his that had the same baton technique was Leon Barzin, and he passed it on to some of his young students, one of who is Hugo Fiorato, who picked up that technique of being very clear and distinct. And yet, what is most amazing is that Bruno Walter hardly had any baton technique, and Szell had none, and yet, they got great performances. Stokowski didn't use any baton at all, and got excellent precision. And so it's something that happens between the orchestra and the conductor. It's sort of a certain mysticism that is created. It's unfortunate that present generations of young musicians haven't had the opportunity to play with him or witness his conducting, and to experience this certain mysticism about Toscanini."

## Rehearsal vs. Performance

Unlike most conductors, Toscanini used smaller physical gestures during performances than he did during rehearsals.

Civetta: "Was there a difference between rehearsal and performance?"
Winter: "He was more restrained at performance."

J. Bernstein: "People who didn't hear or see Toscanini in the rehearsals never saw Toscanini. In the rehearsals he was 50 percent better than in concerts. In rehearsals he used to open his heart; he felt comfortable."

Civetta: "Was he a showman at rehearsals?"
Koutzen: "Yes, but not preconceived. It all came very naturally. He was just into the music. If he had to get on his knees to get what he wanted, he went on his knees. He just poured his whole body into what he was doing, and it was showmanship, but it was not premeditated."

Katims: "As for his behavior on the podium, he used every trick in the book—and some tricks not in the book—to get what he wanted from the orchestra. He exhorted, he demanded, he browbeat, he was bitingly sarcastic, he cajoled, he pleaded, he begged. On that famous occasion when he wanted a passage played as *pianissimo* as if it were coming 'from Brooklyn,' he was on his knees before the orchestra. He used visual illustrations, as when he took out a large white silk scarf and threw it into the air. As it floated gently to the stage, he said, '*Comme ça*,' to show the ethereal quality he sought in Debussy."[8]

Freeman: "In concerts it was more relaxed and it wasn't as showy. Of course his rehearsal conducting was not showmanship. At concerts there wasn't all the hard work doing it. You knew what be wanted; it was a question only of nuances, tempos or expression, and that usually was done very nicely and not overdone. In rehearsals he would overdo it a little to get to you, but in the concerts he was not a dramatic conductor, not a showman, and he was not an exhibitionist. That's why sometimes as members of the orchestra, when we'd get a conductor that was very overdramatic, trying to be a showpiece and all of that, it used to make us laugh, because we knew it wasn't necessary. It was stage play for the audience. For us, stage play wasn't in our bag."

Bloom: "A rehearsal is when a conductor does his work, and that's when you can really see how great the man was. At the concert, a lot of times Toscanini would just be leading and together we would do what we rehearsed. He didn't think of the concert as being an exercise in public relations. He did his work. The concert was a result of it. Almost any symphony musician will tell you that rehearsals are done, very straightforward and then suddenly at the concert the conductor takes on a personality. He starts soaring and making beautiful faces and that's for the public. That's not for anybody else, so that the work of any good conductor is done at the rehearsal. By the time you get to a concert an orchestra should able to go along without a conductor dancing, you know.

"What happens at the concert is nothing. What he does during a rehearsal—that's when you judge a conductor, not at a concert—the way he would rehearse and want certain things. When Toscanini conducted that way and looked that way, you had to play well for him, or you were a very unhappy man—not because you were worried about your job so much as that you didn't want to displease him, because you knew that his ideals were so high."

Haggin wrote about a 1947 rehearsal of Beethoven's Seventh Symphony: "I recall the performance of the finale at a rehearsal. His movements at rehearsal were more uninhibitedly vigorous than they were in the presence of an audience at a concert; and the climax of the last crescendo had him stamping his feet—with results that caused one member of the orchestra to exclaim, 'I've got to get back into my skin.'"[9]

## Dress Rehearsals

A. Shulman: "The dress rehearsals were absolutely extraordinary: In that atmosphere of quiet and intense concentration we were hypnotized, and the 95 men functioned as one."

Bachmann: "The truly great Toscanini performances were hardly ever in front of an audience. The best performance was almost invariably the dress rehearsal. Because once he had on what he called the 'monkey dress,' the 'monkey suit,' or the 'clown's costume,'* it wasn't the same as when he came in and was among his people. This last rehearsal was the most important thing for us and for him because it assured him of a fine performance."

---

* Formal performance attire.

Heiles: "The best performances, [Mischakoff] insisted, were at the dress rehearsals, when the orchestra had already done its arduous work and the Maestro felt free to take risks. Those performances, my father told me, would put chills up your spine. The actual broadcasts were more controlled and careful."[10]

## Chemistry

Brieff: "That man could draw out a phrase with such intensity, with such warmth. I've never seen or heard a more eloquent baton in all my life. And what he had to say with that marvelous, extraordinarily eloquent baton is unbelievable. The control—that baton, it was a Stradivarius! It sang. It sang all the time. Even under wonderful conductors who have great techniques and know everything, there's a chemistry that is needed and Maestro had that chemistry. It was wonderful."

## Complete Command and Control

Novotny: "One of the greatest assets that the Maestro had was the ability to assume complete command of his instrument. It was a matter of complete control. And it was felt all through the orchestra. It was not a group of individuals. Usually no one played anything for the Maestro the way they thought they should play it; they played the way he wanted them to play it, and all he demanded was proper dynamics, proper phrasing, just what was written on the blueprint in front of you. It was a well-coordinated effort because one man was coordinating it. And those commands were given in a very clear and precise manner. He was very, very easy to play for as far as his conducting was concerned."

## Unorthodox Baton Technique

Novotny: "His conducting beats were not completely orthodox. They weren't conducted the way they were supposed to be conducted in the manual. But at no point did we not know where he was."

D. Walter: "Toscanini's conducting movements didn't beat time in accordance with the traditional skeletal configurations of time-beating in conducting manuals; they delineated the musical flow, and in doing this broke the prison of those configurations . . . They were the most expressive movements and gestures of any conductor."[11]

M. Bernstein: "Some of his gestures were most original. I recall very vividly in the Scherzo of Beethoven's Ninth Symphony: Toscanini beat circles. Toscanini conducting circles was really inflammatory to me as a bass player."[12]

Granick: "In much of the music that had a climax, his gesture when the climax extended over a long period of bars, was often circular. At most other times, it was a clear, concise beat, extended somewhat from his body, not too close."

> Toscanini used a circular, whipping motion during passages of rhythmically driving music to spur the orchestra on.

Carelli: "At the performance you didn't see if Toscanini's beat was in four, in three or in two. It was one big continuous movement of shaping the music—music making, and not beating time."

Shaw: "There was [another] time when he changed the tone of a choir of mine. I think it was in *Mefistofele*: He made one of his gestures—remember, where he would go like this? [*Shaw leans forward, points his arm down, and propels it powerfully from side to side*]—and in immediate response to his gesture, the tone of the choir got richer and deeper and broader—a staggering thing which never happened with another conductor. In general, vocal sound, when it's in blocks of sixty people, remains what it is: You can't get a college glee club to change this tone just by gesture; you can do it by exercises or by telling them what you want. But with Toscanini the tone changed in immediate response to his gesture."[13]

D. Walter: "Those large sweeping movements of the right arm . . . were one of the means of getting you involved as intensely as he was: They swept you on."[14]

# Position of Arms

Carelli: "If you see a movie of his conducting, it is very interesting to realize that his arms do not go very high. It's a rather low conducting style. They don't go high up in the air like some modern conductors who do some aerial acrobatics and like to show off. Maestro was a very low-arm conductor. We once saw a photograph, where the hands are so low. And his comment was, 'I never had my arms so low. I did not realize it.' He did not realize that his arms and his beat were lower than opera conductors who are used to conducting up toward a stage, where you have to be a little higher with your arms. Otherwise the people on the stage will not see them. So it never went higher than the shoulder. And he didn't realize it. That was surprising for me, that he saw these pictures and was very unhappy about this. 'I don't keep my arms so low.' Very interesting."

# Different Gestures for Different Sections of the Orchestra

Winter: "His technique was absolutely crystal clear. The stick was quite simple, but he would conduct differently for different sections of the orchestra—entrances for woodwinds would be given differently than entrances for strings. There would be a little curl at the bottom of the beat to give an entrance to a woodwind, to give them a chance to get their breath into the instrument."

# Placement of Gestures

J. Bernstein: "He had for every beat a different position of the body. A scherzo by Haydn or Mozart, the hand higher. In a scherzo by Brahms, the hand went always lower and lower, because the music is getting heavier. The musicians see, without knowing; they see it's lower, it's getting heavier."

> Seeing Toscanini's arms and hands in a low position caused the musicians to play in a heavier manner, mirroring the character of the music. J. Bernstein's statement "without knowing" indicates that the musicians' reactions to Toscanini's gestures were, in this case, subconscious.

Brieff: "I remember one day we were doing the Brahms Second Symphony, and this began with the cellos and basses. He held his baton to the right of him and began, beating down low. 'No.' Then he raised his baton to a higher level, and did the phrase again. Then he turned away from the cellos, until he found a certain space. And I asked him later, 'Maestro, why did you do that?' 'I don't know. It sounded right over here.' Now this is a very curious thing, I mean, to find an area in space where the gesture gave what he thought sounded right."

## No Lessons

A. Berv: "Nothing was ever calculated with him. It was just natural. And everything seemed to fall in the right place."

Posner: "He said he never took a conducting lesson in his life. He said when you feel the music it will come out regardless of the technique. And he had the clearest, most simplest beat in the world to follow, really, and that was all self-taught."

## Mood and Result

Heiles: "Toscanini had insisted that the players think subdivisions of the beat. Mischakoff taught his students these subdivisions and insisted upon them, especially for dotted figures; trying to feel one's way through a beat provoked a 'Subdivide!'"[15]

The musicians explained that in very slow music such as the prelude to *Parsifal* or the beginning of *Death and Transfiguration*, Toscanini would conduct only the very slow broader units of the beat and insist that the musicians think the small subdivisions in their minds because he wanted his gestures to perfectly mirror the mood and atmosphere of the music. Other conductors, even the best ones, thought nothing of breaking the mood by flicking their wrists and sticks in small subdivisions of the beat to ensure precision. Toscanini's ideal way of conducting these very slow passages was often unsuccessful, though, and in rehearsal he criticized the players for being unable to count the subdivisions in their heads and play together without extra help from him. In performance he would start to subdivide in a subtle manner when the orchestra began to lose its precision. However, on those occasions when the orchestra succeeded, Antek wrote that the resulting "elasticity, spaciousness and nobility were tremendously evocative and moving."[16]

Describing the opening of *Death and Transfiguration*, Antek wrote: "All around was the stillness of a tomb . . . We were 'artists,' each adding his daub of paint to a portrait of death . . . How difficult it was to achieve, but what artistic satisfaction, what personal pride in so subtle and expressive an accomplishment!"[17]

# Tone Color

Galimir: "Looking back, there are so many great moments. It's a long time ago; but how many great moments there were, particularly in rehearsals with this man, that I cannot get out of my memory. In French music, for instance: There was a rehearsal of *La valse* by Ravel—and what went on with his hands to get the flavor was incredible. I can't describe it. There was once *Ibéria*—the second movement, 'The Perfumes of the Night': I swear I smelled the perfumes; and I was not the only one."[18]

Antek described rehearsing the ending of the Funeral March of the "Eroica," where Toscanini gave special attention to the first violin part. "'Weeping . . . weeping!' he would cry out in a high, choked wail . . . In a hoarse, tear drenched, bleating voice, he would sing it . . . 'Find the tone—the sound—you have the right one in your instrument. Find it—down on the fingerboard—f-a-a-r away . . . f-a-a-r away . . . in the sky . . . suffering! . . . s-u-u-ffering! . . .'

"We would nod to one another, beaming with satisfaction and almost disbelief at the transformation."[19]

# CHAPTER 9

# Philosophy

*The orchestra should be moved to play with great sonority and excitement because of something that comes from the inner self. He had that.*
—Frank Brieff

Toscanini stated to Valdengo: "Our art opens the road to great, noble sentiments, opens wide the door to the most ambitious aspirations. And even if in the course of a career one meets at times with unpleasant circumstances that can be most serious, there are, however, moments in which one is repaid by a joy that has no limits!

"The artist, who for reasons of temperament or vocation has chosen our art, must always have a religious worship for it, and if one doesn't feel this worship in his innermost soul, it would be better, much better to change his profession. When art is at stake one must never settle for anything less, for any compromise. Remember that it has even an educational function besides existing for recreational purposes, and therefore imposes a great deal of responsibility on every artist. This is the path I have chosen from the beginning, and it has served me well. I have always demanded the same thing, sometimes with severity even, from my orchestral players and singers. All of us have thus found a success together that has filled our spirits with the purest joy."

Civetta: "What was Toscanini's greatest quality?"

Krasnopolsky: "His love of music, first of all. Also his love for the musicians, and love of what he does. Music was his life and love, and he inspired the musicians with his enthusiasm, his love for the music and respect for the composer, and instilled these things in the musicians. He brought them almost to perfection.

"By nature he was a humanitarian. He loved freedom, he loved people, and his greatest passion was music and this passion made us also love . . . I think that when we came to him we became better musicians, better people, and more humble people."

## Composers

Krasnopolsky: "Toscanini was great because . . . he had great respect for the desires and wishes of the composer. To him it was a law."

Valdengo: "To an orchestral player who asked him if at a certain point of a Brahms composition he wanted a crescendo, he responded abruptly, 'It's Brahms who wants this crescendo, not Toscanini!'"

Civetta: "What struck you the most about him?"
A. Shulman: "The music came first. People didn't matter. Toscanini didn't matter. Maybe it did. I mean after all, if you're going to be a conductor of an orchestra, you have to have a strong ego to superimpose your will on a hundred egomaniacs. I have to quote Gregor Piatigorsky in his memoirs, *Cellist*. He talks about the incredible arrogance of some of these conductors who walk around in terribly possessive ways and say, 'Have you heard my Brahms? Have you heard my Beethoven?' as if it's their exclusive property. Well that's a lot of bull. I mean with the Old Man, he prostrated himself at the base of the pedestal of the composer. He worshipped the composer, and he had to be honest. It was not a matter of Toscanini superimposing his will on Beethoven; it was a matter of Toscanini exceeding to Beethoven's wishes."

Winter: "At the end of a performance, if Toscanini was pleased, there would be sort of a benign smile on his face. I watched Solti; at the end of a performance he looked so pleased with himself. That was the difference: Toscanini had the feeling that what he owed Wagner had come through. He had a debt to the composer to make it sound a certain way, and he was pleased that he was able to realize it. He did not pat himself on the back that it turned out so well."

Valdengo: "The irresistible, interminable applause that burst out after every performance left him feeling ill at ease. After every performance, in those moments
when the audience exalted in the performance, he had the sensation that the praise
which only the composer deserved was being squashed."
Toscanini: "The praise should go to whoever created the piece, not to the performers. The only praise I deserve is to intuit what the composer felt at the height of his
inspiration. Nothing more."

# Humility

Winter: "His humility was unique particularly in a conductor who was universally
recognized as the greatest of his time."

Civetta: "What did he think of himself?"
Krasnopolsky: "He didn't think very much of himself. He didn't have the time to
think about himself. He was absorbed by what was going on."

Ugo Ojetti, journalist, quoted Toscanini: "The most important quality in a conductor? Humility, humility . . . If something doesn't go well, it's because I haven't
understood the composer. It's all my fault. Whoever thinks that Mozart, Beethoven,
Wagner, Verdi are mistaken and have to be corrected is an idiot. One must study
more, begin studying again, understand better. They haven't written music in order
to make me look good. It is I who must make them look good by revealing them
as they are, by trying to bring myself and the orchestra closer to them, as much
as I can, so that nothing escapes. The conductor must not create, he must achieve.
Humility, faithfulness, clarity, unity."[1]

Bloom, discussing the 1940 Missa Solemnis preparations: "There were certain
works that he approached with such great reverence. The reverence was born of
awe that these works were so great and so difficult to communicate. It's not an
easy piece. It is not the most grateful piece for the voices, and there were strange
things, even in the orchestra parts, and he had to make this thing come off. When
Toscanini would get a thing like that, he would start building up the tension. We
could tell two or three weeks ahead of time, before we even started working on
it, that he was starting to worry about things. But his worry was always, 'Will I

be able to do it right?' It was his self-examination that he did all the time. He was just a great man."

Heiles: "My father used to speak of Toscanini's humility when approaching Beethoven's music, and how the NBC would start rehearsing a score like the Beethoven Ninth Symphony weeks and even months before its performance."[2]

Shaw recalled Toscanini's comment about conducting Beethoven's Ninth: "He said modestly, 'You know, I have never been able to do this piece well. I am always bad with this piece. It's too big a piece. I don't do it as well as I should.'"

At the first rehearsal for his last performance of the Ninth Symphony in 1952, Toscanini told the orchestra that he had never really done it as well as he had hoped. "Maybe this time," he said. "Today is fifty years that I have conducted the Ninth Symphony. Fifty. I never conduct well."[3]

Hupka: "Macklin Marrow, music director of RCA Victor, told me that after Toscanini did a beautiful performance of the Brahms Second Symphony he said to him, 'Maestro, this is almost greater than the performance you did twenty years ago with the New York Philharmonic.' And Maestro said to him, 'Well in twenty years, don't you think I should have learned something?'"

> Leonard Bernstein visited Toscanini to ask about one of the tempos in Berlioz's *Roméo et Juliette*. Bernstein told Toscanini that when he listened to the maestro's recording, the tempo seemed wrong. During the visit, Toscanini couldn't locate the recording. Upon returning home, Bernstein discovered that it was a recording by Charles Munch, not Toscanini's, that contained the faulty tempo, whereupon Bernstein sent Toscanini a letter of apology. Toscanini wrote to Bernstein explaining that he had found the recording, listened again to it, and that while it didn't seem like a betrayal of Berlioz's tempo marking, it could have been better. Toscanini called himself "stupid" and thanked Bernstein for bringing it to his attention![4]

To Ira Hirschmann, Toscanini's modesty and humility toward music and musicians reminded him of the pianist Arthur Schnabel, who said: "I hope to improve every day," which was Toscanini's philosophy. Hirschmann believed that only a few giants of great accomplishments have had this deep humility, and he included Toscanini among them.[5]

## Ideals

Antek: "We always sensed his frustration in reaching for something—a beauty, an understanding—just beyond his grasp. We sensed his despair and his uncertainty, and we loved him for it."[6]

Bachmann: "He had in his mind something. He never was satisfied with it. Why? Because you cannot re-create an ideal. You can come near it but you can not absolutely re-create it."

## *La mer*

Winter: "There were two pieces he kept recording over and over again that he was never happy with. One was the 'Queen Mab' of Berlioz. The other was Debussy's *La mer*."

Posner: "I recall certain favorite pieces of his, like *La mer* and the 'Queen Mab.' And every time he conducted them he would say, 'Please play it for me once before I die. Play it the way I want to hear it.' And it was played so magnificently each time, I didn't think he could repeat the previous performance."
Civetta: "And yet he was never satisfied."
Posner: "Never satisfied. His state of perfection was so tremendous that it was just unbelievable."

Weber: "Musically he was very intellectual; for instance, admitting that he could not get out of the orchestra and reproduce with actual sound what he had in his mind's ear, that he had thoughts about *La mer*, and never actually could get it."
Civetta: "He had an ideal."
Weber: "That's right, and that's what I mean by 'intellectual.' He had ideals, and in his mind he saw *La mer* as a tone poem. He saw the waves. He saw the wind, and so forth, and he tried to reproduce it. But not only that: He was always a student,

always studying scores. You must realize that the Beethoven symphonies were recorded several times. He was looking for something. I remember one time in *La mer* I heard the Old Man saying, 'I have never been able to do it the way I want it. I have never gotten *La mer* the way I want it to sound. Just once, just once I would like to do it the way I hear it in my mind.'"

Civetta: "He did *La mer* so often."

Weber: "That's right. But he always complained. He said he couldn't capture it, couldn't capture the mood."

Luigi Gaddoni, Toscanini's chauffeur, recounted to Robert Hupka that one day he drove Toscanini to a recording session of *La mer* at two o'clock in the afternoon. During the session, Toscanini listened to a playback and something happened that did not please him, and he kept on trying over and over again until five o'clock. He was disgusted about it because he couldn't get exactly what he wanted and quit without completing the recording that day. On the way back, Gaddoni asked him, "What was the particular point that didn't satisfy you? Is there one person out of a thousand who would be able to detect a technical point that you were so severe about?" He said, "Luigi, I'm surprised at you. Do you think I could possibly let something go that is not absolutely as it should be? It is just for that one person that I would rerecord it." Gaddoni was amazed to witness Toscanini's most severe, honest feeling stemming from his intolerance of imperfection. Gaddoni felt that the hard work Toscanini had gone through to obtain this particular result is generally not known.[7]

## Sincerity

Civetta: "How did Toscanini manage to get such excitement in the response of the orchestra?"

Nathan Gordon: "Because he was honest—simple as that."

Ania Dorfmann, pianist, spoke about audiences' perception of Toscanini's utter sincerity: "He was different from other musicians, in that it was never just another concert for the Maestro. Each one was a new experience. He was like a high priest getting ready with a great sermon, a great message. And when he was walking out, the audience always felt it. He was serving the music he interpreted, and he was so humble before it. And I really think that audiences throughout the world are the same, in that they feel the sincerity of it."

Granick: "In his conducting he was the personification of all the moods. When there was fury, there was fury in his conducting, and every expressive quality in the music was present as a demand which was being made on us. At first one felt that it was the Maestro who was making the demands, but it was really the music that made the demands. The Maestro was merely the personification of it."

Paolucci, in conversation with Hupka: "One of the most fascinating things was that as rigorous a task master as Toscanini was, the musicians felt freer under him than they did under other conductors. He used the individual talent more it seemed."

Hupka: "It was the sincerity of Toscanini, the complete dedication to the music, the selflessness that really conveyed the music. It was music; it was not the conductor. Very often when you listen to a conductor, you are sidetracked by the conductor's ego, who is trying to show off. Toscanini just simply presented music in its purest essence. He was a man of incredible honesty."

Paolucci: "What struck me about him was his humility both on the podium and when he would come out the stage door. You speak of sincerity as being the key to his greatness. What were the other facets that made him so great?"

Hupka: "There was one gift that Maestro had which I never found in any other conductor: The music was simply a means to convey a reality that was on the mind of the composer. The music conveyed something; it was not simply a nice melody that you listen to. He conveyed the reality behind the music. He portrayed life, death, this life, the next life, anything that was in the music. It was simply by re-creating the music, because music is a language without words. It's the most powerful language, and the power of music cannot be fully appreciated unless you hear music in its truest, purest form.

"For example, *The Sorcerer's Apprentice*: the plight of the apprentice who has made the broom fetch water, and the building is being flooded. You have a flood, and water is going higher and higher—the panic. It's real. It's in the music. It's not just notes. It's a catastrophe, a flood.

"I will never forget the rehearsals of Verdi's *Otello*, and I will never forget the death scene of Desdemona, where Otello comes to strangle his wife. I stood right in the orchestra and I thought I'd die myself because expressed in music was the struggle of a human soul at the point of death. It was the struggle to survive, to live, not to be killed. It was such extraordinary realism that no actor, no theatre, no spoken word could ever convey. It's an experience. Everything the man did was the conveying of something: whatever was in the music. The music spoke.

"There are many conductors who have very little to convey, or conduct what they feel and not always pay attention to what the composer had in mind. They betray the composer. The Maestro had a selfless dedication to the composer. He was completely in the service of the composer and would identify himself with the composer. He would re-create from the written symbols in the score into actuality what really was on the mind of the composer which is a very, very difficult thing to do, but he had the genius to recognize it."[8]

# Channel

Brieff: "The most important thing to him was if he could speak the mind of the composer through his music-making, without allowing his own temperament and his own personality to enter into it.

"A conductor should be exactly what the word means, almost like an electrical conductor, through your wire, through your hands, through your body, to relate to the orchestra. The orchestra should be moved to play with great sonority and excitement because of something that comes from the inner self. He had that."

William Paisley, NBC Symphony librarian: "He believed the composer had a definite thing to say and that he indicated what he wanted said. He presented what the composer wanted to say exactly as he wanted to say it. Since the composers were filled with inspiration themselves, the Maestro succeeded in being a channel for that inspiration, got it over to the orchestra and through them to the audience. He forgot himself when he was in the midst of his conducting. He considered himself a channel through which this music poured out. I frankly believe he forgot himself completely."[9]

Bachmann: "These so-called great conductors know every note in the score. What they miss is the beauty between the notes. That's what Maestro realized immediately in a composition, and what he placed his greatest effort on: in between the notes. What did the composer intend within what he wrote down? For instance we discussed for over one hour and a half the *Enigma Variations* of Elgar. And

Maestro said, 'You know Bachmann there is one thing that bothers me about the *Enigma Variations*: One variation is a sentimental piece, but it's much sadder than he wrote in the score, and I would like to know whether I am correct if I think that this is really a heartbreaker. And so I asked Mr. Elgar; and on that occasion Mr. Elgar gave me a list of whom he meant with each variation.' The importance of what I'm telling you is not what Elgar wrote, not that Elgar gave him the list, but the fact that Maestro noticed it and realized it."

## Tchaikovsky's "Pathétique" Symphony

Bloom discussed Toscanini's 1938 performance of Tchaikovsky's "Pathétique" Symphony (the first time the conductor had performed the work in forty years): "He said, 'I don't think I can do it well. I don't think I am sympathetic to this music.' He didn't say he didn't like it. He had probably heard some performances of the 'Pathétique,' you know, sort of wiping the floor and tearing clothes, and he couldn't do that. He wasn't that kind of a musician. He started studying the score and really working on it and he realized that there was great music here if it were to be done the way it was written and not the way we had all been hearing it for years, you know, with people crying. Tchaikovsky was really not that kind of person; Tchaikovsky was a meticulous man. He was not a gypsy. He got to the heart of the music and let the music speak for itself. We did a performance of the 'Pathétique' that was really one of the greatest experiences, because it was like somebody coming in and clearing all the garbage out and suddenly hearing this thing, because Tchaikovsky was a very skillful man and most of his music was just layers and layers of stuff that people had put on top of it, with their own ideas and all the schmaltz and stuff, and suddenly there it was, just the way it was written—it was beautiful."

Valdengo: "At a first rehearsal he expressed it this way to the performers: 'You have performed the music the way it's written . . . It's easy to play this way . . . Now we must give it the spirit, the heat, and the color that the creator of it wanted!

"'If the music is simply performed as it is written, it doesn't come across as it should. Don't ever ignore the delicate passages in the music; in fact, give them value. A strong passage is by definition accentuated, so there's no need to reinforce it, but the delicate passages, on the other hand, need to be given attention.'"

## Music and Painting

Valdengo wrote: "The Maestro often compared music to painting, with which he was in love. 'Music and painting are sisters, and, I would say, twin sisters. However, music also has a close kinship with the other arts that beautify human life. When you admire a beautiful painting, for the blending of the shades of color, for the colors' softness, for the reflection of light in contrast with the shadows, you feel inside yourself the emotional warmth of the artist while intent at the creation of the work. On the contrary, a monochrome painting, even if it's perfect, doesn't succeed in giving you a true emotion. It's the same in music, my dear rascal. We don't have colors, but we have the *pianissimo*, the *forte*, the *crescendo*, the *ritenuto*, etc. . . . We have, that is, a palette no less rich than that of painting. Everything depends on knowing how to manage and control it! Our instruments take the place of the brush . . . My baton is an allegorical brush that rolls in the air and expresses the colors that the performers translate into sound!'"

# CHAPTER 10

# Rehearsal Style

*When I was worn out at the end of a Toscanini rehearsal I didn't mind, because it had been an endlessly fascinating, exciting and instructive experience.*
—**David Walter**

Mischakoff: "He rehearses like one possessed. He never sits down, but he is always inspiring."[1]

Lehmann: "The fanatical frenzy of this extraordinary personality compelled all who worked under him to give their utmost. He wouldn't stand for any slackness or 'routine work.' Every rehearsal was like the actual performance to him, and every performance was a 'festival performance.'"[2]

Marcia Davenport, writer and friend of Toscanini, recalled a rehearsal of *Die Meistersinger*, featuring Lotte Lehmann as Eva, at the 1936 Salzburg Festival: "We who heard that rehearsal and saw it . . . were overwhelmed with emotion. But when the curtain fell on the finale, and then went up again as curtains do at rehearsals for technical reasons, there stood the entire company on stage, every one of them in tears. The Maestro himself stood motionless in his place with his right hand covering his eyes."[3]

H. Berv: "Every rehearsal was looked forward to. At his rehearsals, all your troubles vanished; you couldn't think of anything else. I must say that the incentive you had was brand new all the time, like new blood being injected into you."

Civetta: "What was it about these performances that made them so special?"
Koutzen: "Electricity. Referring back to the rehearsals, the reason they weren't ever boring was because the word rehearsal didn't exist. It was always a performance. It had to be ready."

Barzin: "Rehearsals stuck out most because we were electrified. You never saw the New York Philharmonic sitting back in their seats, this type of lying back and saying, 'Well, it's a rehearsal.' We were right on the edge of the chair."

## "Sing!"

Civetta: "What were the central qualities that Maestro brought to the orchestra?"
Bachmann: "First, it was his absolutely limitless reverence for music, his absolute respect for the wishes of the composer. Then, it was his desire to hear, at every moment singing. Singing. That was his most used word in all the twenty-three years, '*Canta, canta, canta.* Sing, sing.'

"He submerged himself into the music. He begged of you, he cajoled you, he threatened you, he menaced you in every way, shape or form humanly possible to give more and more singing. In other words, he made it human. To him the human voice was the most singing, and you were to transport it onto the instrument.

"When the first orchestra rehearsal of operas took place, after all the singers were well prepared by him, he asked all the principals to take a seat in the front row with their vocal scores. And Maestro went through the entire opera, singing every part of the text, and with such dramatic connotation, that it was moving."

Carelli, in conversation with Guarrera: "At rehearsals he always sang the whole opera himself, sometimes even in the recordings of his performances of *Bohème*, of *Traviata*, you can hear it. He sang, and he knew exactly where you had to breathe, and he was breathing with you, which is the mark of a good conductor, and nobody did it better than Maestro Toscanini."
Guarrera: "Even a symphonic conductor should think in terms of breathing and singing, because instruments sing also. And the greatest conductors do, including Toscanini. He was equally as great as a symphonic conductor as he was as an opera conductor because he treated symphonic music that way."

Carelli: "Yes, and you can hear this on the tapes of rehearsals. One of his favorite expressions was when he turned to the violins, he didn't say louder or softer; he said, '*Cantate! Cantate!*'"

Guarrera: "Which means 'Sing! Sing!'"

Carelli: "Never strict and rigid music-making. Maybe for some people's taste it was a bit fast, or faster than they are used to now, but it was never rigid."

Bachmann: "The one person who forgot himself and said the wisest thing was Jan Peerce. When Maestro sang for him a passage in *La bohème* dramatically, with that shrieking voice of Maestro which was terrible, Jan Peerce said to me, 'You know, Eddy, if I could sing like that I would be the greatest singer in the world.' That was the dramatic greatness of Maestro."

Paolucci: "How was Toscanini able to convey this musical understanding of his to the men in his orchestra?"

Hupka: "It was simplicity: He sang. Instead of like other conductors who would go into great long descriptions about playing soft and loud and this and that, Toscanini simply sang it. I remember in Vienna people were amused. They used to laugh and say, 'Well, he always sings!' And it is the most natural thing, because you have to have music in your soul before you give it to others. When he sang at rehearsals his voice was old and croaky and people laughed. To me it was the most beautiful, expressive voice in the world. No singer with the most gorgeous voice could sing as Toscanini did. He was music personified.

"I remember a wonderful incident at a Missa Solemnis rehearsal in London in 1939. In the Benedictus, there is a beautiful violin solo and then a magnificent sequence of chords by the brass. Maestro stopped them and said to the brass section, 'Do you hear the violin? He sings. You play.' I shall never forget the transformation that took place when they repeated that passage because I never heard a brass choir play with such extraordinary angelic, ethereal beauty. It was just singing. It was one of the outstanding, remarkable characteristics of Toscanini's orchestra: It sang. There was a sonority. It was not just playing."[4]

Toscanini said, during a rehearsal of Beethoven's Ninth Symphony: "This movement is difficult because we never sing; we always play, and we play badly."[5]

Bloom: "There was this way of preserving a line in music. There was no moment when certain notes became unimportant. You started a phrase or a group of notes or a sentence or a line and when you start, every note has its place and there was never any relaxation. Now, when I say that I mean musical relaxation. There was always this wonderful thing, which I like to feel as intensity between notes. You never played two notes; you played an interval. You didn't play one note and then another one. What was in between was the important thing so that you never got to the second note too soon or too late and there was a feeling of traveling from one note to another. He used to say, '*Canta, canta!* Sing, sing, sing.' He wasn't very articulate in describing these things.

"If I'm coaching somebody and a musical line is not coming through, I can explain how to make that musical line. And Toscanini did it by singing with his croaky, ugly voice, which he had in practically a monotone. But he would, just by doing this, give an impression of line with intensity. He wanted this long line that had intensity, which was not an easy thing to do."

Heiles: "Toscanini could throw a tantrum if two grace notes were not articulated enough, exhorting players to take care of the small notes and not 'eat' them; to 'sing,' not to 'play'; and to sustain each note for its fullest value in melodic phrases: '*sostenere*,' '*tenere*,' '*cantare*,' the musicians heard repeatedly.

"My father's innate expression was that singing style, and he frequently enjoined his students to 'Sing!' He often said, 'Don't swallow the little notes' or 'Sing the little notes'; he trained his students to save enough bow, to draw the bow slowly enough, to sing over the full length of the bow."[6]

At a rehearsal of the prelude to Wagner's *Parsifal*, Toscanini insisted that the bow changes be carefully accomplished so as to be inaudible.[7] Violinist Joseph Silverstein explained how this insistence of a sustained line forced the NBC concertmaster, Mischa Mischakoff, to insist on great care in bowing: "Mainly bow distribution was the big thing with Mischakoff. The idea was not to move the bow slower in the upper half of the bow, but to accelerate into the bow change generally. The bow change did not come as a diminuendo; it was not a new sound. Sustaining the sound and keeping the long line was the main concern in his approach to bowing.

"Mischakoff was very much influenced by Toscanini's extremely vocal concept of music: *Cantare! Cantare!* Always sing, sing! He wanted long phrases. He didn't much like choppy stuff, short notes. Studio 8H, of course, was the driest room in the world. To get a singing sound in that hall you really had to sustain the tone."[8]

## Beauty of Sound

Civetta: "Did you have a certain impression of Maestro before you began to work with him?"
Bachmann: "Three things: Perfection was one; balance was another. The other was absolutely incredibly beautiful sound. If you can get the beauty out of a composition and out of an orchestra like he did, then you can do anything, anything."

Bloom: "I can explain what he did, but he didn't want to take the trouble—he wasn't patient enough and he certainly wasn't articulate enough in English. He could be very articulate in Italian when he wanted to swear at somebody. There was a place were he wanted to say *flowing* but couldn't think of the English word and he said *fliessen*, using the German word, and then later when we told him *flowing*, he said, 'Yes, but it's not the same word.' To him, the sound of the German word meant more than it meant in English. He could find words every once in a while. They could be in German, Italian, English, or French."

## Vibrato

Haggin described a 1954 rehearsal of the Prelude to Act I of *Lohengrin*: "[Toscanini] stopped to tell the violins to play the opening A major chords without vibrato, which he said was suitable for *Inferno*, but not for *Paradiso*."[9]

## Oboe Sound

Toscanini discussed oboe playing with Valdengo, who had been an oboist before becoming a singer: "Today, unfortunately, your colleagues on the oboe no longer have the tone of some time ago and then they exaggerate so much with that vibrato that the tone becomes unraveled and as thin as tissue paper.

"The English started and everyone immediately went in their direction. Even in Italy I noticed that many follow this bad custom. In the bassoon, a little, I don't mind, but in the oboe definitely not, or, if we want, only a little is enough.

"Now, you need three oboists to make the sound of your oboe teacher Nori. Today, do you know what they sound like? . . . Bagpipes from the mountains . . . !"

Schoenbach: "He began to tell me about a performance of *Carmen* he had conducted, and about a chord which involved an oboe and three trombones and how the oboe in those days had an almost trumpet-like sound so that it matched those brass instruments."[10]

## Self-Dissatisfaction

Toscanini was rarely satisfied with his performances and was quite reluctant to approve his recordings for publication.

When he was in his seventies, Toscanini told Halina Rodzinski that he hadn't had even one moment of complete artistic satisfaction in his long career. She recalled, "I was thunderstruck. 'I cannot believe [it], Maestro', I told him . . . Here, before me, was the most beloved and famous conductor in the world . . . admired by musicians who had known or worked under Mahler, von Bülow, and Richter. It seemed utterly unbelievable . . . 'Cara [dear], the people who love and make a conductor famous are a crowd, and crowds know nothing. No true musician can be satisfied with his performance, even though an audience is driven to a frenzy. A performance can always be better. We never reach that perfection we strive for. Sometimes I even hate my performances, though the crowd may be clapping in ecstasy.'"[11]

J. Bernstein: "With Italian music he felt comfortable. He could do twenty-five things that were not in the score. He felt this way, and it was beautiful. But in many places in Beethoven he felt he wanted to do something else, but felt, 'Ah! This is not in the score. I cannot do it. It's written this way, and I have to go as written; I cannot do anything else.' He started the 'Pastoral' Symphony four times, and by nature he felt beautiful in the beginning, not ritardando but a little broader. So the arm went broader, but it was not in the score, so he used to break stands and watches and everything. People thought he was mad at musicians. No, he was mad at himself, that he cannot do what he wants. The 'Pastoral' Symphony was always the same, as was the Ninth Symphony; he wanted to do it differently, but as soon as he started to conduct, 'Ah, no; it is not in the score.' But when he conducted *Aida*, and *Bohème,* absolute freedom; do whatever you want. Similarly, Furtwängler took all the liberties in Schumann, Brahms, and Beethoven like Toscanini took in *Aida,* but when Furtwängler had to conduct Verdi he was scared to death! So sometimes he was getting crazy, but not with the musicians—with himself, because it didn't come out as he would like to have it."

Civetta: "So he felt it was his fault."

J. Bernstein: "Absolutely. Absolutely. If somebody took it personally, it was just stupid."

Weber: "I think it was more against himself than anybody else. When he said, 'I would like to do it the way I have it in my mind,' that's the way he approached music. And if he became angry, it was because he couldn't get what he wanted out of the musicians, so that it matched what he had in his mind's ear."

## Perfection and Ideals

Valdengo: "With that very strict man, rehearsals always meant starting over, and redoing everything. He was never satisfied, and I understood that he continually yearned for an ideal form of beauty that he caught a glimpse of in his soul, without being able to attain it."

Toscanini to Haggin: "Always conducting is great suffering for me. At home, with score, when I play piano, is great happiness. But with orchestra is great suffering—*sempre, sempre*! [always] Even when I listen to record I am afraid horn will not play correct, clarinet will make mistake—*sempre, sempre*!"[12]

Antek: "I was always aware of . . . the frustration he felt because of the disparities between the notes on the printed score, the music in his mind's ear, and the sounds that actually came from the orchestra."[13]

Krasnopolsky: "His outbursts were not admonishments. It was just an outcry for perfection. He was a perfectionist and he wanted everybody to adopt the same attitude. Very often he used to say, 'I suffer and I want you to suffer, too.' He said,

'Music is my life.' Very often when he was very angry, he'd beat the side of his thigh with the stick. Very often I would say it was letting off steam."

Mischakoff: "Toscanini was a taskmaster: He expected perfection, even at the first rehearsal. When he didn't get it, he would hit the ceiling."[14]

Many musicians related that superior playing was expected and accepted without praise.

## Tantrums

Valdengo wrote: "The Maestro suffered when he heard it said that his severity and inflexibility at work was labeled as nastiness, arrogance, or even worse, cruelty." Toscanini: "You see, I am severe with the soloists and with the musicians, because I want everyone to give their best. Only in this manner does one serve art. If you only knew how I identify with the struggle and the attempts of every artist and musician, and how much I suffer with them as they practice their most difficult parts!"

D. Walter: "He had gotten terribly upset at one point and then after we played something there was an intermission and he stood there in his black alpaca jacket, quite warm—I mean warm both in perspiration and in the aftermath of his anger—and we felt rather sorry that he had to go through such agony to get what he wanted, and one of the musicians said, 'Maestro, you must try to be more calm. You get so angry and your blood pressure goes up.' 'Don't worry, is good for my blood when I get angry.' [*Laughs*] I do understand that. His circulation was beautiful."

Bachmann: "On one occasion he really blew up. After he threw out this poison, he went into his room and he broke down and cried like a baby. And he called in the principal string players: Mischakoff, Miller, myself, and Carlton Cooley. When we came in, he got a hold of both Mischakoff and myself and he said, 'I'm a bad man, heh? You know, when I take that *sporco* baton [that dirty stick] in my hand, I'm not a human being. I'm a devil. I want everything perfect. Why am I angry with you or with you when you don't play 100 percent? Because I know you can. So don't give me 90 percent. I don't want 90 percent. I want 100 percent. That's why I picked you, because I know I can depend on you.'"

Galimir: "That's why he got so angry: when he showed and they didn't do what he showed. Actually he got angry only when—either he felt one was not prepared, or was negligent; or when he felt one was inattentive, that he showed something and one didn't respond. I understand that; and I think he was right: He always was justified when he blew up—sometimes a little overblown, but always justified."[15]

> One of the things that Toscanini would not accept was carelessness or inattentiveness. With temper tantrums, he was able to immediately change musicians' halfhearted attitudes or a rehearsal's lax atmosphere.

Bachmann: "I don't recall one moment, even a fleeting moment, when Maestro allowed himself the luxury of taking it easy. He never forgave anybody who showed signs of taking it easy. He said, 'I am an aged man, and I work like a beaver, and it's up to you to work the same way. Give me every second, everything you have. I give you everything I have.'"

Toscanini admonished the orchestra during a rehearsal of Beethoven's *Coriolan* Overture: "Give of yourselves. I give *everything* I have."[16]

J. Bernstein: "One thing disturbed him: If you made a mistake or you didn't play so terrific, it wouldn't be bad. He hated it when you didn't follow him. His famous expression was, 'Fol-low me, fol-low me!' Always, 'Fol-low me!' He could break music stands if you didn't. Most of the musicians sometimes don't follow, and that's when he was breaking his watches and so on, but this had nothing to do with the musicians personally, absolutely not! I played with many conductors in my life; he was the easiest, most convenient one to work with. He didn't ask for much—play well, and do what he wants. And to do what he wants, you have to be a good musician, to feel what he feels, I mean, this is the whole story. What is the secret of conducting? The big international orchestras, they can play the standard repertoire without a conductor. Who needs a conductor? They can play everything, sometimes better than with the conductor. He had beautiful musical taste and expression. And the way he could transmit a fantastic power on musicians was something that only Toscanini could achieve. To bring over to them a concept, this is so difficult. I always say that to conduct is the easiest thing, and the most difficult thing, nothing in between."

> During rehearsals, he would become impatient with repeated mistakes.

Mischakoff: "He hated 'stupid musicians' and could heap invectives on them during rehearsals but feel sorry afterward."[17]

S. Shulman: "When we didn't get it after two or three attempts, we were building toward an explosion. With Toscanini you could make a mistake, always; a second one he just couldn't understand; but God forbid, a third one? Well, it was like a baseball player striking out. He just climbed the walls; three times was unbelievable to him.

"And at such times he was capable of great cruelties—though I'm convinced he wasn't aware of them as such. His dedication to his art was so intense that he couldn't think of anything else, including human feelings; and so he rode roughshod over many musicians. When things went well, it was heaven; when they went badly, it was hell, and we ran scared."

Toscanini commented to Haggin: "Last week they play for me record of rehearsal of *Tod und Verklärung*. I do not know why they make this record. All my life I have bad temper: is impossible for me to understand why orchestra cannot play correct. But when I hear this record I am ashamed."[18]

## Intense Concentration

Mischakoff: "He often got so deep into the music that if a musician asked a question, he sometimes failed to understand, almost as though he were being forced to come back from another world."[19]

Bernard Shore, violist and writer: "He enters into another world, taking the orchestra with him. It is frequently noticeable at rehearsal that when he is deeply engaged upon a line of thought and anything unexpectedly happens to snap it, he reacts violently."[20]

Hupka: "He was so dedicated to his art and totally involved that anything else was secondary. He had a violent temper. He had to, because in order to create the great performances that he did you can't just be a normal human being with an ordinary disposition."[21]

# Line

When Toscanini guest conducted an orchestra, he allowed the orchestra to play through each movement without interruption. And he often did the same at the first rehearsal and dress rehearsal with any orchestra he conducted. He conveyed how he wanted the music played through his gestures and kept his talking to a minimum. This was the opposite of conductors whose rehearsal style is to frequently stop the orchestra to talk and explain, restart, stop again, explain further, start over, and continue starting and stopping endlessly. When he invited George Szell to guest conduct the NBC Symphony, Toscanini attended Szell's rehearsals and was angered at Szell's frequent interruptions.

Freeman: "He said to Szell, 'What do you think this is, a school?'"

A. Shulman: "Harvey Shapiro and I were sitting on the third desk and kept tabs. Szell stopped fifty-seven times in the slow movement of the 'Eroica' Symphony, which is enough to lose any musician's span of interest. You see, when a musician plays in a symphony orchestra he doesn't like to be interrupted every two minutes, because he loses his span of concentration; he loses his sense of line and continuity; and the talking should be done with the stick, not the mouth. And that goes for today, because too many conductors are just enamored of the sound of their own voice. They're just knocked over by their rhetoric. Maestro talked with the stick. Maestro was so angry at the rehearsal that at intermission time, he went backstage and he chewed into Szell for having the nerve to exhaust his orchestra."

Several musicians recounted that the first bassoon player, William Polisi, kept track of the number of times Szell stopped the orchestra: 117 times in Schubert's Ninth Symphony, and 97 times in *Till Eulenspiegel*. This infuriated Toscanini, who was listening to the rehearsals.

Freeman: "One thing about Toscanini that was unusual about him compared to other conductors: You give a conductor a two-and-a-half-hour rehearsal, and he'll use every minute of the two and a half hours. Give him three hours and he'll use three. You can give him ten and he'll use ten. But with Toscanini it was different. You had a two-and-a-half hour rehearsal, and it comes to the last rehearsal. He went through many spots and tried many things; but he was one of the few conductors who knew when he had what he wanted, and he would just stop the rehearsal and say, 'Thank you,' and we were through. He did know when he had what he wanted. The Beethoven Ninth was that way. We came to the last rehearsal and he was satisfied. He stopped the rehearsal at least an hour and a half before we were supposed to quit. *Traviata*—final rehearsal, the same thing: We went right through it, and he said, 'Thank you,' and we just sat there waiting, and he left the stage. We were sitting there maybe four or five minutes, and the contractor came out and said, 'The Maestro says the orchestra is dismissed.' Some very unusual things about him. He never wasted a lot of time. As I say, it was a facility that most conductors know nothing about or have: knowing when you've got what you want from the orchestra and leaving it alone. He was a fantastic person that way. Also he could get what he wanted out of you."

A. Shulman: "He came prepared. He knew what he wanted. He knew how to rehearse. So at the end of an hour, when we were scheduled for two and a half hours, he'd say, '*Alla casa* [To home]'. He was satisfied. 'Go home. Rest. You've done your thing.' But on the other hand, if we didn't do our job, then all hell broke loose, and let's face it—not without justification.

"There was an honesty too in his dealing with us . . . what was important was that he was fair: He knew his scores; he came prepared; he knew what he wanted and how to go about getting it; and he wasn't satisfied until he got it—he wouldn't compromise for half. But once he got it, that was it; and this made him the least demanding of any of the conductors we worked with—by which I mean that he believed in not wearing his orchestra out. If we were scheduled for a two-and-a-half-hour rehearsal—and if after the two and a half hours he hadn't achieved what he wanted, he had no qualms about keeping us overtime until he was satisfied—but if he was satisfied at the end of an hour he would dismiss us."[22]

## Afternoon Rehearsals Preferred

Heiles: "The NBC rehearsals were mostly in the late afternoon at Toscanini's insistence. At one time, the managers tried to reschedule the rehearsals to run from 11 a.m. to 1:30 p.m., but Toscanini balked at this 'early' a rehearsal."[23]

## No Recriminations after Performances

A. Shulman: "One thing I must say: If we didn't deliver at a rehearsal, there could be an explosion; but if there was a slip-up at a performance—this was the human factor, it could happen to anyone, and there never were any postmortem recriminations, not even a mention of it. This, to me, was evidence of understanding and tolerance; and I point to it because all the public heard about was intolerance and temper."

Weber: "One thing that I admired about Toscanini was his sense of orchestral psychology. During a performance, if something went amiss, or there was a wrong note, he never stared at the man. He never looked a player down and never gave any recognition that there was anything wrong. He knew that if you make an issue of it at a performance, you're going to upset the musician, and sure enough, you're gonna have another accident right after. So it was remarkable, at a performance, he would never recognize an error; he just went on and conducted."

# Psychology

Galimir: "He was a fantastic psychologist on how to put his will and personality over to the musicians."

Civetta: "You came under his wrath once on the road. Was this the 1950 tour?"
Freeman: "Yeah. It was my birthday coming up, and it was the first trombone player's birthday, Neal Di Biase. Both of us were May 3. We were coming from Texas and going to New Orleans. The train stopped somewhere on the desert; they said they were getting water. Actually, Toscanini had someone call ahead and order cakes and all kinds of things, champagne, whiskey, you name it. And it was all put on board the train. It was a surprise party for Neal and myself that Toscanini gave. The *New York Times* was there, *Time* magazine and others. He ran this big party and treated us so royally, and went through a tremendous expense because it was not only for the orchestra: It was for all the publicity people who traveled with us, all the managers, NBC people, and RCA record people. They all took pictures of Toscanini's cutting the cake and holding our hands. It was a terrific thing. Neal and I went into his own private car—very luxurious. Toscanini had

his own chef on the train with him. We thanked him and told him how surprised and pleased we were.

"The next day we arrived in New Orleans. We never had too many rehearsals on the tour. The longest rehearsal was maybe an hour. When we got to a new place, he would usually go in to hear the acoustics, to get the feel of the hall, and, we'd quit. He said, 'Daphnis et Chloé.' Well, that opens up with two clarinets. That's one piece that all first clarinet players are happy that they're not second clarinet players, because that part is much harder than the first. We played it and he stopped the orchestra and yelled, 'Ancora [again].' We played it again. And then he stopped and he asked for it again, and we played it again, just the two clarinets alone. Then he said, 'Second clarinet alone.' I played it. And he said, 'Again.' Played it again—didn't find anything wrong; I guessed he was fishing. So after about six times going over and over it with him alone, he was at a loss for words, didn't say anything, but progressively was getting angrier, and started to scream at me, not about the music or anything, but just started to scream. So we all sat there all amazed, and he yelled and yelled. And when he got through he threw his baton down and said, 'Go home.' So we all left. I was pretty upset about it, so all of us tried to figure out what it was. 'Well, it was your birthday. He made a party for you guys, had a good time. Now he's taking the polish off, he's getting you back to the way you were.' That was the only time I ever had a run-in with him; and I think that in seventeen years it was a good record, because I sat there many times feeling horrible about the way it was being dished out to some of the people. When he was on the stand he was one kind of a person, and when he was off he was a very bashful man, very kind, very easy-going."

Bachmann: "He knew very well when people were in the hall at rehearsals, listening. He knew that when he put on an act of anger, people were looking. He knew darn well what he was doing. It wasn't 100 percent through and through. But when he was through and through, when that wrath really came out, then he was wonderful. He got hold of his jacket that had twenty-five military buttons from top to bottom. And he gave it one yank and all the twenty-five buttons went flying in twenty-five different directions. That was Maestro. That's when he didn't know about the people listening to the rehearsal in the dark hall."

Katims: "Sometimes I felt that an explosion was really manufactured—that it was really one of his methods (a sort of shock tactic) to get what he wanted. I'm sure that if standing on his head would have led to a more perfect performance, he would

have done just that. He had a habit, when we were nearing the end of a long movement and he wanted to go over it again, of exploding over something—anything, in
order to be able to say, 'Da capo! Da capo tutto! [From the beginning! All of it from
the beginning!]' I remember his picking up on something wrong near the end of the
Schubert C Major and exploding. He really was angry at something—it wasn't an
act—but at the same time you sensed that he'd been looking for something like this
in order to have a reason for going back to the start [of the movement]. Finally he
said, 'Da capo!' Beginning."[24]

## Forgiven by Musicians

D. Walter: "Our timpanist was Karl Glassman, who had been possibly the most
noted timpanist in the United States since 1905. He had been around a long time,
and one day Mr. Toscanini said to him, 'Oh, Glassman, you are getting old, and you
are not my old friend Glassman. You don't play so well anymore.' And he criticized
him very bitterly in front of everybody. And it was, of course, rather horrifying for
those of us like myself who were very young in the orchestra, who loved Mr. Glassman, that this older gentleman should be so abused. So I did go up to him during
the intermission of our rehearsal and expressed my regret. I said, 'It's too bad, Karl,
that he has to shout at you and abuse you that way, and I think it's terrible.' And he
said, 'Don't worry about it. I would tell him off if he weren't right.'"

Freeman: "When he went off on one of his tantrums, it was rather justified. To the
extreme that he went, I don't know if it was justified.

   "He would describe portions of passages where he was trying to get something
and I thought he had it, or else it was pretty close; but then he would talk about love
and two people in love. He would try to give you a mental picture, but was rather
impatient about it because he couldn't believe you didn't understand it, because he
did, and why should it be so one-sided?"

Bloom: "He was terribly impatient, but the saving thing about him was that he was
just as impatient about himself. Many times when he was rehearsing he'd stop and
say, 'Toscanini, you're a fool,' because he didn't like what he was doing. You see, if
an orchestra wasn't doing what he wanted them to do, it was his fault, which was a
very, very unusual and still is an unusual attitude for conductors."

Shaw recalled Toscanini speaking about Beethoven's Ninth Symphony: "He said, 'You know, I have never had a good performance of this work. Sometimes the chorus is bad; sometimes the orchestra is bad; many times the soloists are bad; and many times I am terrible.' It was this fantastic modesty that was part of the way he moved people. And I also think it was the thing that made his tantrums easy to take. They were childish; but they weren't: 'You are crucifying me; you are being cruel to me.' It was: 'You're being cruel to Beethoven; you are being cruel to Verdi.'"[25]

Civetta: "Was he always giving of himself?"
Brieff: "Oh my God, absolutely! He was more demanding of himself, in a way. He never stopped probing himself and asking himself and demanding of himself as much as he demanded from the musicians. This is why I personally felt that despite all the grumblings that might have gone on as far as his attitude toward the orchestra was concerned—and at times it could have been different, he could have withheld his temper—I forgave him these things because he was very hard on himself."

Winter: "Most of the time he was very easy to rehearse with. He was not a fusspot; he didn't bother with minute details. He always went for the main point of the piece, or things that he knew from experience didn't come off at performance, things that he wanted to hear."

D. Walter: "The stories were true, but I think the emphasis is misplaced. It's much more dramatic to tell about a man grabbing a baton and breaking it in anger than it is to tell about a man holding a baton and giving a magnificent round gesture which made everybody play with the most exquisite vibrato and beautiful phrasing, so most of the stories deal with his anger and his tirades. But actually most of the time he was very calm; he was a very good workman. I have some recordings of rehearsals that we did, in which you hear him singing, talking, and conducting, and you can visualize him conducting. And I would say that 1 percent of the time he was living the life of the anecdotes about his anger and that 99 percent of the time he was just doing a good and efficient job of making very beautiful music and teaching very marvelous concepts. But, of course, they make good stories for late at night over a drink!"

# Humanism

Emmons: "Melchior worked on *Tristan* daily and privately with Toscanini. He insisted that the Italian conductor was paternal, kindly, generous, patient, and forgiving to those singers he respected."[26]

A. Shulman: "It wasn't hard work if we could satisfy him; it was when we didn't satisfy him musically that it was hard. We'd turn a phrase, and it wasn't exactly right, so we'd do it again—and possibly a third and a fourth time—until we hit it; and then it was as though the clouds broke and the sun came through, and he'd smile, and with the tension broken the whole orchestra would relax and breathe again."

Bloom: "As far as I know, in the six years that I was with him, there were people in that orchestra that were not pleasing him because they just didn't have the talent, but he never fired anybody from that orchestra. If anybody was fired, NBC would sort of push him to do it. He never did—there was one particular member of the orchestra that used to drive him crazy, but he would just stick with it and just try to make him play. He figured it was his failure if a musician didn't play his best, which was, at least if not unique, it certainly isn't usual these days.

"I don't think I have ever been so anxious to please anybody in my life as I was Toscanini because the man had such tremendous standards and I didn't want to disappoint him. And right from the beginning he treated me very well. He used to call me 'dear.' He treated me more like a son and I thought of him as a father. He was a great teacher—that's what he was. In fact, he used to say, 'A conductor has to be a teacher. That is the first thing that he has to be.'"

Mischakoff: "To see Toscanini directing our orchestra with such intensity and fire, one would suppose him to be formidable, unapproachable . . . but those of us who are privileged to work with him love him . . . for Toscanini never would have attained the pedestal he now occupies if he were not the kind and sympathetic, thoughtful and understanding man we know him to be."[27]

Ghignatti: "Having played in his orchestra for forty years, and always felt I was not up to what I should be as a musician, I never feared talking to him whenever necessary, and he always listened, understood, and appreciated my frankness and sincerity."[28]

Valdengo: "Those who didn't know Toscanini well couldn't have an idea of his greatness of spirit and kindness. Terribly severe in artistic work, he was very human in private life.

"When teaching, he didn't have endearments for anyone and brutally gave Caesar what Caesar deserved. Even if there had been a storm, after the rehearsal he was just as much a friend as before, without hard feelings toward anyone, always quick to help out and benevolent toward those who deserved his attention.

"One day I was attending an orchestral rehearsal and noticed that one of the best musicians wasn't succeeding in performing a passage. Toscanini began to get nervous and said, 'But, my friend, you've always played it. We've performed this piece a hundred times; try again.' Nothing helped; the passage still didn't work out, and after a few notes, there was always the same mistake.

"Toscanini waited for a break, and called the player into his studio. He addressed him in the following way: 'Listen, I can't cut this piece from the program; you're simply not at your best; let's say that you are sick, and don't worry about it.'

"The musician did this and everything went on without anyone finding out about it. Toscanini had been an instrumentalist and so understood these things well; he didn't want to fluster the player further and possibly expose him, because of a minor incident, to the criticism of a lot of people. A generous heart, displaying solidarity with other artists!"

Valdengo: "One day during a rehearsal, a soloist misplayed a passage. Two other players laughed, winking at each other, and Toscanini saw it. At a certain point he stopped the orchestra and said, 'Let me hear this scale played by the two orchestra members up there who were laughing at their colleague's mistake a little while ago.'

"I'll never forget the tragicomic scene that followed: The two instrumentalists didn't succeed in hitting a single note of the scale and so Toscanini said, 'Who's laughing now? I now authorize you to add to your business card, under your name, the title of jackass.' When the rehearsal ended I said to the Maestro, 'You fixed those two.' And he, looking at me, responded, 'Sometimes I am cruel; even I understand that. It's something that that I don't like, but it's the only way to get the point across that everyone can make a mistake and that one must never laugh behind others' backs.'"

Jerome Hines, bass, described Toscanini being very patient, kind, and understanding when the singer had a very bad cold on the day of a recording session with the Maestro.[29]

Lehmann's monthly period started on the day of her first orchestral rehearsal with Toscanini. She told him about it upon arriving at the rehearsal. He immediately had a chair brought out for her, asked her to remain seated, and told her to relax—that it was unnecessary for her to prove her talent, of which, he said, he was already well aware.[30]

Mischakoff: "People thought he was a devil—but only onstage. He was the sweetest man off stage—like a lamb . . . He would give parties for the whole orchestra and the wives."[31]

Weber: "He was a wonderful host. He was running things and was all over the house, shaking hands and talking to people, talking to musicians and having a wonderful time. He had a sense of humor; he was kind; he was generous; he remembered. I know for a fact that even in the New York Philharmonic days he would remember musicians' birthdays, particular musicians, and even their wives, and presented them with gifts. So he was very human. Some people paint him as a tyrant and enraged lion at times, but he was very gentle. And he had to be kind and gentle and understanding, otherwise the music wouldn't have come out the way it did because I believe that a person can only reproduce what he is capable of, and what his mind has, and what he has in his heart and soul. He plays what he is; he can't play what he's not. If a musician plays cold, he is a cold person. Toscanini was far from being cold. He could be, can I say, schmaltzy in Puccini? He was very warm and sentimental in Puccini, and he was warm and sentimental personally, too."

Valdengo wrote about Toscanini's recollection of his engagement at the Municipal Theatre in Casale Monferrato in 1887: "'I found myself in that beautiful theatre built in the same baroque style as the Carignano Palace of Turin, with a local orchestra that was not entirely satisfactory, but the players were so willing to learn, that within a few rehearsals I succeeded in molding it the way I wanted it, and bringing it to a good point. We achieved a noteworthy success with that intelligent audience of connoisseurs, but what impressed me was the manifestation of intense and warm affection from those orchestra players. When I took my leave of them, I was moved to tears. It is one of the beautiful memories of my life!'"

## After Toscanini

> Several of the musicians said they refused to continue playing in orchestras after Toscanini. Harry Glantz said he would prefer to work as a gas station attendant.[32]

Civetta: "What conductor today comes close to Toscanini?"
Krasnopolsky: "Nobody. Not one of the conductors I would like to say came near Toscanini in any way. It was impossible. In general, I gave everybody credit and I think everybody has the right to conduct in any position, but so far [1978] they don't have my respect. No. I wouldn't like to play with them even if they gave me millions of dollars."

H. Berv: "There were a lot of times when he'd chop me down to a toothpick like he did many other men. He was a great disciplinarian, and I say if I had my orchestra days to live over again, I wouldn't want them with anybody else but him, even with all the rugged things we went through during the rehearsals."
Civetta: "Who comes the closest to Toscanini today?"
H. Berv, after a very long pause: "I can't answer that question."

# CHAPTER 11

# Recordings

*In 1936 I make "Rhine Journey" with Philharmonic . . . In Carnegie Hall is right tempo, when I hear record is wrong tempo. Last year I am in bed, and a friend telephone to me: "Maestro, listen to radio." I listen: is "Rhine Journey"; is good—is right tempo—IS MY "RHINE JOURNEY"! In 1936 is wrong tempo; now is right tempo! Ah,* Dio santo!
    —Toscanini

Toscanini's first recordings were made with the La Scala Orchestra in 1920. He made several recordings with the New York Philharmonic in the 1920s and '30s, with the BBC Symphony in the '30s, as well as with the Philadelphia Orchestra in the early '40s. His performances with several European, Scandinavian, and South American orchestras were also recorded. The majority of his recordings were made with the NBC Symphony between 1938 and 1954. In addition to these, recordings were made of nearly all of his concerts with the NBC Symphony, which were broadcast live.

The recording techniques varied, as did the quality of the results. Unfortunately, many of the maestro's recordings are not accurate representations of his art. However, not all of the recordings are flawed; several of them are excellent. Fortunately, we can be thankful to Arthur Fierro, for his dedicated efforts to restore Toscanini's recordings, as artistic supervisor of many of the recordings that were remastered for CD in the BMG Toscanini Collection.

## Alteration of Acoustics

Some of the producers attempted to change the acoustics of NBC's Studio 8H and Carnegie Hall. Sometimes the microphones were placed at a significant distance from the orchestra to capture more of the resonance of the room. This resulted in recordings that lacked presence and the aggressive, powerful sonority that Toscanini succeeded in obtaining when the character of the music called for it. At other recording sessions, draperies were placed over the side boxes and parquet of Carnegie Hall to reduce the natural reverberation of the hall. Many of the recordings had electronic reverberation added to the final mix, sometimes with very unsatisfactory results.

## Dynamics Destroyed

One huge challenge for the engineers was the enormous dynamic range Toscanini elicited from orchestras he conducted. This was true whether the music was that of Mozart or Beethoven, a Rossini crescendo, the music of Wagner and Verdi, or that of Debussy and Respighi. This wonderful dynamic range of his recordings was sometimes electronically compressed, resulting in the quieter passages being recorded to sound louder in volume, and the louder passages, reduced in volume. The justification was twofold: The average home listening equipment of the day was not sophisticated enough to satisfactorily reproduce Toscanini's enormous dynamic range. If not compressed, the speaker volume would have had to be loud enough to hear the quietest passages but wouldn't have been able to reproduce the loudest ones without distortion or damage to the equipment.

In addition, so many of the recordings were made on acetate discs before the advent of tape. The stylus's coming into contact with the imperfections on the surface of the revolving discs produced a hissing, crackling noise. Therefore, when recording quiet music it was thought necessary to raise the volume to have an acceptable music-to-noise ratio. This necessitated lowering the recording volume level back to normal during the louder passages, resulting in the destruction of the dynamics Toscanini and the orchestra worked so hard to achieve.

Freeman: "During a playback he used to hit the ceiling and we finally found out why. He said he spent many hours, many days trying to figure out a crescendo, starting from what and to go where. He finally got it, and thought it was beautiful in his mind, and on the playback it was all at one level. He couldn't understand why. He asked, Is he getting old, is he getting deaf, is he getting crazy, what is it? But he found that the engineer was watching that needle in there, and he kept that needle at one level all the time. So when the orchestra started working for the crescendo, the engineer just kept turning it right back down again."

## Equalization

Another problematic aspect of Toscanini's recordings is the equalization that was often added to suit the subjective tastes of the various recording producers, with sometimes dismal results.

## Microphone Placement

Hupka explained that early on in the NBC Symphony era, there was one engineer, Robert Johnston, who for the purpose of broadcasting the concerts used a single microphone, as opposed to multiple microphones. Just as crucial was his choice of location for this microphone: By being positioned a few feet above and behind Toscanini's head, it basically picked up the orchestra the way Toscanini heard it while standing on the podium. Hupka called this the "optimum position" for the placement of the microphone. This contrasted with the typical multiple microphone setup, whereby the engineers in the control room could vary the volume level of each microphone, thereby changing the balance that Toscanini worked so hard to achieve.

Hupka made it a practice to immediately go into the control room after a concert to compare the recording that had just been made of the event with the actual sounds of the orchestra "still ringing in my ears." And to his delight, the recordings of Johnston beautifully matched what he had heard in the hall. They were, as Hupka put it, "an accurate representation of what the orchestra sounded like. It was the only intelligent way to record Toscanini's unique sound."

## Single Mic vs. Multiple Mics

The recordings of the early NBC broadcasts derived from this single-mic setup that reproduced the orchestra with a presence and impact that is not heard on some of the other recordings where multiple-mic setups were used, especially when the mics were placed farther back in the hall, away from the orchestra. To demonstrate, Hupka played me side-by-side comparisons of two recordings of the opening of the second movement of Beethoven's Ninth Symphony with Toscanini conducting the NBC Symphony with the same timpanist, Karl Glassman. The first was a recording of the performance from 1938 in an audience-filled Carnegie Hall. It was recorded with Johnston's setup that utilized the single mic in the optimum position. The second one was from the recording sessions of 1952 in an empty Carnegie Hall with a multiple-microphone setup. One would assume with the passage of fourteen years of advancement in recording technology—especially the advent of tape, as well as the freedom of having an empty Carnegie Hall to set up in, and the opportunity of recording several takes, that the results of the 1952 recording sessions would certainly produce a superior recording. Yet it is in the 1938 version that the impact and incisiveness of the orchestra are captured—especially the timpani solo in bar 5. The same passage from the 1952 recording is rather weak in comparison, sounding like a different orchestra, and different hall.

## Balance

Haggin described the NBC microphone placements for some of the Carnegie Hall broadcasts of the 1950s: "Solo woodwinds were louder than tuttis, and other balances so laboriously worked out by Toscanini were similarly destroyed."[1]

A. Shulman recalled the recording session of the Mozart Bassoon Concerto: "After they recorded the Mozart Divertimento [K. 287], there was about three-quarters of an hour of the session left—time enough for one take; and so there was only one take. This attitude was the thing that bothered me about recording, and I believe it was responsible for Toscanini's hating recording. He felt it never did justice to his tonal palette and balances; and he was right, because when it came to balancing the orchestra I remember that Charles O'Connell, the recording director, was concerned with only one thing—that the session did not go [into] overtime. So everything was great: 'Sounds fine, Maestro.' Then the Old Man would listen to the playback and say, 'I don't hear the oboe; I don't hear the second bassoon'; and they'd say, 'Oh, but it sounds different upstairs. It's wonderful, Maestro.' But when he got the test pressing he still didn't hear the second bassoon; and so he came to detest recording. For us, of course, even if the bassoon can't be heard there is the nobility of concept, the rhythmic force, the tremendous drive."

Civetta: "Do you think the Maestro liked recording?"
Brieff: "He hated it. I remember going up into the control room at Carnegie Hall, when the orchestra would have an intermission, and they would play this thing back, and he would tear his hair out. 'What happened to the harp? What happened to the second oboe? I cannot hear! *Terribile! Terribile!*' Actually, if he were alive today, we wouldn't see so many of the things he did published, because he didn't agree to allow many recordings to go out, in the time that I was with him at NBC from '48 to '52. He was very unhappy with the sound; he was very unhappy with the quality. 'No sound like that! I don't hear! I don't like sound!' I don't think he was happy with the recordings. Occasionally maybe some things pleased him, but I don't think basically that he was happy with the sound."

## Clarity

Marek: "He wanted the orchestra at recording sessions to sit exactly as they did at the concerts. He just wanted a portrayal of the concerts, and he strove for clarity of individual instruments. So his recordings do not by any means do him justice."

Sarser: "He liked the orchestra to sound on recordings the way it sounded to him when he stood on the podium. Now, this is not always what recordings turn out to be. It's not what record manufacturers feel is commercial. But this is what he listened to all his life. His spot when he listened to an orchestra was on the podium, where the sound of an orchestra jells. A conductor, after all, balances an orchestra. He mixes the voices of the orchestra and he's responsible for making this sound balanced and the way the score is written. And we must assume that if he's satisfied, it sounds that way where he is standing. For pure symphony-type recording, if you put a mic slightly above and behind him approximately where he is, you should get a good balance. When we did use this technique, he seemed to be the most satisfied. From my experience, having watched him listen to recordings of many performances, the ones that he liked the best were the ones that were picked up in the simplest manner and had the truest sound with the least amount of room tone added."

# Dubbing

Lora described Toscanini's recording of Beethoven's *Leonore* Overture No. 3: "The Maestro was not satisfied with the balance or the presence of the solo flute and had refused to allow the release of the record. I dubbed in several flute spots that seemed to be weak. The reinforced version later received the Maestro's blessing and the record was released! Thus my first collaboration with Toscanini was in absentia [not present]!"

> Lora subsequently was principal flutist with Toscanini at NBC from 1947 to 1952.

# Self-Dissatisfaction

Haggin: "During the break in a Debussy recording session with the Philadelphia Orchestra in 1942, Walter [Toscanini's son] invited me to visit his father in his dressing room, where we found him fanning himself and worrying about the difficulty of recording. 'I make *pianissimo* in *La mer*: in hall is correct; on record is *not* correct! In 1936 I make "Rhine Journey" with Philharmonic . . . In Carnegie Hall is right tempo, when I hear record is wrong tempo. Last year I am in bed, and a friend telephone to me: "Maestro, listen to radio." I listen: is "Rhine Journey"; is good—is right tempo—IS MY "RHINE JOURNEY"! In 1936 is wrong tempo; now is right tempo! Ah, *Dio santo!*' And he hurled the fan at the wall in despair."[2]

> The same recording may seem slower or faster than one's expectations, depending on many variables, such as one's current pulse rate, metabolism, or state of mind.

Arthur Fierro, administrative assistant to Toscanini's son, Walter, explained: "After hearing recordings at his home in 1953 of the early takes of the Kyrie of Beethoven's

Missa Solemnis, Toscanini insisted on conducting another take in which he animated the tempo of the second part of the Kyrie in a manner different from previous performances, the recent broadcast, and early takes. It is this version he approved for publication."

> It was not always a matter of tempos changing over the years, but of hearing, in this case, a new take, and deciding to change the tempo.

Bloom: "I was at his house when he played a whole string of test records that he had made with the Philadelphia Orchestra, because he did a lot of recording with them. And he played recordings for me that I thought were just wonderful, and he would say, 'No. I took the wrong tempo.' To me they sounded perfect. But you see, when he got a chance to hear back, he had some ideas about what he wanted to do, and it didn't always come off. Now, at a concert, it's a spur-of-the-moment thing. But on a recording, he had a chance to reexamine his music with an aural microscope, you might say, and he would find things that he didn't like. It was very seldom a thing that the orchestra did. He didn't like what he did and he rejected an awful lot of recordings that I am sure were then released after he died. I remember what he used to insist on and what he tried to do—and I know that poor man would have been very unhappy to know people were judging his work from those recordings because he was already dead when they were released."

## Recording in Five-Minute Segments

> In the days of 78 rpm records (78s), the maximum duration of one side of a disc was approximately five minutes. Therefore, all of the music Toscanini conducted at recording sessions was played in five-minute segments. Matching the tempos between segments and achieving an unbroken architectural line was an extraordinarily difficult task.

Freeman: "There was no such thing as splicing; it was all done on acetate discs, and if something was wrong either you had to go back to the beginning of a movement or to where the orchestra made a stop [the end of a five-minute passage]. It was a lot more difficult recording on 78s, with acetates, than it is now."

## Listening at Home

Hupka: "In listening to a playback he would often conduct. He wouldn't go through the violent motion of course, but you could see he was completely carried away in a trance. And it was a great experience to watch him listening to a playback."[3]

Sarser designed and installed Toscanini's home sound system: "We made him a home system that would reproduce the orchestra as loud as possible without distortion. He liked big volume. He liked to have it sound exactly the way it was when he stood before the orchestra. The sound level at that point was quite intense, plenty of decibels. For instance, in a work like the *Manfred* Symphony, there are times, sitting in the orchestra, when you almost reach the threshold of pain. And it was necessary to make the Maestro hear his orchestra at home when he sat in that chair, the same as if he was at the rehearsal. Although it was not *always* necessary to reproduce what he heard when he conducted. He would be satisfied to listen to a tiny portable radio out in the garden, and he would provide the ambience and presence in his mind.

"We had no tone controls. We used a flat response. We had equalizers available, but most of the time we used a flat response because our speaker had good response at all frequencies and it was used at sufficiently high levels, which enabled us to play back the sound exactly the same as it was recorded in the studio. Everything was flat with all frequencies amplified equally. The system was large enough and the low-frequency speakers were large enough that they gave out the true bass sound without having to be boosted. The highs should be there with no distortion. That's the most important thing. If it sounded like the orchestra, that was right.

"He eventually ended up with four professional tape recorders and a resident engineer for transferring discs to tape, making recordings off the air, listening to broadcasts, listening to recordings he made at RCA, helping him with the editing; and one great thing was to help him reminisce about past performances and study scores.

"We installed the complete Voice of the Theater speaker in the corner in the main hall of the house where he used to sit and listen. And there was another chair right by him where a friend would sit.

"In his retirement, Maestro listened to music and studied scores, and listened to music and studied scores. That was his whole life. And he did it to the very end. If there was something that RCA wanted to release, then all the available previous performances were gotten together, and they'd be put on tape and played for Maestro. That was really the only work he did after he retired, and he'd select the ones he liked best. And then they would splice the better parts together and play them for him to try to come up with something they could release."

## Recorded Legacy

Hupka instigated a policy at NBC whereby several hundred hours of rehearsals were recorded during the last several years of Toscanini's career. He also was responsible for salvaging many recordings of Toscanini's concerts that had been discarded. And he was a tireless crusader for the restoration of the films of Toscanini's ten televised concerts, which Hupka worked on in preparation for their publication on videocassette and DVD. Fortunately, these rehearsal recordings and all of Toscanini's NBC Symphony broadcasts—as well as performances he conducted with other orchestras—can be heard at the New York Public Library at Lincoln Center's Rodgers and Hammerstein Archives of Recorded Sound.

As with other aspects of Toscanini's art, it is difficult to make generalizations about his recordings. They provide an extensive record of his work, especially during the last eighteen years of his sixty-eight-year career, and demonstrate that interpretively, he was an ever-evolving artist.

# CHAPTER 12

# Conclusion

*After the concert I just couldn't bear to go into the subway; and so I walked for blocks and blocks to my home with the sounds of the performance ringing in my mind.*
—Fred Zimmermann

## Toscanini's Opinions of Other Conductors

Toscanini often criticized other conductors, but there were many whom he spoke well of. Artur Rodzinski was chosen by Toscanini to assemble and train the NBC Symphony at its inception in 1937. He also liked Ernest Ansermet, Fritz Busch, Erich Kleiber, Pierre Monteux, Fritz Reiner, Enrico Piazza, Robert Shaw, William Steinberg, Bruno Walter, and his protégé, Guido Cantelli.

Toscanini: "Cantelli is a born orchestra conductor and has what it takes to become a great conductor . . . I am not eternal."*

He recommended that Furtwängler succeed him as music director of the New York Philharmonic in 1936. His break with the German conductor was not over artistic differences, but over Furtwängler's decision to conduct

---

* Quotations from Toscanini that are not otherwise attributed are translations from Valdengo's *Scusi, conosce Toscanini?*

in Germany during the Nazi regime. (See page 7 regarding Toscanini and Furtwängler.)

Toscanini repeatedly pointed out that some of his colleagues seemed to enjoy their own performances, smiling while they conducted. And he contrasted this attitude with his own, which he described as one of suffering to attain the ideal in his mind's ear. "I'm like a *woman giving birth!*"[1]

Burghauser: "Toscanini . . . talked about the shortcomings of Furtwängler and Walter and this and that—how it's never *all* good and therefore it's really *never* good: It's good enough, but never perfect, so it's *not* good. But there was one who was good: [Arthur] Nikisch. And Ernst von Schuch in Dresden: 'I heard things—I was transported.' . . . So Toscanini admitted always: There were conductors; but they were not here now; and those who are here now—sorry, it's good enough, but not really good."[2]

Haggin: "He spoke with especial warmth of Schuch, the one-time director of the Dresden Opera; he spoke of Nikisch as a good conductor, but criticized him for his occasional insufficient study of the score and for the acting on the podium others have told me Nikisch indulged in; similarly, he spoke well of De Sabata but disapprovingly of his violent gesticulation."[3]

Toscanini considered Victor De Sabata to be an excellent conductor, but criticized him for often changing tempos.

Bachmann: "He told me he thought Hans Richter was a great conductor."

Valdengo: "One day Toscanini, seeing me reading, asked me what it was. I replied that it was the libretto of *Otello*, which I employed to commit the words to memory and from there, the part. 'A good idea. Who suggested it to you?' I replied that it was Antonio Guarnieri. Hearing the name of Guarnieri, the Maestro immediately exclaimed, 'What a beautiful baton . . . He was born to conduct. He was with me at La Scala for several years and I will never forget the *Francesca da Rimini* of Zandonai conducted by him. He was a great conductor, who didn't use gestures in excess.'

"He was happy to know when a soloist or a conductor distinguished himself in a performance. When RCA Victor published the recording of *Il trovatore* conducted by Maestro Renato Cellini, he immediately said, 'You know, rascal, I heard the records of *Trovatore* conducted by your friend from Torino, the son of that stage director that was with me at the Regio. He is really a good conductor. His recorded *Trovatore* is excellent. The colors of the orchestra are so intuitive . . . the transitions of the tempos . . . wonderful!'

"Of Maestro Molinari-Pradelli, whom he heard on the radio in Italy, he said, 'I heard a very good young conductor certain to make a big career.'"

Toscanini also encouraged the conducting careers of several orchestral musicians who played with him at NBC and the New York Philharmonic, including Samuel Antek, Leon Barzin, Frank Brieff, Milton Katims, Frank Miller, and Alfred Wallenstein. He assisted the careers of Erich Leinsdorf, Georg Solti, and William Steinberg.

Wallenstein: "In my early years of conducting on the radio, when I had some technical problem, I could call on him and his knowledge of all those problems: 'Oh yes, you mean the place so many bars after this theme. Watch out, because you feel this and you must do that.' And after the broadcasts he'd call up to tell me this was fine but that wasn't good . . . When I look back I think that those of us who were privileged to know and work with Maestro and benefit by his all-round knowledge were the luckiest people in the world; and the years in the Philharmonic were the happiest years of my life . . . He remained as a father and a sort of father confessor. Toscanini was the greatest musical influence in my life."[4]

Katims: "Backstage, before my first NBC Symphony guest appearance, he hovered over me like a mother hen, arranging my pocket handkerchief and adjusting my tie . . . Afterwards he came back to my dressing room and embraced me. All I could think of were all those little mishaps, but he said, 'Oh, my dear, something always happens.' One of the greatest moments of my life was when Maestro embraced me after that broadcast."[5]

Taubman: "He is especially curious about conductors, past and present. He watches the young fellows coming up [1951], insisting that their principal shortcoming is that they do not study hard enough. 'I conducted more than a dozen operas at the start,' he once said, 'but I didn't puff up with my importance as a conductor. I kept on studying and I thought of myself as a cellist, not a conductor.'"[6]

Grossman: "I presumed upon him to go over some of these things that I was about to conduct, if he had the time. I remember we discussed *Carmen*. Then I was going to do *Butterfly* with the NBC Opera Theatre . . . and we had something like a five- or six-hour session on *Butterfly* interspersed with his comments and playing the piano, and illustrations, and even playing of some recordings where he wanted to hear things."[7]

## Influence

In 1978, I asked Harold Coletta whether Toscanini had influenced the star conductors of the day.

Coletta: "No. Bernstein is very talented, but he gushes too much and distorts. I can't think of anyone who has Toscanini's stature, his knowledge, background, his taste, or his magnetic personality. They're all like children in comparison with him. I don't think I've been moved by any except Karajan, who I admire a great deal."

Koutzen: "The whole artistic scene seems to be much more—I don't have a correct word to use—bad serious. The vibrant, magnetic personality in music is becoming more and more rare. And Toscanini represented that kind of magnetism. That's something you're born with."

## Inspiration

Mischakoff: "You were never bored when you rehearsed with Toscanini, and that's a blessing for a musician. When you play Brahms and Tchaikovsky thousands of times, it's very boring unless the conductor inspires you. Toscanini had that quality."[8]

> Many of the musicians considered performing with Toscanini to be the high point of their careers. String players often aspire to and train for glamorous careers as soloists or chamber musicians. They don't plan on becoming members of string sections.

Mischakoff: "Perhaps one in one-thousand musicians can be a soloist."[9]

Orchestral musicians are required to play according to the tastes of whoever is conducting. The scenario is void of individual artistic expression and they often become jaded, playing somewhat mechanically at a job that bears no resemblance to the dreams and visions they had during their student years when they practiced several hours each day to master their instruments. Historically, orchestra players have often been subjected to the arrogance and condescending behavior of conductors. Yet many of the musicians told me that when playing with Toscanini, musicians—even those who disliked their orchestral career, having aspired to be soloists—felt they were individual artists again.

Antek wrote about being "stimulated, challenged to give your best . . . working toward ideals often long forgotten."[10] "This set apart the experience of playing with Toscanini from that of playing with any other conductor . . . Compared with our Old Man . . . others seemed little more than apprentices."[11]

Bachmann: "You will always hear this expression and it's well merited: 'He played under this conductor, he played under that conductor.' You hear that all the time. You never should hear that about Maestro Toscanini. You never played under Toscanini; you played *with* him. You were his equal and he made you feel that.

"His respect for musicians—if they showed the right amount of talent and achievement and, above all, good musical taste—was unbounded. He considered every musician his equal. There was nobody who was lesser than him in his eyes, and he meant it. He was able to convey, not only to the orchestra but . . . to every listener, a sense that this is a man who is conducting just for me. It's my performance. That was the great secret of Maestro's great performances."

According to Antek, a rehearsal of the NBC Symphony with Toscanini was scheduled on the day Hitler had invaded the Sudetenland in the northwestern part of Czechoslovakia. The musicians were indifferent; the rehearsal seemed completely unimportant compared to the gravity of the invasion. Antek wrote that as soon as the musicians began playing, Toscanini mesmerized the orchestra. "No conductor I ever worked with could create quite this feeling of ecstasy."[12]

Zimmermann: "We felt his love for the music, his excitement . . . and we reacted to his excitement with our own excitement about the music and the performance.

And there were marvelous performances. The one that stands out in my memory is the Schubert Ninth: It was an experience. After the concert I just couldn't bear to go into the subway; and so I walked for blocks and blocks to my home with the sounds of the performance ringing in my mind. Wagner, too: It was deeply stirring, deeply spiritual; and being part of it was a transcendent experience."[13]

## Lessons Learned

One of the most inspiring lessons I have learned from Toscanini is the humility with which he approached his work throughout his life. I am impressed by his habit of self-reflection, asking others what they thought of a particular performance or detail, and his constant striving for self-improvement, even in his eighties.

One lesson that has become a recurring theme throughout the interviews is that it's easy to make generalizations about various aspects of Toscanini's style. Yet there are many exceptions that weaken the strength of these generalizations.

Gavazzeni reported Toscanini's own words on the subject: "They say that I've always been the same. Nothing more foolish has ever been uttered about me. I've never been the same—not even from one day to the next. I knew it even if others didn't."[14]

Toscanini possessed a superb memory, highly trained ears, and a magnetic personality. He worked incredibly hard, demanding of himself as much as he did of the artists with whom he made music. And most revealing of all was to learn how thoroughly he prepared himself before the first rehearsal of any composition, even if it was one he had been conducting for fifty years.

Daisaku Ikeda compared Toscanini to Tsunesaburo Makiguchi (1871–1944), educational theorist and author of *The System of Value-Creating Pedagogy*. Dr. Ikeda observed that they both lived during roughly the same period. Standing up to Japanese militarism, Makiguchi fought for freedom and justice, and died in prison as a result.

Dr. Ikeda stated, "Both were individuals of remarkable courage and unwavering belief," asserting that "their heroic achievements served as an example to others—teaching people that hope is the light of the heart; hard work, the royal path of the spirit; and hardship, the beautiful melody of the soul."[15]

# Appendix of Names

This appendix does not attempt to summarize the numerous achievements of the individuals profiled but instead to convey the nature of their relationship with Toscanini and highlight some of the achievements they were best known for.

The musicians listed as having played in the NBC Symphony, did so with Toscanini.

When an artist is credited as having sung at the Metropolitan and La Scala, one can imagine that these artists may have also sung in many of the world's other opera houses. The Metropolitan Opera is referred to as the "Met."

An asterisk next to a name indicates that the author interviewed the person, whether or not the interview is excerpted in this book. Interviews by others with the same person may also be quoted in the text.

**Abell, Arthur**, European musical correspondent for several American journals and newspapers; conducted in-depth interviews, and published *Talks with Great Composers: Candid Conversations with Brahms, Puccini, Richard Strauss and Others.*

**Accorinti, Michele**, tenor, voice teacher, who taught Giuseppe Valdengo.

\***Albanese, Licia**, soprano; sang regularly with the Met and in Toscanini's last performances of *La bohème* and *La traviata*, both of which were recorded.

**Ansermet, Ernest**, founder and conductor of L'Orchestre de la Suisse Romande; guest conducted the NBC Symphony.

**Antek, Samuel**, conductor and violinist; played with the NBC Symphony throughout its entire seventeen-year existence. He was the music director of the New Jersey Symphony and is the author of *This Was Toscanini*, with eighty-four photographs by Robert Hupka.

**Antonicelli, Giuseppe**, conducted at La Scala and the Met.

**Assandri, Virginio**, tenor; sang Cassio in Toscanini's last performance of *Otello.*

**Baccaloni, Salvatore**, bass; sang with Toscanini at La Scala in the 1920s. Despite a huge repertoire, he was most celebrated for his performances of comic roles at the Met.

\***Bachmann, Edwin**, violinist; played with Toscanini for twenty-three years at the New York Philharmonic and was the principal second violinist of the NBC Symphony for the entirety of Toscanini's tenure.

\***Barzin, Leon**, founder and conductor of the National Orchestra Association, founding music director of the New York City Ballet, and principal violist of the New York Philharmonic with Toscanini.

**Battistini, Mattia**, baritone; was admired by Toscanini for his legato and mastery of the bel canto style.

\***Bernstein, Jascha**, cellist; played with Toscanini with the NBC Symphony.

**Bernstein, Leonard**, one of the most successful conductors of the twentieth century; best remembered for the telecasts of his Young People's Concerts, and as composer of *West Side Story*.

**Bernstein, Martin**, bass player with the New York Philharmonic with Toscanini; taught at New York University for several decades.

\***Berv, Arthur**, principal horn of the Philadelphia Orchestra and the NBC Symphony; taught at the Manhattan School of Music.

\***Berv, Harry**, horn player in the Philadelphia Orchestra and in the NBC Symphony; taught at Juilliard, Columbia University, and New York University, and is the author of *A Creative Approach to French Horn*.

\***Bloom, Robert**, oboist; played in the Philadelphia Orchestra from 1930 to 1936 and was the principal oboist in the NBC Symphony from 1937 to 1943. He was later a principal member of the Bach Aria Group, recorded with the RCA Victor Symphony and the Columbia Symphony, and taught at Juilliard and Yale University.

**Boito, Arrigo**, best known as the composer of *Mefistofele* and as the librettist of Verdi's operas *Otello* and *Falstaff*. As vice president of La Scala's administrative council, he recommended that Toscanini become its conductor in 1898.

\***Bolognini, Remo**, conductor, violinist and pupil of Eugène Ysaÿe; was concertmaster of the Philharmonic in Buenos Aires, assistant concertmaster of the Chicago Symphony and the New York Philharmonic, third assistant concertmaster of the NBC Symphony, and assistant conductor of the Baltimore Symphony. He played with Toscanini for more than twenty years, including as soloist in the Mendelssohn Concerto with the New York Philharmonic.

\***Brieff, Frank**, violist with the NBC Symphony, music director of the New Haven Symphony; guest conducted the NBC Symphony.

**Bülow, Hans von**, conductor, pianist, and composer; was soloist in the world premiere of Tchaikovsky's First Piano Concerto and conducted the world premieres of *Tristan und Isolde*, *Die Meistersinger*, *Siegfried*, and *Götterdämmerung*.

\***Burghauser, Hugo**, bassoonist with the Metropolitan and the Vienna Philharmonic; as chairman of the Vienna Philharmonic, he was responsible for Toscanini's appearances with the orchestra in Vienna and Salzburg.

**Busch, Fritz**, principal conductor of the Danish National Symphony, and music director of the Glyndebourne Festival; conducted at the Met, and guest conducted the NBC Symphony.

**Calusio, Ferruccio**, conductor; was Toscanini's musical assistant at La Scala and one of the primary conductors at the Teatro Colón in Buenos Aires throughout much of the twentieth century.

**Cantelli, Guido**, young conductor; was admired and enthusiastically promoted by Toscanini. He was killed in an airplane crash at age thirty-six, one week after his appointment as music director of La Scala.

*****Carassy, Howard**, librarian for the NBC Symphony.

**Carboni, William**, violist in the NBC Symphony; subsequently played with the New York Philharmonic until 1983.

*****Carelli, Gabor**, tenor with the Met; sang the role of Dr. Caius with the NBC Symphony in Toscanini's last performance of *Falstaff*.

**Caruso, Enrico**, one of the most famous tenors in history; performed with Toscanini at La Scala and the Met.

**Casals, Pablo**, composer, conductor, and the pre-eminent cellist of the first half of the twentieth century.

**Cellini, Renato**, conductor whose recording of *Il trovatore* was praised by Toscanini.

*****Coletta, Harold**, violist with the NBC Symphony and later with the New York Philharmonic.

**Cooley, Carlton**, composer; was the principal violist of the Cleveland Orchestra and the NBC Symphony.

*****Copland, Aaron**, composer, whose *El Salón México* was performed by Toscanini.

**Cotogni, Antonio**, legendary baritone and voice teacher who was admired by Verdi. His pupils included Beniamino Gigli, Giacomo Lauri-Volpi, and Mariano Stabile.

*****Crisara, Ray**, principal trumpet player of the Met and associate first and third trumpet with the NBC Symphony.

*****Cusumano, Robert**, played extra trumpet with Toscanini in the NBC Symphony.

**Dal Monte, Toti**, soprano; sang at the Met, and at La Scala with Toscanini.

**Dalla Rizza, Gilda**, one of Puccini's favorite sopranos; sang at the Met and with Toscanini at La Scala.

**Danise, Giuseppe**, baritone and teacher; sang at La Scala and the Met.

**Davenport, Marcia**, author and music critic.

**De Angelis, Nazzareno**, bass; sang at La Scala, and was much admired by Toscanini.

**De Luca, Giuseppe**, one of Toscanini's favorite baritones. He sang at La Scala and at the Met from 1915 to 1945; sang in the world premieres of *Adriana Lecouvreur*, *Madama Butterfly*, and Massenet's *Don Quichotte*; and taught at Juilliard.

**De Lucia, Fernando**, tenor; sang at the Met and La Scala, was admired by Toscanini.

**De Sabata, Victor**, composer and conductor who succeeded Toscanini at La Scala. His recording of *Tosca* with Callas, di Stefano, and Gobbi was called "one of the finest of all operatic recordings" by Paul Gruber in *The Metropolitan Opera Guide to Recorded Opera*.

**Di Stefano, Giuseppe**, enormously admired tenor; sang at La Scala and the Met and with Toscanini for the maestro's last performance of Verdi's Requiem.

**Dolan, James**, head librarian of the NBC Symphony and the Los Angeles Philharmonic.

\***Dorfmann, Ania**, pianist; performed Beethoven's *Choral Fantasia*, Triple Concerto, and First Piano Concerto with Toscanini, and taught at Juilliard.

**Downes, Edward**, music critic and musicologist.

**Elmo, Cloë**, mezzo-soprano who sang at the Met and in Toscanini's last performance of *Falstaff*.

**Emmons, Shirlee**, soprano, voice teacher, and author of several books, including *Tristanissimo: The Authorized Biography of Heroic Tenor Lauritz Melchior*.

\***Falcone, Frank**, second trumpet player in the NBC Symphony.

\***Fierro, Arthur**, administrative assistant to Toscanini's son Walter in the 1960s; was artistic supervisor of many of Toscanini's recordings that were remastered for CD in the BMG Toscanini Collection.

\***Frank, Mortimer**, author of *Arturo Toscanini: The NBC Years*.

**Frank, Philip**, violinist, student of Leopold Auer and Efrem Zimbalist; played in the NBC Symphony.

\***Freeman, Harold**, E-flat clarinetist and third clarinetist in the NBC Symphony.

**Furtwängler, Wilhelm**, widely considered to have been one of the greatest conductors of the twentieth century.

**Galeffi, Carlo**, baritone; sang at La Scala and the Met, and sang in the world premieres of *Il tabarro* and *Gianni Schicchi*.

\***Galimir, Felix**, violinist. He played with Toscanini in the Palestine Orchestra and the NBC Symphony; was a prominent chamber musician and coach; and taught at the Curtis Institute, Juilliard, and the Mannes College of Music.

**Gavazzeni, Gianandrea**, conducted at the Met and was artistic director of La Scala from 1965 to 1972.

**Ghignatti, Filippo**, English horn player with Toscanini for more than forty years, including at the Orchestra Sinfonica di Milano, La Scala, and the NBC Symphony.

**Giacosa, Giuseppe**, dramatist who collaborated with Luigi Illica on the librettos of Puccini's *La bohème*, *Tosca*, and *Madama Butterfly*.

\***Gingold, Josef**, violinist, pupil of Ysaÿe; played with Toscanini in the NBC Symphony, was concertmaster of the Detroit Symphony, and for many years, was concertmaster of the Cleveland Orchestra under George Szell. He was a prominent teacher at the University of Indiana into old age.

**Glantz, Harry**, principal trumpet for the Philadelphia Orchestra; the San Francisco Symphony; the New York Philharmonic from 1923 to 1942, including Toscanini's years from 1926 to 1936;

and the NBC Symphony from 1942 to 1954. Glantz taught at the University of Miami after Toscanini's retirement, and stated that he would prefer to work as a gasoline station attendant rather than play with other conductors.

**Glassman, Karl**, timpanist at the Met, the New York Philharmonic, and, for seventeen years, the NBC Symphony.

*****Goldsmith, Harris**, pianist, teacher, and music critic.

*****Goodman, Saul**, timpanist for the New York Philharmonic for forty-six years, including Toscanini's tenure from 1926 to 1936; was an instructor at Juilliard for forty-one years.

*****Gordon, Nathan**, music director of the Dearborn Symphony in Michigan and violist with the NBC Symphony.

**Graf, Herbert**, stage director who worked with Toscanini at Salzburg and directed operas at the Met and Zurich Opera.

*****Granick, Arthur**, principal violist of the National Symphony, violist with the NBC Symphony and for many years with the New York Philharmonic.

**Grauer, Ben**, announcer for many of the NBC Symphony radio concerts; was announcer and interviewer for the NBC Radio series *Toscanini: The Man Behind the Legend*, which ran from 1963 to 1967.

**Grossman, Herbert**, conductor of the NBC Opera Theatre and the Great Neck Symphony.

**Guarnieri, Antonio**, conductor; succeeded Toscanini at La Scala in 1929, and was admired by Toscanini.

*****Guarrera, Frank**, baritone who sang with Toscanini at La Scala after World War II, at the NBC Symphony, and for many years at the Met.

**Gustavson, Eva**, contralto; sang at the Met and sang the role of Amneris in Toscanini's last performance of *Aida*.

*****Haggin, B. H.**, music critic for *The Nation* and *The New Republic* and author of fourteen books, including *Conversations with Toscanini* and *The Toscanini Musicians Knew*, which were republished as *Arturo Toscanini: Contemporary Recollections of the Maestro*, edited by Thomas Hathaway.

**Heifetz, Jascha**, legendary violinist who played as a soloist with Toscanini at the New York Philharmonic and the NBC Symphony.

**Heiles, Anne Mischakoff**, biographer of her father, violinist protagonist of *Mischa Mischakoff: Journeys of a Concertmaster*.

**Hines, Jerome**, celebrated basso throughout the world, including forty-one years with the Met; sang in Toscanini's last performance and recording of Beethoven's Missa Solemnis.

**Hirschmann, Ira**, friend of Toscanini's, vice president of Saks Fifth Avenue and Blooming-dale's, founder of the American Friends of Music, and author of *Obligato: Untold Tales from a Life with Music*; was responsible for saving the lives of tens of thousands of Eastern European Jews during the Holocaust.

**Horowitz, Vladimir**, legendary pianist and husband of Toscanini's daughter, Wanda Toscanini Horowitz.

**Horowitz, Wanda Toscanini**, daughter of Arturo Toscanini and wife of Vladimir Horowitz.

**Horszowski, Mieczysław**, pianist; had the longest known career in the history of the performing arts, playing until his ninety-ninth year, and died one month before his 101st birthday. He played Martucci and Mozart concertos with Toscanini and the NBC Symphony.

**Huberman, Bronisław**, Polish violinist. In 1936 he founded the Palestine Orchestra, which is now known as the Israel Philharmonic.

*****Hunter, Ralph**, choral conductor; prepared the chorus for Toscanini's final performances of Cherubini's Requiem and Verdi's Requiem.

*****Hupka, Robert**, photographer; attended Toscanini's rehearsals, recording sessions, and concerts in Vienna, London, and New York from 1934 to 1954. He worked at RCA as a record librarian and audio technician, and as a CBS television cameraman. He took 1,500 photographs of Toscanini in rehearsal and at recording sessions, many of which were published on LP, CD, and video covers, as well as in Samuel Antek's book *This Was Toscanini*. He was an indefatigable crusader for the preservation of the Toscanini broadcast archives, as well as the restoration and publication of the Toscanini telecasts. He introduced the author to several of the musicians that are featured in this book and personally recorded some of the interviews. He also published *Michelangelo: Pièta*, a book of 150 of his photographs of Michelangelo's statue.

**Ikeda, Daisaku**, Buddhist philosopher, poet, and peace activist; president, Soka Gakkai International, and founder of Soka University, Min-On Concert Association, and the Fuji Art Museum.

**Illica, Luigi**, co-librettist with Giuseppe Giacosa of Puccini's most popular operas.

**Karajan, Herbert von**, one of the most successful and often recorded conductors of the twentieth century.

*****Katims, Milton**, associate principal violist of the NBC Symphony, music director of the Seattle Symphony; guest conducted the NBC Symphony.

**Kipnis, Alexander**, bass; sang throughout the world, including performances with Toscanini at Bayreuth and Salzburg and with the NBC Symphony.

**Kleiber, Erich**, conductor in the world's major opera houses; guest conducted the NBC Symphony, and was admired by Toscanini.

**Klemperer, Otto**, one of the leading conductors of the twentieth century.

*****Koutzen, George**, cellist with the NBC Symphony.

*****Krasnopolsky, Michael**, double bass player, pupil of Alexander Glazunov; played with the Chicago Symphony and the NBC Symphony.

**Legge, Walter**, record producer; founded the Philharmonia Orchestra, produced many famous recordings, and was the husband of soprano Elisabeth Schwarzkopf.

**Lehmann, Lotte**, legendary soprano chosen by Richard Strauss to sing the world premieres of *Ariadne auf Naxos*, *Die Frau ohne Schatten*, and *Intermezzo*; sang with Toscanini at the New York Philharmonic and the Vienna Philharmonic in concert and in staged operas at the Salzburg Festival.

**Leinsdorf, Erich**, longtime guest conductor at the Met, music director of the Boston Symphony; assisted Toscanini at the Salzburg Festival, and guest conducted the NBC Symphony.

**Levine, James**, music director of Chicago Symphony's Ravinia Festival and the Boston Symphony Orchestra, artistic director of the Met, and chief conductor of the Munich Philharmonic.

***Lora, Arthur**, principal flutist of the Met and the NBC Symphony; for many years, he taught at the Juilliard School.

**Mainardi, Ada**, one of Toscanini's mistresses. Extant are approximately one thousand letters written to her by Toscanini during the 1930s.

**Makiguchi, Tsunesaburo**, educational theorist and author of *The System of Value-Creating Pedagogy*, founder of the Soka Gakkai; died while imprisoned during World War II for his opposition to the Japanese government's militarism.

***Marek, George**, vice president and general manager of RCA, and author of several biographies, including *Toscanini*.

**Maurel, Victor**, baritone who sang the world premieres of *Otello* and *Falstaff*.

**Melchior, Lauritz**, legendary Wagnerian tenor who sang at the Met, with Toscanini at Bayreuth, and with the NBC Symphony.

**Menuhin, Yehudi**, world-renowned violinist and conductor; appeared as soloist with Toscanini.

**Merrill, Robert**, leading baritone at the Met for many years; sang in Toscanini's last performances of *Un ballo in maschera* and *La traviata* with the NBC Symphony.

**Merriman, Nan**, mezzo-soprano; sang five roles with Toscanini and the NBC Symphony.

***Miller, Frank**, cellist and conductor. He played in the Philadelphia Orchestra, and was principal cellist of the Minneapolis Symphony, of the Chicago Symphony for twenty-six years, and of the NBC Symphony with Toscanini for fifteen years. He was also music director of the Orlando and Evanston Symphonies.

**Mischakoff, Mischa**, violinist, student of Leopold Auer; was soloist with the Bolshoi Opera and concertmaster of the Moscow Philharmonic, Saint Petersburg Philharmonic, Warsaw Philharmonic, New York Symphony, Philadelphia Orchestra, Chicago Symphony, NBC Symphony (from 1937 to 1952), Detroit Symphony, Chautauqua Symphony, and Baltimore Symphony.

**Moldavan, Nicolas**, violist with the Flonzaley and Coolidge Quartets and the NBC Symphony.

**Molinari-Pradelli, Francesco**, conductor; was admired by Toscanini.

**Montesanto, Luigi**, baritone; sang at the Met and La Scala and sang the role of Michele in the world premiere of Puccini's *Il tabarro*.

**Monteux, Pierre**, conductor of the San Francisco Symphony, the Boston Symphony, and the Concertgebouw; conducted the world premieres of Stravinsky's *Petrushka* and *Le sacre du printemps*, and Ravel's *Daphnis et Chloé*. He also guest conducted the NBC Symphony, and conducted it in its first concert.

*****Mordino, Joseph**, tenor; recorded *Wozzeck* with Mitropoulos, and as a student at La Scala was Toscanini's neighbor.

**Muzio, Claudia**, soprano; sang with Toscanini at the Met and La Scala.

**Nelli, Herva**, soprano; sang with Toscanini at La Scala after World War II and at NBC for Toscanini's last performances of Verdi's *Otello*, *Aida*, *Falstaff*, Requiem, and *Un ballo in maschera*.

**Nissen, Hermann**, bass-baritone; sang at La Scala and the Met, and with Toscanini at Salzburg.

**Novotná, Jarmila**, soprano; sang *Die Zauberflöte* with Toscanini at Salzburg, sang Beethoven's Ninth Symphony and Debussy's *La damoiselle élue* with him at the NBC Symphony, and sang at the Met from 1940 to 1956.

*****Novotny, Joseph**, principal tuba of the NBC Symphony, and later, at the New York Philharmonic.

**Oltrabella, Augusta**, soprano and mezzo-soprano; sang at La Scala and with Toscanini at Salzburg.

**Osvath, Julie**, soprano; sang *Die Zauberflöte* with Toscanini at Salzburg.

**Paisley, William**, NBC Symphony librarian.

**Paolucci, Bridget**, writer and lecturer; author of *Beverly Sills, Opera Singer*.

**Parikian, Manoug**, concertmaster of the Philharmonia during Toscanini's appearances with the orchestra in 1952.

**Pasero, Tancredi**, much-admired bass; sang at La Scala and the Met.

**Patti, Adelina**, legendary soprano of the latter half of the nineteenth century.

**Peerce, Jan**, tenor; sang at the Met, and sang with Toscanini at the NBC Symphony on fifteen occasions.

**Pelletier, Wilfrid**, friend of Toscanini; conducted at the Met, and was married to soprano Rose Bampton.

**Pertile, Aureliano**, tenor; sang at the Met and Covent Garden, and was Toscanini's preferred tenor at La Scala.

**Piatigorsky, Gregor**, principal cellist of the Bolshoi Theatre and the Berlin Philharmonic before commencing his celebrated solo career; performed in trios with Heifetz and Horowitz, and later, with Nathan Milstein and Arthur Rubinstein. He taught at Curtis and at the University of Southern California.

**Pini-Corsi, Antonio**, baritone; sang in the world premieres of *Falstaff* and *La bohème*.

**Poliakine, Raoul**, violinist with the Lucerne Festival Orchestra with Toscanini.

**\*Posner, Selig**, violist with NBC Symphony, and later, the New York Philharmonic.

**Primrose, William**, violist, pupil of Ysaÿe, member of the NBC Symphony, founder of the Primrose Quartet, and celebrated soloist; commissioned Bartók's Viola Concerto.

**Reiner, Fritz**, best remembered as conductor of the Chicago Symphony; guest conducted the NBC Symphony.

**Rethberg, Elisabeth,** widely acclaimed soprano admired by Toscanini; sang at La Scala and the Met.

**Rodzinski, Artur**, music director of the Los Angeles Philharmonic, the Cleveland Orchestra, the Chicago Symphony, and the New York Philharmonic. At Toscanini's request, Rodzinski chose and rehearsed the members of the NBC Symphony at its inception in 1937, and appeared with it as a guest conductor.

**Rodzinski, Halina**, wife of Artur Rodzinski and author of *Our Two Lives*.

**Rosé, Arnold**, concertmaster of the Vienna Court Opera and the Vienna Philharmonic from 1881 to 1938, and husband of Gustav Mahler's sister.

**\*Rostal, Leo**, cellist with the NBC Symphony.

**Rubinstein, Arthur**, legendary pianist; played Beethoven's Third Piano Concerto with Toscanini and the NBC Symphony.

**Ruffo, Titta**, baritone; sang at Covent Garden, La Scala, and the Met.

**\*Sachs, Harvey**, author; has written four books about Toscanini.

**Salvemini, Gaetano**, anti-Fascist politician, historian, and writer.

**Sargeant, Winthrop**, music critic; was a violinist in the New York Philharmonic with Toscanini.

**\*Sarser, David**, violinist with the NBC Symphony, audio engineer, and electronics pioneer; designed Toscanini's home audio system.

**Sayão, Bidú**, soprano; sang at the Met and with Toscanini at the New York Philharmonic. Villa-Lobos wrote his *Bachianas Brasileiras* for her.

**Schoenbach, Sol**, principal bassoonist of the Philadelphia Orchestra, including during Toscanini's concerts and recordings with that orchestra; taught at the Berkshire Music Center, the Curtis Institute, and the New England Conservatory.

**Schonberg, Harold C.**, senior music critic of the *New York Times* and author of thirteen books.

**Scotti, Antonio**, internationally acclaimed baritone; sang over 1,200 performances with the Met.

**\*Shaw, Robert**, conductor of the Atlanta Symphony and Chorus; prepared the choruses for most of Toscanini's choral and operatic performances at NBC from 1945 to 1954.

**Shore, Bernard**, violist and writer; was principal violist for Toscanini in the BBC Symphony.

*Shulman, Alan, cellist, arranger, and composer; played in the NBC Symphony, cofounded the Stuyvesant Quartet, and taught at Juilliard.

*Shulman, Sylvan, violinist with the NBC Symphony, and cofounder of the Stuyvesant Quartet.

Silverstein, Joseph, violinist and conductor, for many years concertmaster of the Boston Symphony, and music director of the Utah Symphony.

Stabile, Mariano, baritone; sang many performances with Toscanini at La Scala and Salzburg.

Stokowski, Leopold, one of the twentieth century's legendary conductors; guest conducted the NBC Symphony.

Steinberg, William, conductor, trained the Palestine Orchestra at its inception; guest conducted the NBC Symphony, best remembered as the music director of the Pittsburgh Symphony.

Stracciari, Riccardo, baritone; sang in many of the world's major opera houses.

Szell, George, best remembered as conductor of the Cleveland Orchestra; guest conducted the NBC Symphony.

Tagliavini, Ferruccio, tenor; sang at the Met and La Scala.

Tamagno, Francesco, tenor; sang the title role at the world premiere of Verdi's *Otello*.

Tassinari, Arrigo, principal flute player at La Scala with Toscanini in the 1920s.

Taubman, Howard, music and drama critic for the *New York Times*, and author of *Toscanini: The Maestro*.

Tebaldi, Renata, soprano; sang in the world's major opera houses, including La Scala with Toscanini after World War II.

Tess, Giulia, soprano and mezzo-soprano; sang with Toscanini at La Scala.

Tetrazzini, Luisa, soprano; sang with Toscanini at the Met.

Toscanini, Carla, Toscanini's wife.

Toscanini, Walter, Toscanini's son and a liaison between his father and the NBC. Credited for overcoming Toscanini's reluctance to record, he collected memorabilia of his father's career, as well as collecting and preserving Toscanini's entire recorded legacy, which was donated by the family to the New York Public Library in the 1980s.

Tucker, Richard, greatly celebrated tenor; sang at La Scala, at the Met, and with the NBC Symphony for Toscanini's last performance of *Aida*.

Valdengo, Giuseppe, baritone; sang at La Scala and the Met, and sang the leading baritone roles in Toscanini's last performances of *Aida*, *Falstaff*, and *Otello*. He is the author of a book about his experiences with Toscanini, *Scusi, conosce Toscanini?* (Excuse Me, Do You Know Toscanini?).

*Vardi, Emanuel, assistant principal violist of the NBC Symphony, conductor, and painter.

**Vinay, Ramón**, tenor, whose recording of *Otello* with Toscanini has become legendary.

**Wagner, Siegfried**, Richard Wagner's son.

**Wagner, Winifred**, Siegfried Wagner's wife.

**Wallenstein, Alfred**, principal cellist of the New York Philharmonic with Toscanini, music director of the Los Angeles Philharmonic; taught conducting at Juilliard.

**Walter, Bruno**, world-renowned conductor of the premieres of Mahler's Ninth Symphony and *Das Lied von der Erde*; guest conducted the NBC Symphony.

*****Walter, David**, principal bass player of the Pittsburgh Symphony; played with Toscanini at the NBC Symphony, and taught at Juilliard and the Manhattan School of Music.

*****Weber, David**, clarinetist with the NBC Symphony; taught at Juilliard.

**Weill, Kurt**, composer, best known for *The Threepenny Opera*.

*****Winter, Paul**, violinist in the NBC Symphony.

**Ysaÿe, Eugène**, legendary violinist, composer, and conductor.

**Zimmermann, Fred**, bass player at the New York Philharmonic with Toscanini.

# Notes

## Preface

1. B. H. Haggin, *Conversations with Toscanini* (Garden City, NY: Doubleday, 1959), 30.
2. Harvey Sachs, *Toscanini* (London: Weidenfeld & Nicolson, 1978), 146.
3. Denis Matthews and Ray Burford, *Arturo Toscanini* (Tunbridge Wells, Kent: Midas Books, 1982), 41.
4. Harvey Sachs, *Arturo Toscanini from 1915 to 1946: Art in the Shadow of Politics* (Torino: E.D.T. Edizioni di Torino, 1987), 135.

## Chapter 1. Toscanini Defies Mussolini and Opposes Hitler

1. Arturo Toscanini to Ada Mainardi, April 2, 1937, in Arturo Toscanini and Harvey Sachs, *The Letters of Arturo Toscanini* (New York: Alfred A. Knopf, 2002), 244.
2. Daisaku Ikeda, "Recollections of My Meetings with Leading World Figures: Carlo Maria Badini, Superintendent of La Scala," translated from *Seikyo Shimbun* (Tokyo), October 22, 2000.
3. B. H. Haggin, *The Toscanini Musicians Knew* (New York: Horizon Press, 1967), 54.
4. Toscanini to Mainardi, March 19, 1938, 327–328.
5. Shirlee Emmons, *Tristanissimo: The Authorized Biography of Heroic Tenor Lauritz Melchior* (New York: Schirmer Books, 1990), 98.
6. Ibid., 104.
7. Harvey Sachs, *Reflections on Toscanini* (New York: Grove Weidenfeld, 1991), 74.
8. Clara Clemens, *My Husband Gabrilowitsch* (New York: Harper and Brothers, 1938), 206.
9. Sachs, *Reflections on Toscanini*, 118.
10. Ibid.
11. Sachs, *Reflections on Toscanini*, 119.
12. Sachs, *Toscanini*, 251.
13. Toscanini to Mainardi, January 4, 1937, 229.
14. Sachs, *Toscanini*, 252.
15. America-Israel Cultural Foundation, *Arturo Toscanini: A Commemorative Tribute by the America-Israel Cultural Foundation on the Occasion of the Centenary of His Birth, the 10th Anniversary of His Death, and the 30th Anniversary of the Israel Philharmonic Orchestra*, ed. Barry Hyams (New York: America-Israel Cultural Foundation, 1967).
16. Howard Taubman, *The Maestro: The Life of Arturo Toscanini* (New York: Simon and Schuster, 1951), 217.

17. Harvey Sachs, "Toscanini and Wagner, Salzburg 1937"; liner notes for *Wagner: Die Meistersinger von Nürnberg/Toscanini, Salzburg 1937*, compact disc (Andante Records, AND3040, 2003), 32.

18. Taubman, *The Maestro: The Life of Arturo Toscanini*, 217.

19. Sachs, *Reflections on Toscanini*, 126.

20. Sachs, *Reflections on Toscanini*, 127.

21. Taubman, *The Maestro: The Life of Arturo Toscanini*, 218.

22. Telephone conversation with Ada Mainardi, n.d., in Toscanini and Sachs, *The Letters of Arturo Toscanini*, 343.

23. George R. Marek, *Toscanini* (New York: Atheneum, 1975), 186.

24. Toscanini to Mainardi, October 12, 1938, 347.

25. Toscanini to Mainardi, November 2, 1938, 350–351.

26. Taubman, *The Maestro: The Life of Arturo Toscanini*, 319.

27. Toscanini to Mainardi, August 10, 1940, 375.

28. Toscanini to Mainardi, September 4, 1940, 377.

29. Toscanini to Mainardi, May 16, 1941, 379.

30. Arturo Toscanini, editorial, "To the People of America," *Life* magazine, September 13, 1943, 32.

31. Ikeda, "Recollections of My Meetings with Leading World Figures," October 22, 2000.

32. Ibid.

33. Lanfranco Rasponi, *The Last Prima Donnas* (New York: Alfred A. Knopf, 1982), 252.

34. Ikeda, "Recollections of My Meetings with Leading World Figures," October 22, 2000.

## Chapter 2. Inner Power and Charisma

1. Mischa Mischakoff, "My 'Strad' and I with Toscanini," *Band World* 1, no. 2 (Spring 1938), 4.

2. Ethel Peyser, "92 Men and—Toscanini: NBC Plays Santa Claus to American Music Lovers," *Scholastic*, February 5, 1938, 8.

3. Haggin, *The Toscanini Musicians Knew*, 29.

4. Harry Glantz, interview by Mortimer Frank, *The Toscanini Legacy*, WFUV, 1970s.

5. Matthews and Burford, *Arturo Toscanini*, 117.

6. Peter Rosen, *Toscanini: The Maestro*, Peter Rosen Productions, 1984.

7. Ibid.

8. Raoul Poliakine, interview by Mortimer Frank, *The Toscanini Legacy*, WFUV, 1970s.

9. Glantz, interview by Mortimer Frank, *The Toscanini Legacy*, WFUV, 1970s.

10. Haggin, *The Toscanini Musicians Knew*, 131.

11. Ibid., 139.

12. Lotte Lehmann, interview by Ben Grauer, *Toscanini: The Man Behind the Legend*, NBC Radio, November 20, 1963.

## Chapter 3. Work

1. Manoug Parikian, undated interview of unknown origin.

2. Haggin, *The Toscanini Musicians Knew*, 192.

3. Ibid., 19.
4. Ibid., 21.
5. Taubman, *The Maestro: The Life of Arturo Toscanini*, 247.
6. Wilfrid Pelletier, monologue recorded at the Manhattan School of Music, late 1970s.
7. Marek, *Toscanini*, 40–42.
8. Halina Rodzinski, *Our Two Lives* (New York: Scribner, 1976), 131.
9. Toscanini to Mainardi, August 23, 1937, 278.
10. Lotte Lehmann, *Midway in My Song: The Autobiography of Lotte Lehmann* (Indianapolis: Bobbs-Merrill, 1938), 232.
11. Bruno Walter, *Theme and Variations* (New York: Alfred A. Knopf, 1946), 179.
12. Elisabeth Rethberg, interview by Edward Downes, Metropolitan Opera radio intermission broadcast, March 25, 1967.
13. Andrea Della Corte, *Toscanini, visto da un critico* (Torino: ILTE, 1958), 281–282.
14. Harold C. Schonberg, *Horowitz: His Life and Music* (New York: Simon & Schuster, 1992), 141–142.
15. Ibid., 138.
16. Haggin, *Conversations with Toscanini*, 102.
17. Ibid., 49.
18. Sachs, *Arturo Toscanini from 1915 to 1946: Art in the Shadow of Politics*, 134.
19. Igor Stravinsky, *Stravinsky: An Autobiography* (New York: Simon & Schuster, 1936), 129–130.
20. Glantz, interview by Mortimer Frank, *The Toscanini Legacy*, WFUV, 1970s.
21. Haggin, *The Toscanini Musicians Knew*, 255.
22. Ibid., 198–199.
23. Licia Albanese, interview by Edward Downes, Metropolitan Opera radio intermission broadcast, March 25, 1967.
24. Haggin, *The Toscanini Musicians Knew*, 21.
25. Philip Frank, "Do We Know More?," *Music Magazine*, February 1979, 29.
26. Haggin, *The Toscanini Musicians Knew*, 200.
27. Peter Rosen, *Toscanini: The Maestro*, 1984.
28. James Dolan, interview by Ben Grauer, *Toscanini: The Man Behind the Legend*, NBC Radio, August 28, 1965.
29. Haggin, *The Toscanini Musicians Knew*, 32.
30. Ibid., 87–88.
31. Marek, *Toscanini*, 196.
32. Francis Robinson, interview by Ben Grauer, *Toscanini: The Man Behind the Legend*, NBC Radio, April 1, 1964.
33. Haggin, *The Toscanini Musicians Knew*, 257.
34. Marek, *Toscanini*, 5.
35. Haggin, *The Toscanini Musicians Knew*, 180.

## Chapter 4. Tempo

1. Haggin, *The Toscanini Musicians Knew*, 169.
2. Emmons, *Tristanissimo: The Authorized Biography of Heroic Tenor Lauritz Melchior*, 99.
3. Marek, *Toscanini*, 176.

4. Schonberg, *Horowitz: His Life and Music*, 143–144.
5. Glantz, interview by Mortimer Frank, *The Toscanini Legacy*, WFUV, 1970s.
6. Ibid.
7. Emmons, *Tristanissimo: The Authorized Biography of Heroic Tenor Lauritz Melchior*, 100.
8. Haggin, *The Toscanini Musicians Knew*, 56.
9. Ibid., 196–197.
10. Ibid., 168–169.
11. Haggin, *Conversations with Toscanini*, 99–100.
12. Haggin, *The Toscanini Musicians Knew*, 83.
13. Haggin, *Conversations with Toscanini*, 131.
14. Ibid., 19.
15. Haggin, *The Toscanini Legacy*, WFUV, 1970s.
16. Rodzinski, *Our Two Lives*, 143.
17. Haggin, *The Toscanini Musicians Knew*, 74.
18. Anne Mischakoff Heiles, *Mischa Mischakoff: Journeys of a Concertmaster*, Detroit Monographs in Musicology/Studies in Music No. 46 (Sterling Heights, MI: Harmonie Park Press, 2006), 280.
19. Haggin, *The Toscanini Musicians Knew*, 170.
20. Marek, *Toscanini*, 250.
21. Haggin, *The Toscanini Musicians Knew*, 205.
22. Ibid., 229.
23. Milton Katims, interview by Ben Grauer, *Toscanini: The Man Behind the Legend*, NBC Radio, January 15, 1964.
24. Haggin, *Conversations with Toscanini*, 172.
25. Sachs, *Reflections on Toscanini*, 147.
26. Gianandrea Gavazzeni, *Non eseguire Beethoven e altri scritti* (Milano, Italy: Il saggiatore, 1974), 96.
27. Martin Bernstein, interview by Mortimer Frank, *The Toscanini Legacy*, WFUV, 1970s.
28. Schonberg, *Horowitz: His Life and Music*, 139–140.
29. Haggin, *The Toscanini Musicians Knew*, 16.
30. Ibid., 16–17.
31. Ibid., 16.
32. Haggin, *Conversations with Toscanini*, 34–35.
33. Haggin, *The Toscanini Musicians Knew*, 200–201.
34. NBC Symphony rehearsal recordings, archived at New York Public Library at Lincoln Center's Rodgers and Hammerstein Archives of Recorded Sound.
35. Haggin, *The Toscanini Musicians Knew*, 106.
36. Sachs, *Toscanini*, 235.
37. Schonberg, *Horowitz: His Life and Music*, 135–136.
38. Ibid., 141.
39. Rasponi, *The Last Prima Donnas*, 127–128.
40. Ibid., 483.

## Chapter 5. Opera

1. Haggin, *The Toscanini Musicians Knew*, 49.

2. Arthur Abell, *Talks with Great Composers: Candid Conversations with Brahms, Puccini, Strauss, and Others* (New York: Carol Publishers Group, 1994), 124–125.
3. Ibid.
4. Filippo Ghignatti, interview by Ben Grauer, *Toscanini: The Man Behind the Legend*, NBC Radio, 1960s.
5. William Weaver and Simonetta Puccini, *The Puccini Companion* (New York: W.W. Norton & Co., 1994), 122.
6. B. H. Haggin, "Vienna's Great Conductors," *Ovation*, December 1980.
7. Taubman, *The Maestro: The Life of Arturo Toscanini*, 279.
8. Robert Merrill, interview by Robert Sherman, *The Listening Room*, WQXR, 1980s.
9. Erich Leinsdorf, *Cadenza: A Musical Career* (Boston: Houghton Mifflin, 1976), 41–42.
10. Lehmann, *Midway in my Song: The Autobiography of Lotte Lehmann*, 232.
11. Marek, *Toscanini*, 202.
12. Francis Robinson, interview by Ben Grauer, *Toscanini: The Man Behind the Legend*, NBC Radio, April 1, 1964.
13. Mario Labroca and Virgilio Boccardi, *Arte di Toscanini* (Torino: Edizioni RAI Radio-televisione Italiana, 1966), 99–100.
14. Antonietta Meneghel, *Una voce nel mondo, di Toti dal Monte* (Milano: Longanesi, 1962), 107.
15. Ibid.
16. Ibid., 119.
17. Labroca and Boccardi, *Arte di Toscanini*, 99–100.
18. Meneghel, *Una voce nel mondo, di Toti dal Monte*, 118.
19. Giovanni Martinelli, "Singing Verdi," *Musical America*, March 1963.
20. Sachs, *Toscanini*, 153.
21. Rasponi, *The Last Prima Donnas*, 533.
22. Haggin, *The Toscanini Musicians Knew*, 157.
23. Ibid., 60.
24. Haggin, *Conversations with Toscanini*, 115.
25. Rasponi, *The Last Prima Donnas*, 347.

# Chapter 6. Musical Architecture

1. Haggin, *The Toscanini Musicians Knew*, 228.
2. Ibid., 197.
3. Ibid., 74–75.
4. Ibid., 167–168.
5. Ibid., 83–84.

# Chapter 7. Balance

1. Toscanini, quoted by Milton Katims in Haggin, *The Toscanini Musicians Knew*, 228.
2. David Dalton and William Primrose, *Playing the Viola: Conversations with William Primrose* (New York: Oxford University Press, 1988), 99.
3. Robert Hupka, interview by Bridget Paolucci, *The Toscanini Legacy*, WFUV (originally recorded for CBC, 1967), 1978.

4. Haggin, *Conversations with Toscanini*, 134–135.
5. Ibid., 196.
6. Parikian, interview.
7. Ira Arthur Hirschmann, *Obligato: Untold Tales from a Life with Music* (New York: Fromm International Pub. Corp., 1994), 44–45.
8. Ira Arthur Hirschmann, interview by Ben Grauer, *Toscanini: The Man Behind the Legend*, NBC Radio, December 11, 1963.
9. Haggin, *Conversations with Toscanini*, 14–15.
10. Martin Bernstein, interview by Mortimer Frank, *The Toscanini Legacy*, WFUV, 1970s.
11. Schonberg, *Horowitz: His Life and Music*, 138–139.
12. Haggin, *Conversations with Toscanini*, 29–30.
13. Ibid.
14. Saul Goodman, interview by Rick Mattingly, *Modern Drummer*, December 1981.
15. Erich Leinsdorf, *The Composer's Advocate: A Radical Orthodoxy for Musicians* (New Haven: Yale University Press, 1981), 131.
16. Ibid., 200.
17. Samuel Antek and Robert Hupka, *This Was Toscanini* (New York: Vanguard Press, 1963), 134.
18. Heiles, *Mischa Mischakoff: Journeys of a Concertmaster*, 280–281.
19. Haggin, *Conversations with Toscanini*, 125–126.
20. Ibid., 147.
21. Antek and Hupka, *This Was Toscanini*, 174–177.

## Chapter 8. Baton Technique

1. Haggin, *The Toscanini Musicians Knew*, 74.
2. Poliakine, interview by Mortimer Frank, *The Toscanini Legacy*, WFUV, 1970s.
3. Robert Hupka, WFUV Radio documentary.
4. *Toscanini: The Man Behind the Legend*, NBC Radio, 1960s.
5. Bernstein, interview by Mortimer Frank, *The Toscanini Legacy*, WFUV, 1970s.
6. Haggin, *Conversations with Toscanini*, 197–198.
7. Bernstein, interview by Mortimer Frank, *The Toscanini Legacy*, WFUV, 1970s.
8. Haggin, *The Toscanini Musicians Knew*, 220.
9. Haggin, *Conversations with Toscanini*, 84.
10. Heiles, *Mischa Mischakoff: Journeys of a Concertmaster*, 145.
11. Haggin, *The Toscanini Musicians Knew*, 20.
12. Bernstein, interview by Mortimer Frank, *The Toscanini Legacy*, WFUV, 1970s.
13. Haggin, *The Toscanini Musicians Knew*, 83.
14. Ibid., 20.
15. Heiles, *Mischa Mischakoff: Journeys of a Concertmaster*, 280.
16. Antek and Hupka, *This Was Toscanini*, 52.
17. Ibid., 149.
18. Haggin, *The Toscanini Musicians Knew*, 199.
19. Antek and Hupka, *This Was Toscanini*, 52.

# Chapter 9. Philosophy

1. Sachs, *Toscanini*, 200.
2. Heiles, *Mischa Mischakoff: Journeys of a Concertmaster*, 145.
3. *Toscanini: The Man Behind the Legend*, NBC Radio, May 26, 1965.
4. Marek, *Toscanini*, 295.
5. Hirschmann, interview by Ben Grauer, *Toscanini: The Man Behind the Legend*, NBC Radio, December 11, 1963.
6. Antek and Hupka, *This Was Toscanini*, 19.
7. Hupka, interview by Bridget Paolucci, *The Toscanini Legacy*, WFUV (originally recorded for CBC, 1967), 1978.
8. Ibid.
9. William Paisley, interview by Ben Grauer, *Toscanini: The Man Behind the Legend*, NBC Radio, November 17, 1965.

# Chapter 10. Rehearsal Style

1. J. Dorsey Callaghan, "Mischakoff Wants the City to Be a Music Leader," *Detroit Free Press*, September 17, 1951.
2. Lehmann, *Midway in My Song: The Autobiography of Lotte Lehmann*, 232.
3. Marcia Davenport, *Too Strong for Fantasy* (New York: Scribner, 1967), 195.
4. Hupka, interview by Bridget Paolucci, *The Toscanini Legacy*, WFUV (originally recorded for CBC, 1967), 1978.
5. *Toscanini: The Man Behind the Legend*, NBC Radio, December 23, 1964.
6. Heiles, *Mischa Mischakoff: Journeys of a Concertmaster*, 280.
7. NBC Symphony rehearsal recordings, archived at New York Public Library at Lincoln Center's Rodgers and Hammerstein Archives of Recorded Sound.
8. Heiles, *Mischa Mischakoff: Journeys of a Concertmaster*, 233.
9. Haggin, *Conversations with Toscanini*, 137.
10. Haggin, *The Toscanini Musicians Knew*, 130.
11. Rodzinski, *Our Two Lives*, 128–129.
12. Haggin, *Conversations with Toscanini,* 81.
13. Antek and Hupka, *This Was Toscanini*, 78.
14. Callaghan, "Mischakoff Wants the City to Be a Music Leader."
15. Haggin, *The Toscanini Musicians Knew*, 197.
16. NBC Symphony rehearsal recordings, archived at New York Public Library at Lincoln Center's Rodgers and Hammerstein Archives of Recorded Sound.
17. Heiles, *Mischa Mischakoff: Journeys of a Concertmaster*, 160.
18. Haggin, *Conversations with Toscanini,* 81–82.
19. Heiles, *Mischa Mischakoff: Journeys of a Concertmaster*, 160.
20. Bernard Shore, *The Orchestra Speaks* (London: Longmans, 1938).
21. Hupka, interview by Bridget Paolucci, *The Toscanini Legacy*, WFUV (originally recorded for CBC, 1967), 1978.
22. Haggin, *The Toscanini Musicians Knew*, 27.
23. Heiles, *Mischa Mischakoff: Journeys of a Concertmaster*, 157.

24. Haggin, *The Toscanini Musicians Knew*, 226.
25. Ibid., 80–81.
26. Emmons, *Tristanissimo: The Authorized Biography of Heroic Tenor Lauritz Melchior*, 99.
27. Mischakoff, "My 'Strad' and I with Toscanini," 4.
28. Ghignatti, interview by Ben Grauer, *Toscanini: The Man Behind the Legend*, NBC Radio, 1960s.
29. Jerome Hines, interview by Ben Grauer, *Toscanini: The Man Behind the Legend*, NBC Radio, December 18, 1963.
30. Marek, *Toscanini*, 158.
31. Heiles, *Mischa Mischakoff: Journeys of a Concertmaster*, 160.
32. Glantz, interview by Mortimer Frank, *The Toscanini Legacy*, WFUV, 1970s.

## Chapter 11. Recordings

1. Haggin, *Conversations with Toscanini*, 146.
2. Ibid., 22.
3. Hupka, interview by Bridget Paolucci, *The Toscanini Legacy*, WFUV (originally recorded for CBC, 1967), 1978.

## Chapter 12. Conclusion

1. Toscanini to Mainardi, August 25, 1938, 279.
2. Haggin, *The Toscanini Musicians Knew*, 173.
3. Haggin, *Conversations with Toscanini*, 106.
4. Haggin, *The Toscanini Musicians Knew*, 185.
5. Ibid., 230–231.
6. Taubman, *The Maestro: The Life of Arturo Toscanini*, 294.
7. Haggin, *The Toscanini Musicians Knew*, 173.
8. Herbert Grossman, interview by Ben Grauer, *Toscanini: The Man Behind the Legend*, NBC Radio, May 20, 1964.
9. Ibid., 281.
10. Antek and Hupka, *This Was Toscanini*, 74.
11. Ibid., 61.
12. Ibid., 18.
13. Haggin, *The Toscanini Musicians Knew*, 42.
14. Sachs, *Reflections on Toscanini*, 17.
15. Daisaku Ikeda, "An Invincible Spirit Is the Key to Realizing Ultimate Victory in Life" (graduation speech, Soka University, Hachioji, Japan, March 18, 1992).

# Bibliography

Abell, Arthur. *Talks with Great Composers: Candid Conversations with Brahms, Puccini, Strauss, and Others*. New York: Carol Publishers Group, 1994.

Albanese, Licia. Interview by Edward Downes. Metropolitan Opera radio intermission broadcast, March 25, 1967.

America-Israel Cultural Foundation. *Arturo Toscanini: A Commemorative Tribute by the America-Israel Cultural Foundation on the Occasion of the Centenary of His Birth, the 10th Anniversary of His Death, and the 30th Anniversary of the Israel Philharmonic Orchestra*. Edited by Barry Hyams. New York: America-Israel Cultural Foundation, 1967.

Antek, Samuel, and Robert Hupka. *This Was Toscanini*. New York: Vanguard Press, 1963.

Bernstein, Martin. *The Toscanini Legacy*. WFUV radio series. Interview by Mortimer Frank. 1970s.

Callaghan, J. Dorsey. "Mischakoff Wants the City to Be a Music Leader." *Detroit Free Press*, September 17, 1951.

Clemens, Clara. *My Husband Gabrilowitsch*. New York: Harper and Brothers, 1938.

Dalton, David, and William Primrose. *Playing the Viola: Conversations with William Primrose*. New York: Oxford University Press, 1988.

Davenport, Marcia. *Too Strong for Fantasy*. New York: Scribner, 1967.

Della Corte, Andrea. *Toscanini, visto da un critico*. Torino: ILTE, 1958.

Dolan, James. *Toscanini: The Man Behind the Legend*. NBC Radio series. Interview by Ben Grauer. August 28, 1965. Archived at New York Public Library at Lincoln Center's Rodgers and Hammerstein Archives of Recorded Sound.

Emmons, Shirlee. *Tristanissimo: The Authorized Biography of Heroic Tenor Lauritz Melchior*. New York: Schirmer Books, 1990.

Frank, Philip. "Do We Know More?" *Music Magazine*, February 1979.

Gavazzeni, Gianandrea. *Non eseguire Beethoven e altro scritti*. Milano, Italy: Il saggiatore, 1974.

Ghignatti, Filippo. *Toscanini: The Man Behind the Legend*. NBC Radio series. Interview by Ben Grauer. 1960s. Archived at the New York Public Library at Lincoln Center's Rodgers and Hammerstein Archives of Recorded Sound.

Glantz, Harry. *The Toscanini Legacy*. Interview by Mortimer Frank. WFUV radio series. 1970s.

Goodman, Saul. Interview by Rick Mattingly. *Modern Drummer*, December 1981.

Grossman, Herbert. *Toscanini: The Man Behind the Legend*. NBC Radio series. Interview by Ben Grauer. May 20, 1964. Archived at the New York Public Library at Lincoln Center's Rodgers and Hammerstein Archives of Recorded Sound.

Haggin, B. H. *Conversations with Toscanini*. Garden City, NY: Doubleday, 1959.

———. *The Toscanini Musicians Knew*. New York: Horizon Press, 1967.

———. "Vienna's Great Conductors." *Ovation*, December 1980.

———. *The Toscanini Legacy*. WFUV radio series. Monologue. 1970s.

Heiles, Anne Mischakoff. *Mischa Mischakoff: Journeys of a Concertmaster*. Detroit Monographs in Musicology/Studies in Music No. 46. Sterling Heights, Mich.: Harmonie Park
Press, 2006.

Hines, Jerome. *Toscanini: The Man Behind the Legend*. NBC Radio series. Interview by Ben
Grauer. December 18, 1963. Archived at the New York Public Library at Lincoln Center's
Rodgers and Hammerstein Archives of Recorded Sound.

Hirschmann, Ira Arthur. *Obligato: Untold Tales from a Life with Music*. New York: Fromm
International Pub. Corp., 1994.

———. *Toscanini: The Man Behind the Legend*. NBC Radio series. Interview by Ben Grauer.
December 11, 1963. Archived at the New York Public Library at Lincoln Center's Rodgers
and Hammerstein Archives of Recorded Sound.

Horowitz, Wanda Toscanini. Interview by Edward Downes. Metropolitan Opera radio intermission broadcast. March 25, 1967.

Hupka, Robert. *The Toscanini Legacy*. WFUV radio series. Interview by Bridget Paolucci,
(originally recorded for CBC radio in 1967). 1978.

Ikeda, Daisaku. "An Invincible Spirit Is the Key to Realizing Ultimate Victory in Life." Soka
Gakkai, trans. Summary of graduation speech given at Soka University, Hachioji, Tokyo,
March 18, 1992.

———. "Recollections of My Meetings with Leading World Figures: Carlo Maria Badini,
Superintendent of La Scala." Translated from *Seikyo Shimbun* (Tokyo), October 22, 2000.

Katims, Milton. *Toscanini: The Man Behind the Legend*. NBC Radio series. Interview by Ben
Grauer. January 15, 1964. Archived at the New York Public Library at Lincoln Center's
Rodgers and Hammerstein Archives of Recorded Sound.

Labroca, Mario, and Virgilio Boccardi. *Arte di Toscanini*. Torino: Edizioni RAI Radiotele-
visione Italiana, 1966.

Lehmann, Lotte. *Midway in My Song: The Autobiography of Lotte Lehmann*. Indianapolis:
Bobbs-Merrill, 1938.

———. *Toscanini: The Man Behind the Legend*. NBC Radio series. Interview by Ben Grauer.
November 20, 1963. Archived at the New York Public Library at Lincoln Center's Rodgers
and Hammerstein Archives of Recorded Sound.

Leinsdorf, Erich. *Cadenza: A Musical Career*. Boston: Houghton Mifflin, 1976.

———. *The Composer's Advocate: A Radical Orthodoxy for Musicians*. New Haven: Yale
University Press, 1981.

Marek, George R. *Toscanini*. New York: Atheneum, 1975.

Martinelli, Giovanni. "Singing Verdi." *Musical America*, March 1963.

Matthews, Denis, and Ray Burford. *Arturo Toscanini*. Tunbridge Wells, Kent: Midas Books,
1982.

Meneghel, Antonietta. *Una voce nel mondo, di Toti dal Monte* [pseud.]. Milano: Longanesi,
1962.

Merrill, Robert. *The Listening Room*. Interview by Robert Sherman. WQXR radio series.
1980s.

Mischakoff, Mischa. "My 'Strad' and I with Toscanini." *Band World* 1, no. 2 (Spring 1938).

NBC Symphony rehearsal recordings, archived at New York Public Library at Lincoln Center's
Rodgers and Hammerstein Archives of Recorded Sound.

Paisley, William. *Toscanini: The Man Behind the Legend*. NBC Radio series. Interview by Ben Grauer. November 17, 1965. Archived at the New York Public Library at Lincoln Center's Rodgers and Hammerstein Archives of Recorded Sound.

Parikian, Manoug. Undated interview of unknown origin.

Pelletier, Wilfrid. Monologue recorded at the Manhattan School of Music, late 1970s.

Peyser, Ethel. "92 Men and—Toscanini: NBC Plays Santa Claus to American Music Lovers." *Scholastic*, February 5, 1938.

Poliakine, Raoul. *The Toscanini Legacy*. WFUV radio series. Interview by Mortimer Frank. 1970s.

Rasponi, Lanfranco. *The Last Prima Donnas*. New York: Alfred A. Knopf, 1982.

Rethberg, Elisabeth. Interview by Edward Downes. Metropolitan Opera radio intermission broadcast. March 25, 1967.

Robinson, Francis. *Toscanini: The Man Behind the Legend*. NBC Radio series. Interview by Ben Grauer. April 1, 1964. Archived at the New York Public Library at Lincoln Center's Rodgers and Hammerstein Archives of Recorded Sound.

Rodzinski, Halina. *Our Two Lives*. New York: Scribner, 1976.

Rosen, Peter. *Toscanini: The Maestro*. Documentary film. Peter Rosen Productions, 1984.

Sachs, Harvey. *Arturo Toscanini from 1915 to 1946: Art in the Shadow of Politics: Homage to the Maestro on the 30th Anniversary of His Death*. Torino: EDT/Musica, 1987.

———. *Reflections on Toscanini*. New York: Grove Weidenfeld, 1991.

———. "Toscanini and Wagner, Salzburg 1937." *Wagner: Die Meistersinger von Nürnberg/Toscanini, Salzburg 1937*, Andante Records, AND3040, 2003, compact disc. Recorded 1937. Liner notes.

———. *Toscanini*. London: Weidenfeld & Nicolson, 1978.

Schonberg, Harold C. *Horowitz: His Life and Music*. New York: Simon & Schuster, 1992.

Shore, Bernard. *The Orchestra Speaks*. London: Longmans, 1938.

Stravinsky, Igor. *Stravinsky: An Autobiography*. New York: Simon & Schuster, 1936.

Taubman, Howard. *The Maestro: The Life of Arturo Toscanini*. New York: Simon and Schuster, 1951.

Toscanini, Arturo. Editorial, "To the People of America." *Life* magazine, September 13, 1943.

Toscanini, Arturo, and Harvey Sachs. *The Letters of Arturo Toscanini*. New York: Alfred A. Knopf, 2002.

Valdengo, Giuseppe, and Renzo Allegri. *Scusi, conosce Toscanini?* Aosta: Musemeci Editore, 1984.

Walter, Bruno. *Theme and Variations*. New York: Alfred A. Knopf, 1946.

Weaver, William, and Simonetta Puccini. *The Puccini Companion*. New York: W.W. Norton & Co., 1994.

# Index

Abell, Arthur, 90
Accorinti, Michele, 94
*Adagio for Strings. See under* Barber, Samuel
*Aida. See under* Verdi, Giuseppe
Albanese, Licia, 37, 44, 96, 149
*Andrea Chénier. See under* Giordano, Umberto
Ansermet, Ernest, 71, 221
Antek, Samuel, 152, 153, 175, 181, 195, 223, 225
Antonicelli, Giuseppe, 97
Arrau, Claudio, 60
Assandri, Virginio, 99–100

Baccaloni, Salvatore, 97
Bachmann, Edwin, xvi, 18, 23, 25, 26, 48, 50, 53, 54, 61, 81, 110, 111, 139, 141, 144, 158, 170, 181, 184, 190, 191, 193, 196, 197, 202, 222, 225
Barber, Samuel
*Adagio for Strings*, xv
*Barber of Seville, The* (*Il barbiere di Siviglia*). *See under* Rossini, Gioachino
Barenboim, Daniel, 60
Barzin, Leon, 54, 79, 81, 168, 190, 223
Battistini, Mattia, 103, 104
Bayreuth, xvii, xxi, 2, 4–5, 7, 39, 40, 55
BBC Symphony Orchestra, xvii, xxi, 43, 211
Beethoven, Ludwig van, xvi, 19, 49, 41, 42, 43, 44, 46, 48, 54, 60, 62, 63, 66, 69, 70, 75, 77, 78, 126, 139, 145, 146, 147, 148, 149, 150, 178, 179, 180, 182, 194, 195, 212
*Coriolan* Overture, 74, 197
*Fidelio*, 33, 38, 99
*Leonore* Overture No. 3, 48, 216
Missa Solemnis, 136, 179, 191, 216–217

Piano Concerto No. 5, "Emperor," 82
Septet, 145
String Quartets Op. 18, 54
Symphony No. 3, "Eroica," 17, 44, 45, 67, 75, 77, 85, 146, 164, 175, 199
Symphony No. 4, 43, 44, 146
Symphony No. 5, 43, 47, 74, 81
Symphony No. 6, "Pastoral," 146, 194–195
Symphony No. 7, 46, 66–67, 70, 78, 170
Symphony No. 9, 74, 75, 80, 116, 133–134, 143, 146, 148, 172, 180, 191, 195, 200, 204, 214
Violin Concerto, 41
Bellini, Vincenzo, 79, 94
*La sonnambula*, 94
*Norma*, 94
Bellison, Simeon, 149
Berlioz, Hector, 69
*Harold in Italy*, 69
*La damnation de Faust*, xv
"Queen Mab Scherzo," 181
*Roméo et Juliette*, 180
Bernstein, Jacob (Jascha), 26, 28, 66, 75, 157, 161, 169, 173
Bernstein, Leonard, 64, 70, 159, 160, 180, 224
Bernstein, Martin, 75, 145, 166, 168, 172
Berv, Arthur, 17, 22, 23, 38, 43, 47, 151, 159, 163, 164, 174
Berv, Harry, 17, 18, 155, 189, 208
Berv, Jack, 17, 151
Bizet, Georges
*Carmen*, 113–114, 120, 194, 224
Bloom, Robert, 19, 47, 51, 64, 76, 77, 81, 140, 146, 160, 164, 170, 179, 185, 192, 193, 203, 205, 217
Boito, Arrigo
*Mefistofele*, 12, 117

*Boléro. See under* Ravel, Maurice

Bolognini, Remo, 19, 34, 44, 52, 65, 144

Bonci, Alessandro, 107

*Boris Godunov. See under* Mussorgsky,
    Modest

Brahms, Johannes, 16, 17, 31, 48, 54, 60, 63,
    66, 71, 76, 83, 134, 135, 139, 142, 173,
    178, 195, 224
    *Liebesliederwalzer*, 73
    Piano Concerto No. 1 in D minor, 60
    Piano Concerto No. 2, 82
    Symphony No. 1 in C minor, 16, 49, 60
    Symphony No. 2, 48, 174, 180
    Symphony No. 3, 48, 66
    Symphony No. 4, 135
    *Tragic Overture*, xv

Brieff, Frank, 17, 21, 25, 26, 27, 28, 43, 45, 46,
    49, 80, 144, 159, 161, 162, 171, 174, 177,
    184, 204, 215, 223

Bruckner, Anton, 40

Bülow, Hans von, 194

Burghauser, Hugo, 44, 59, 60, 62, 71, 73, 84,
    116, 134, 135, 222

Busch, Fritz, 36, 221

Busoni, Ferruccio, 73, 74

Calusio, Ferruccio, 35

Cantelli, Guido, 51, 89, 145, 155, 162, 168, 221

Carassy, Howard, 147

Carboni, William, 1, 65

Carelli, Gabor, 20, 22, 36, 40, 65, 160, 172,
    173, 190–191

*Carmen. See under* Bizet, Georges

Carnegie Hall, xvii, 7, 48, 76, 79, 149, 151,
    211, 212, 214, 215, 216

Caruso, Enrico, 92–93, 105, 107, 108, 113–114

Casa di Riposo (Verdi Rest Home), xviii,
    7, 11

Castelbarco, Wally Toscanini, xxi

Castelnuovo-Tedesco, Mario
    Cello Concerto, 52

Cellini, Renato, 223

"Chanson à boire." *See under* Ravel,
    Maurice

Charpentier, Marc-Antoine
    *Louise*, 73, 83

Cherubini, Luigi
    Requiem, 73–74

Cliburn, Van, 60

Coletta, Harold, 21, 42, 71, 80, 141, 224

Cooley, Carlton, 81, 196

Copland, Aaron, 42, 148
    *El Salón México*, 42, 148

*Coriolan* Overture. *See under* Beethoven,
    Ludwig van

Cotogni, Antonio, 102

Crisara, Ray, 22, 28, 44

*Cristoforo Colombo. See under* Franchetti,
    Alberto

Cusumano, Robert, xvi, 80

Dal Monte, Toti, 91, 104, 107, 109, 110

Dalla Rizza, Gilda, 83, 109, 110

Danise, Giuseppe, 122, 127

*Danse macabre. See under* Saint-Saëns,
    Camille

*Daphnis et Chloé. See under* Ravel, Maurice

Davenport, Marcia, 189

De Angelis, Nazzareno, 101

De Luca, Giuseppe, 20, 104, 105, 106, 114

De Lucia, Fernando, 101

De Sabata, Victor, 168, 222

*Death and Transfiguration (Tod und
    Verklärung). See under* Strauss,
    Richard

Debussy, Claude, xvi, 140, 149, 169, 212,
    216
    *Ibéria*, 72, 175
    *La mer*, xvi, 140, 147, 149, 167, 181–182,
    216
    *Le martyre de Saint-Sébastien*, xv
    *Pelléas et Mélisande*, xv, 112
    *Prelude to the Afternoon of a Faun*, 140

Di Stefano, Giuseppe, 93

*Die Meistersinger von Nürnberg. See under*
    Wagner, Richard

*Die Moldau. See under* Smetana, Bedřich

*Die Walküre. See under* Wagner, Richard

*Die Zauberflöte (The Magic Flute). See
    under* Mozart, Wolfgang Amadeus

"Dixie," 18

Dolan, James, 50

*Don Juan. See under* Strauss, Richard

*Don Pasquale* Overture. *See under*
    Donizetti, Gaetano

*Don Quichotte à Dulcinée. See under* Ravel,
    Maurice

*Don Quixote. See under* Strauss, Richard

Donizetti, Gaetano, 79, 98
  *Don Pasquale* Overture, 41
  *L'elisir d'amore*, 97, 98
  *Linda di Chamounix*, 113
  *Lucia di Lammermoor*, 104, 109, 110, 112
Dorfmann, Ania, 182
Dukas, Paul
  *The Sorcerer's Apprentice*, 183

*Ein Heldenleben. See under* Strauss,
  Richard
*El Salón México. See under* Copland,
  Aaron
Elgar, Edward, 185
  *Enigma Variations*, 184–185
  *Introduction and Allegro for Strings*, 81
Elmo, Cloë, 106, 111
Emmons, Shirlee, 65, 205
*Enigma Variations. See under* Elgar,
  Edward
*Ernani. See under* Verdi, Giuseppe
"Eroica" Symphony. *See under* Beethoven,
  Ludwig van
*Eugene Onegin. See under* Tchaikovsky,
  Peter Ilyich
*Euryanthe. See under* Weber, Carl Maria
  von

Falcone, Frank, 25
*Falstaff. See under* Verdi, Giuseppe
*Faust. See under* Gounod, Charles
*Feste Romane. See under* Respighi, Ottorino
*Fidelio. See under* Beethoven, Ludwig van
Fierro, Arthur, 211, 216
Fiorato, Hugo, 168
Firkušný, Rudolf, 60
*Francesca da Rimini. See under* Zandonai,
  Riccardo
Franchetti, Alberto
  *Cristoforo Colombo*, xv
Frank, Mortimer, 24
Frank, Philip, 47
Freeman, Harold, 39, 84, 142, 157, 159, 167,
  169, 199, 201, 203, 212, 217
Furtwängler, Wilhelm, 7, 18, 23, 59, 62, 67,
  71, 135, 162, 195, 221–222, 222

Gabrilowitsch, Ossip, 3, 82
Gaddoni, Luigi, 182

Galeffi, Carlo, 91
Galimir, Felix, 23–24, 26, 31, 38, 43, 48,
  66–67, 79, 134, 142, 146, 156, 168, 175,
  197, 201
Gavazzeni, Gianandrea, 226
Ghignatti, Filippo, 91, 205
Giacosa, Giuseppe, 124
Gingold, Josef, 27
Giordano, Umberto
  *Andrea Chénier*, 123
Glantz, Harry, 20, 25, 42, 61, 65, 208
Glassman, Karl, 214
Goldsmith, Harris, 74, 149
Goodman, Saul, 64, 143, 148
Gordon, Nathan, 62, 79, 162, 164, 182
*Götterdämmerung. See under* Wagner,
  Richard
Gounod, Charles
  *Faust*, 93, 100, 112
Graf, Herbert, 36, 111
Granick, Arthur, 61, 68, 73, 78, 134, 156, 157,
  158, 172, 183
Grauer, Ben, 72–73
Grossman, Herbert, 163, 224
Guarnieri, Antonio, 222
Guarrera, Frank, 20, 23, 64, 96, 144, 160,
  190–191
*Guillaume Tell. See under* Rossini,
  Gioachino
Gustavson, Eva, 116

"Haffner" Symphony. *See under* Mozart,
  Wolfgang Amadeus
Haggin, B. H., xvi, 18, 32, 41, 42, 55, 59, 66,
  68, 69, 76, 77, 78, 95, 125, 136, 142,
  145, 147, 151, 170, 193, 195, 198, 214,
  216, 222
*Harold in Italy. See under* Berlioz, Hector
Haydn, (Franz) Joseph, 40, 77, 145, 173
Heifetz, Jascha, 62, 64, 161
Heiles, Anne Mischakoff, 71, 151, 171, 174,
  180, 192, 200
Hines, Jerome, 207
Hirschmann, Ira, 143, 180
Hitler, Adolf, xxi, xxii, 1, 4, 5, 7, 8, 9, 10, 225,
  239
Horowitz, Vladimir, xxi, 40, 41, 60, 75, 80,
  82, 147
Horowitz, Wanda Toscanini, xxi, 6, 82

Horszowski, Mieczysław, 80
Huberman, Bronisław, 5, 6, 8
Hunter, Ralph, 73, 163
Hupka, Robert, xvii, 19, 26, 78, 84, 140, 159, 162, 180, 182, 183, 191, 198, 213, 214, 218, 219

*I pagliacci. See under* Leoncavallo, Ruggero
*I vespri siciliani* Overture. *See under* Verdi, Giuseppe
*Ibéria. See under* Debussy, Claude
Ikeda, Daisaku, 1, 11, 12, 226
*Il barbiere di Siviglia* (*The Barber of Seville*). *See under* Rossini, Gioachino
*Il trovatore. See under* Verdi, Giuseppe
Illica, Luigi, 124
*Introduction and Allegro for Strings. See under* Elgar, Edward
Israel Philharmonic, xvii, xxii, 5, 6, 8

Johnston, Robert, 213, 214

Karajan, Herbert von, 62, 64, 224
Katims, Milton, 72, 73, 133, 169, 202, 223
Kipnis, Alexander, 116
Kleiber, Erich, 221
Klemperer, Otto, xvi, 223
Koussevitzky, Serge, 21, 69–70, 166
Koutzen, George, 18, 69, 168, 169, 190
Krasnopolsky, Michael, 15, 17, 25, 27, 82, 84, 156, 160, 161, 165, 167, 178, 179, 195, 208

*La bohème. See under* Puccini, Giacomo
*La Cenerentola* Overture. *See under* Rossini, Gioachino
*La damnation de Faust. See under* Berlioz, Hector
*La fanciulla del West. See under* Puccini, Giacomo
*La forza del destino. See under* Verdi, Giuseppe
*La gazza ladra* Overture. *See under* Rossini, Gioachino
*La Gioconda. See under* Ponchielli, Amilcare
*La mer. See under* Debussy, Claude
La Scala, xv, xvi, xxi, xxiii, 2, 7, 9, 11, 12, 33, 34, 35, 41, 55, 73, 88, 90, 98, 104, 107,

109, 110, 111, 112, 115, 120, 124, 126, 151, 211, 222
*La sonnambula. See under* Bellini, Vincenzo
*La traviata. See under* Verdi, Giuseppe
*La valse. See under* Ravel, Maurice
Lange, Hans, 143
*Le martyre de Saint-Sébastien. See under* Debussy, Claude
*Le rossignol. See under* Stravinsky, Igor
Legge, Walter, 17
Lehmann, Lotte, 20, 27, 38, 84, 99, 109, 189, 207
Leinsdorf, Erich, 99, 150, 223
*L'elisir d'amore. See under* Donizetti, Gaetano
"Leningrad" Symphony. *See under* Shostakovich, Dmitri
Leoncavallo, Ruggero, 113, 123
    *I pagliacci*, xv, 105, 113, 114, 123–124
*Leonore* Overture No. 3. *See under* Beethoven, Ludwig van
Levine, James, 49
*Liebesliederwalzer. See under* Brahms, Johannes
*Linda di Chamounix. See under* Donizetti, Gaetano
*Lohengrin. See under* Wagner, Richard
Lora, Arthur, 15, 26, 216
*Louise. See under* Charpentier, Marc-Antoine
Lucerne Festival, xvii, xxii, 8–9
*Lucia di Lammermoor. See under* Donizetti, Gaetano

*Madama Butterfly. See under* Puccini, Giacomo
*Magic Flute, The* (*Die Zauberflöte*). *See under* Mozart, Wolfgang Amadeus
Mahler, Gustav, xxi, 31, 41, 146, 194
Makiguchi, Tsunesaburo, 226
*Manfred* Symphony. *See under* Tchaikovsky, Peter Ilyich
*Manon Lescaut. See under* Puccini, Giacomo
Marek, George, 215
Marrow, Macklin, 180
Martinelli, Giovanni, 110
Martucci, Giuseppe, 3
Maurel, Victor, 119, 129

*Mefistofele. See under* Boito, Arrigo
Melchior, Lauritz, 3, 60, 65, 205
Mendelssohn, Felix, 7, 148
  *A Midsummer Night's Dream*, 64, 141, 148
  Symphony No. 5, "Reformation," 76
Mengelberg, Willem, xxi, 75
Menuhin, Yehudi, 41
Merrill, Robert, 97
Merriman, Nan, 120
Metropolitan Opera, xvii, xxi, 39, 52, 92, 93,
  97, 108, 110, 112, 121
*Midsummer Night's Dream, A. See under*
  Mendelssohn, Felix
*Mignon. See under* Thomas, Ambroise
Miller, Frank, 71, 81, 162, 163, 196, 223
Mischakoff, Mischa, 16, 71, 81, 150–151, 152,
  171, 189, 192, 196, 198, 205, 207, 224
*Missa Solemnis. See under* Beethoven,
  Ludwig van
Mitropoulos, Dimitri, 24, 64, 162
*Moldau, The (Die Moldau). See under*
  Smetana, Bedřich
Moldavan, Nicolas, 55, 70, 134, 158
Molinari, Enrico, 104
Molinari-Pradelli, Francesco, 223
Montesanto, Luigi, 113
Monteux, Pierre, 21, 51, 145, 156, 165, 221
Monteverdi, Claudio, 102
Mordino, Joseph, 34
*Mosè in Egitto. See under* Rossini, Gioachino
Mozart, Wolfgang Amadeus, 16, 40, 41, 68,
  77, 140, 145, 173, 179, 212
  Bassoon Concerto, 214
  *Die Zauberflöte (The Magic Flute)*,
    78–79, 80, 95
  Divertimento K. 287, 214
  Piano Concerto No. 20 in D minor, 41
  Piano Concerto No. 23 in A major, 41
  Symphony No. 35, "Haffner," 67, 75, 145
Munch, Charles, 180
Mussolini, Benito, xxi, 1, 2, 3, 4, 8, 9–10, 11
Mussorgsky, Modest
  *Boris Godunov*, xv, 117
  *Pictures at an Exhibition*, 155
Muzio, Claudia, 105

*Nabucco. See under* Verdi, Giuseppe
National Broadcasting Company (NBC), 1,
  8, 36, 37, 49, 76, 88, 94, 104, 115, 121,

151, 152, 157, 180, 200, 201, 205, 212,
  214, 215, 216, 219, 223, 224
NBC Opera Theatre, 224
NBC Symphony Orchestra, xvi, xvii, xxii,
  10, 15, 16, 17, 18, 19, 45, 50, 70, 76, 140,
  144, 147, 150, 162, 184, 192, 199, 211,
  213, 221, 225
Nelli, Herva, 24, 121
Nikisch, Arthur, 222
Nissen, Hermann, 20
*Norma. See under* Bellini, Vincenzo
Novotná, Jarmila, 22
Novotny, Joseph, 19, 39, 150, 167, 171

*Oberon* Overture. *See under* Weber, Carl
  Maria von
Ogdon, John, 60
Oltrabella, Augusta, 126
Ormandy, Eugene, 25
Osvath, Julie, 95
*Otello. See under* Verdi, Giuseppe

Paisley, William, 184
Palestine Orchestra, xvii, xxii, 5, 6, 8, 9
Paolucci, Bridget, 140, 159, 183, 191
Parikian, Manoug, 31, 142
*Parsifal. See under* Wagner, Richard
Pasero, Tancredi, 91
"Pastoral" Symphony. *See under* Beethoven,
  Ludwig van
"Pathétique" Symphony. *See under*
  Tchaikovsky, Peter Ilyich
Patti, Adelina, 94
Peerce, Jan, 37, 191
*Pelléas et Mélisande. See under* Debussy,
  Claude
Pelletier, Wilfrid, 33
Pertile, Aureliano, 91, 98, 104
Philadelphia Orchestra, xvii, 17, 25, 27, 68,
  163, 211, 216, 217
Philharmonia Orchestra, xvii, 17, 31, 142
Piatigorsky, Gregor, 52, 178
Piazza, Enrico, 221
*Pictures at an Exhibition. See under*
  Mussorgsky, Modest
*Pines of Rome, The. See under* Respighi,
  Ottorino
Pini-Corsi, Antonio, xv
Poliakine, Raoul, 24, 162

Ponchielli, Amilcare
  *La Gioconda*, 92–93
Posner, Selig, 23, 51, 64, 174, 181
*Prelude to the Afternoon of a Faun. See
  under* Debussy, Claude
Primrose, William, 139
Puccini, Giacomo, xv, xvi, 90–91, 120, 124,
  148, 207
  *La bohème*, xv, xxi, 37, 90, 96, 110, 120,
    148, 190, 191, 195
  *La fanciulla del West*, xv, 33
  *Madama Butterfly*, 33, 105, 120, 124, 224
  *Manon Lescaut*, 12, 33, 90–91, 113, 120,
    130
  *Turandot*, xv

*Quattro pezzi sacri. See under* Verdi,
  Giuseppe

Rachmaninoff, Sergei, 40
  Symphony No. 2, 40
Raff, Joachim
  String Quartet No. 5, 53
Ravel, Maurice
  *Boléro*, xv, 15, 64, 65
  "Chanson à boire," 95
  *Daphnis et Chloé*, 61–62, 64, 202
  *Don Quichotte à Dulcinée*, 95
  *La valse*, 175
RCA, xvii, 180, 201, 218, 222
"Reformation" Symphony. *See under*
  Mendelssohn, Felix
Reiner, Fritz, 21, 24, 64, 159, 165, 221
Respighi, Ottorino, 212
  *Feste romane*, xv
  *The Pines of Rome*, 61
Rethberg, Elisabeth, 39
Richter, Hans, 2, 194, 222
*Rigoletto. See under* Verdi, Giuseppe
Rodzinski, Artur, 21, 35, 70, 221
Rodzinski, Halina, 35, 70, 194
*Romeo and Juliet. See under* Tchaikovsky,
  Peter Ilyich
*Roméo et Juliette. See under* Berlioz, Hector
Roosevelt, Franklin D., 11
Rosé, Arnold, 60
Rossini, Gioachino, 69, 70, 84, 134, 212
  *Il barbiere di Siviglia* (*The Barber of
    Seville*), 76, 94, 103, 126

*Guillaume Tell*, 12, 93
*La Cenerentola* Overture, 32
*La gazza ladra* Overture, 12
*Mosè in Egitto*, 12, 101
*Semiramide* Overture, 43
Rostal, Leo, 34, 48, 77, 83, 166, 167
Rubinstein, Arthur, 60
Ruffo, Titta, 93, 105–106, 107

Saint-Saëns, Camille, xv
  *Danse macabre*, xv
*Salome. See under* Strauss, Richard
Salvemini, Gaetano, 7
Sargeant, Winthrop, 95–96
Sarser, David, 22, 23, 45, 59, 69, 70, 161, 215,
  218
Sayão, Bidú, 97
Schipa, Tito, 107
Schippers, Thomas, 62
Schnabel, Arthur, 144, 180
Schoenbach, Sol, 194
Schonberg, Harold C., 60, 75, 82
Schubert, Franz
  Symphony No. 8, "Unfinished," 68,
    143–144
  Symphony No. 9 in C Major, 68, 81, 135,
    199, 203, 226
Schuch, Ernst von, 222
Schumann, Robert, 62, 195
Scotti, Antonio, 104–105
*Semiramide* Overture. *See under* Rossini,
  Gioachino
Shakespeare, William, 109
  *Henry VI*, 11
Shaw, Robert, 26, 53, 68, 133, 135, 136, 148,
  172, 180, 204, 221
Shore, Bernard, 198
Shostakovich, Dmitri, 52
  Symphony No. 7, "Leningrad," xv, 10,
    51–52, 147
Shulman, Alan, 16, 18, 19, 45, 51, 63, 76, 141,
  144, 164, 170, 178, 199, 200, 201, 205,
  214
Shulman, Sylvan, 21, 62, 63, 140, 156, 159,
  161, 198
Sibelius, Jean
  Symphony No. 2, 146
  Symphony No. 7, 49
*Siegfried. See under* Wagner, Richard

Silberstein, Ernst, 164
Silverstein, Joseph, 192
Smetana, Bedřich
    Die Moldau (The Moldau), 142, 147
Sorcerer's Apprentice, The. See under Dukas,
    Paul
Stabile, Mariano, 35, 91, 127
Stalin, Joseph, 1
"Star-Spangled Banner, The," 147–148
Steinberg, William, 54, 221, 223
Stokowski, Leopold, xvi, 17, 21, 24, 61, 85,
    149, 163, 168
Stracciari, Riccardo, 113
Stradivarius, Antonio, 21, 168, 171
Strauss, Richard, xvi, 59, 61, 62, 63, 83, 84,
    141, 145, 149
    Don Juan, 63
    Don Quixote, 81
    Salome, xv, 115
    Till Eulenspiegel's Merry Pranks, 63–64,
        140–141, 149, 199
    Tod und Verklärung (Death and
        Transfiguration), 143, 149, 174, 175,
        198
Stravinsky, Igor, 41
    Le rossignol, 41–42
Szell, George, 135, 166, 168, 199

Tagliavini, Ferruccio, 97–98
Tamagno, Francesco, xv, 93
Tannhäuser. See under Wagner, Richard
Tassinari, Arrigo, 90
Taubman, Howard, 9, 223
Tchaikovsky, Peter Ilyich, 40, 185, 224
    Eugene Onegin, xv
    Manfred Symphony, 32, 218
    Romeo and Juliet, 141
    Symphony No. 4, 160–161
    Symphony No. 6, "Pathétique," 9, 18, 69,
        76, 185
Teatro Regio, xxi, 87, 223
Tebaldi, Renata, 12, 93
Tess, Giulia, 115
Tetrazzini, Luisa, 93, 110
Thomas, Ambroise
    Mignon, 70–71, 101–102
Till Eulenspiegel's Merry Pranks. See under
    Strauss, Richard

Tod und Verklärung (Death and
    Transfiguration). See under Strauss,
    Richard
Toscanini, Carla, xxi, 6, 35
Toscanini, Giorgio, xxi
Toscanini, Wally. See Castelbarco, Wally
    Toscanini
Toscanini, Walter, 43, 147, 216
Toscanini, Wanda. See Horowitz, Wanda
    Toscanini
Toscanini Institute, xxiii
Tragic Overture. See under Brahms,
    Johannes
Tristan und Isolde. See under Wagner,
    Richard
Tucker, Richard, 116
Turandot. See under Puccini, Giacomo

Un ballo in maschera. See under Verdi,
    Giuseppe

Valdengo, Giuseppe, xviii, xxiii, 4, 20, 34,
    37, 38, 53, 88–89, 93, 94, 95, 97, 98, 99,
    100, 101, 102, 103, 104, 106, 107, 108,
    111, 112, 113, 115, 116, 117, 118–119, 120,
    121, 122, 123, 125, 127, 128, 129, 130, 177,
    178, 179, 185, 186, 193, 195, 196, 206,
    207, 221, 222
Valentino, Francesco, 37
Vardi, Emanuel, 22, 40, 43, 49, 63, 140, 144,
    158, 165, 166
Veneziani, Vittore, 11
Verdi, Giuseppe, xv, xxiii, 7, 11, 37, 40, 65,
    72, 79, 89, 90, 96, 97, 99, 100, 109,
    110, 116, 117, 119, 121, 122, 125, 126,
    127, 128, 149, 150, 151, 179, 195, 204,
    212
    Aida, 38, 96, 98–99, 115, 116, 121–123, 195
    Ernani, 103–104
    Falstaff, xv, 35–37, 40, 65, 93, 96, 101,
        106–108, 109, 111, 115, 117, 125–130, 151
    I vespri siciliani Overture, 12
    Il trovatore, 98, 103, 106, 110, 125, 126,
        222–223
    La forza del destino, 108, 117
    La traviata, 44, 84–85, 97, 103, 109, 110,
        126, 149, 190, 200
    Nabucco, 12

*Otello*, 33, 37, 53, 97, 99–100, 106–107,
    109, 114, 115, 116–121, 122, 123, 126,
    130, 150, 183, 222
*Quattro pezzi sacri*, xv
Requiem, 22, 93, 73
*Rigoletto*, 103, 106, 109, 114, 117, 125, 126
Te Deum, xv, 12, 72
*Un ballo in maschera*, 53, 97–98
Verdi Rest Home. *See* Casa di Riposo
Vienna Philharmonic, xvii, xxii, 5, 7, 31,
    44, 60
Vinay, Ramón, 106, 114, 121

Wagner, Richard, 40, 54, 55, 56, 59, 60, 61,
    62, 63, 64, 65, 90, 94, 111, 116, 124,
    134, 139, 141, 145, 164, 167, 178, 179,
    212, 226
*Die Meistersinger von Nürnberg*, xvi, 20,
    59, 71, 84, 111, 189
*Die Walküre*, 62
*Götterdämmerung*, 39, 52–53, 64, 76, 141
*Lohengrin*, 2, 8, 76, 193
*Parsifal*, 4, 40, 59, 65, 76, 83, 164, 174,
    192
*Siegfried*, 54
*Tannhäuser*, 2, 3, 4, 55–56, 83, 116, 205

*Tristan und Isolde*, xv, 2, 33, 55, 76, 83,
    116, 205
Wagner, Siegfried, xv, xxi, 2, 3, 5, 55, 56, 116
Wagner, Winifred, 5
Wallenstein, Alfred, 55, 223
Walter, Bruno, 7, 16, 21, 23, 24, 39, 41, 60, 62,
    135, 156, 162, 168, 221, 222
Walter, David, 16, 31, 32, 46, 48, 54, 76–77,
    78, 133, 150, 160, 165, 172, 189, 196,
    203, 204
Weber, Carl Maria von, 152–153
    *Euryanthe*, xv
    *Oberon* Overture, 152–153, 164
Weber, David, 26, 27, 42, 63, 139, 140, 141,
    143, 146, 148, 149, 155, 164, 165, 166,
    167, 168, 181–182, 195, 201, 207
Weill, Kurt, 73, 74
Weingartner, Felix, 62, 135, 145–146
Weizmann, Chaim, 8
Winter, Paul, 16, 19, 61, 70–71, 77, 139, 148,
    159, 167, 169, 173, 178, 181, 204

Zandonai, Riccardo
    *Francesca da Rimini*, 222
Zimerman, Krystian, 60
Zimmermann, Fred, 88, 221, 225

# About the Author

Cesare Civetta has conducted over sixty orchestras in sixteen countries, including performances at Lincoln Center and Madison Square Garden. The Swedish Radio, the South African Broadcasting Company, and Voice of America have carried his concerts abroad live. ABC, CBS, and NBC news telecasts have featured Civetta's concerts in the United States with the Buffalo Philharmonic, and National Public Radio has featured his performances with the Cincinnati Philharmonia.

A native New Yorker, Civetta studied at the Accademia Musicale Chigiana in Siena, Italy; the Aspen Music Festival; Fordham University; the Juilliard School; Manhattanville College (BA in music education); and the University of Cincinnati (MA in orchestral conducting). His teachers included Vincent La Selva, Walter Levin (founder of the La Salle Quartet), Gerhard Samuel, Paul Vermel, and Italo Tajo. He has participated in master classes with Franco Ferrara, Lukas Foss, Carlo Maria Giulini, Louis Lane, Leonard Slatkin, and Otto Werner Müller.

Civetta conducted his first orchestral concert at age eighteen, led his first opera production at age nineteen, and at twenty-three was appointed conducting fellow of the Buffalo Philharmonic. He first conducted in Europe at master classes of Franco Ferrara with the Orchestra Filarmonica di Russe, Bulgaria. Within the following two years, Civetta made his New York City debuts at Madison Square Garden, Alice Tully Hall at Lincoln Center, and Town Hall. Each of his New York appearances has sold out, including opera galas with Aprile Millo, Leo Nucci, Licia Albanese, Ferruccio Tagliavini, and the Queens Symphony.

His debut in Sweden was with the KammarensembleN, the Swedish Ensemble of New Music. The all-American program was broadcast live over Swedish radio throughout Scandinavia. Civetta made his continental European debut in Wałbrzych, Poland, where he introduced a rarely heard late Schubert work, the "Grand Duo" Op. 140, orchestrated by Joachim. In China, he was the first foreign-born conductor to conduct at the Wuhan Conservatory of Music. He has also given master classes and lectures, and conducted the orchestras of the Shanghai and Shenyang conservatories. In Durban, South Africa, Civetta led the Natal Philharmonic Orchestra in a series of concerts broadcast live by the South African Broadcasting Company. Civetta has the unique distinction of being the first American to conduct twenty orchestras in transcontinental tours of the former Soviet Union. He has toured Russia six times, conducting at the Pushkin Opera and Ballet Theatre (Gorky), the Pacific Symphony (Vladivostok), the Irkutsk Philharmonic, and the Novosibirsk Philharmonic, among others.

Cesare Civetta lives in New York City and is music director of the Beethoven Festival Orchestra.